THE LOGIC OF THE TRANSFER TAXES

A GUIDE TO THE FEDERAL TAXATION OF WEALTH TRANSFERS

■ ■ ■

Laura E. Cunningham
Professor of Law
Benjamin N. Cardozo
School of Law

Noël B. Cunningham
Professor of Law
New York University
School of Law

AMERICAN CASEBOOK SERIES®

WEST
ACADEMIC
PUBLISHING

American Casebook Series is a trademark registered in the U.S. Patent and Trademark Office.

© 2018 LEG, Inc. d/b/a West Academic
  444 Cedar Street, Suite 700
  St. Paul, MN 55101
  1-877-888-1330

West, West Academic Publishing, and West Academic are trademarks of West Publishing Corporation, used under license.

Printed in the United States of America

ISBN: 978-1-64020-497-3

To Professor Leo Schmolka,
Our teacher, mentor, colleague and, most importantly
our dear friend

ACKNOWLEDGMENTS

We are extremely grateful to Professor Miranda Perry Fleischer for her generous devotion of time to reviewing and commenting on drafts of this book. Her assistance was invaluable and greatly appreciated.

Financial support was generously provided by NYU's Filomen D'Agostino Faculty Research Fund and the Benjamin N. Cardozo School of Law, Yeshiva University.

SUMMARY OF CONTENTS

TABLE OF CONTENTS

TABLE OF CASES

TABLE OF CODE SECTIONS

TABLE OF REGULATIONS

TABLE OF REVENUE RULINGS

THE LOGIC OF THE TRANSFER TAXES

A GUIDE TO THE FEDERAL TAXATION OF WEALTH TRANSFERS

CHAPTER ONE

TRANSFER TAX FUNDAMENTALS: POLICY, HISTORY & STRUCTURE

■ ■ ■

Current federal law imposes three separate taxes on the gratuitous transfer of wealth. The estate tax is imposed on wealth transfers made at death. The gift tax taxes transfers of wealth made during life. Finally, the tax on generation-skipping transfers (we'll refer to this tax throughout this book as "the GST tax") imposes a tax on particular transactions that fall between the cracks of the estate and gift tax. The estate and gift taxes act as excise taxes on the act of transferring wealth: the tax is imposed on the transferor, measured by the total amount transferred.[1]

Two basic policy questions arise at the outset. The first is to consider whether the federal government should tax gratuitous transfers of wealth in the first place. As we will see below, this is an extremely controversial question, and Congress has struggled mightily with it over the years. If one decides that taxation of wealth transfers is appropriate, the second question is whether the current system is the most appropriate means to accomplish that goal. While one option is the current estate and gift tax model, which taxes the *transferor*, another possibility would be to tax the *recipients* of gratuitous transfers. The latter model is generally referred to as an "inheritance tax" or sometime an "accessions tax."[2] The two models differ from each other in a very fundamental way: the estate and gift tax is imposed on the transferor, based upon the entire value of all property transferred, regardless of the number of recipients. In contrast, an inheritance tax is imposed on the recipients of the transfer, and each is taxed only the amount he or she receives.

---

[1] The GST tax operates somewhat differently. We will delay discussion of its complexity until *Chapter Nine*.

[2] An inheritance tax can take many different forms. It is very often a separate tax imposed on gratuitous transfers on an annual or cumulative basis with its own exemptions and rates. Rather than creating a separate tax, we could simply include gratuitous transfers in income by repealing Code § 102, which exempts gifts and inheritances from the income tax. This has sometimes been referred to as the "income inclusion approach." Joseph C. Dodge, *Beyond Estate and Gift Tax Reform: Including Gifts and Estates in Income*, 93 Harvard Law Rev. 1177 (1978). One of the more recent proposals for an inheritance tax was made by Professor Lily Batchelder in *Taxing Privilege More Effectively: Replacing the Estate Tax with an Inheritance Tax*, 63 Tax L. Rev. 1 (2009). In this article, Professor Batchelder argues for a hybrid approach, one that combines some attributes of a cumulative accessions tax and the income inclusion approach. All code references in this book are to the Internal Revenue Code of 1986, as amended.

In this chapter we explore these questions, and briefly describe the history leading up to current law.

Part A. Policy Aspects of the Transfer Taxes

In this section we will explore some of the policy arguments made for and against the federal transfer taxes. The two sides break down fairly consistently along political lines, with proponents on the left and opponents on the right. As with the study of all taxes, an understanding of the policy implications of the tax helps us understand current law and predict where the law may go.

Revenue

Like all other federal taxes, the transfer taxes contribute to total federal revenue, and one of the obvious arguments in favor of the transfer taxes is that they represent a significant and necessary source of federal revenue. Historically this was certainly true. As discussed below, the modern estate tax originated in response to revenue needs caused by World War I, yet Congress did not repeal it following the war. Instead, Congress strengthened and expanded it, and added a gift tax during the depression years. During the 1930s, the estate and gift taxes accounted for between 5% and 10% of all federal revenue. Yet the share of revenue contributed by the transfer taxes has fallen dramatically since then. In 1972, the transfer taxes accounted for 2.6% of federal revenue, and that represented the highest percentage of any year post World War II. In 2006, that share had dropped, to 1.2% of total revenue, or $27.8 billion. Following the most recent law changes the amount has dropped even more, in 2014 the transfer taxes contributed a mere .6% of total revenue, or $19.3 billion.[3]

Transfer tax proponents argue that the amounts involved, while small as a percentage matter, are far from trivial. The taxes are projected to raise as much as $200 billion over the next ten years, and if they were repealed the lost revenue would have to be raised elsewhere, presumably from taxes that would be borne by the less wealthy.[4]

Transfer tax opponents argue that the current amount of revenue raised is indeed trivial, and is not sufficient to justify what they perceive as other negative aspects of the taxes.[5] Opponents argue that this is even more true given the enormous amount of time and expense spent by

---

[3] Joint Committee on Taxation, *History, Present Law, and Analysis of the Federal Wealth Transfer Tax System* (JCX-52-15), March 16, 2015 ("*Joint Committee Report*").

[4] See Michael J. Graetz, *It's Fair, and We Need the Revenue*, Wall Street Journal September 20, 2010 ("Graetz, *It's Fair*"). Professor Graetz notes that the amounts involved are hardly "chump change", and that the revenue raised by the transfer taxes in 2008 was sufficient to fund approximately three fourths of the expenditures of the Department of Homeland Security.

[5] See *Costs and Consequences of the Federal Estate Tax, an Update*, Joint Economic Committee, Republican Staff Study, July 25, 2012 ("*Republican Report*").

wealthy taxpayers in planning around the taxes, and the cost to the government of administering the taxes.

Thus, while revenue is important, both proponents and opponents turn to other arguments to justify or oppose the transfer taxes.

Wealth Accumulation & Democracy

An early argument in favor of the estate tax was that it was necessary to prevent excessive accumulation of wealth in the hands of a few. In 1935 President Roosevelt argued that "Such inherited economic power is as inconsistent with the ideals of this generation as inherited political power was inconsistent with the ideals of the generation which established our government." So very early on, the transfer taxes were justified on political philosophy grounds as necessary to the preservation of democracy, by breaking up large estates as they move from one generation to the next.

Those same arguments are made today in favor of the transfer taxes. Proponents of the taxes point to increasing income and wealth inequality, and assert that it poses a threat to our democratic values by placing too much political power in the hands of the wealthy.[6] The argument is that with the dramatic increases in the disparities in income and wealth between the rich and the middle class, and the enormous political contributions made by some of the wealthiest persons in the country, the political influence of the wealthy is apt to grow, an argument that is difficult to ignore given recent Supreme Court decisions striking down campaign finance restrictions.[7] Passing wealth down from generation to generation, proponents argue, is akin to passing political power from generation to generation, something antithetical to the founders' ideals.

Similarly, proponents argue that transferring accumulated wealth from one generation to the next violates the democratic principle of equality of opportunity. It is hardly a level playing field, they argue, when one citizen begins life with a head start of millions (or billions) of dollars.

In its 2012 report, the Republican staff of the Joint Economic Committee counters these arguments by noting that the transfer taxes can do little to reduce inequality, and they point to the fact that most of the wealthiest individuals in the country did not inherit their wealth, but earned it. It is indeed true that no transfer tax can protect against large accumulations of wealth by the "self-made" man or woman. Yet the point

---

[6]   See James Repetti, *Democracy, Taxes and Wealth*, 76 NYU L. Rev. 825 (2001). In his recent best-selling book, CAPITAL IN THE 21ST CENTURY, Belknap Press (2014), Professor Thomas Piketty argues that inequality will continue to increase unless it is checked. He advocates a wealth tax.

[7]   *Citizens United v. FEC* 558 U.S. 310 (2010), *McCutcheon v. FEC* 134 S.Ct. 1434 (2014).

of the estate tax is not to prevent the creation of self-made billionaires, but to prevent their wealth from passing tax-free to future generations.[8]

Equity

On top of the anti-democratic effect of wealth accumulation, the argument in favor of the transfer taxes can be couched in term of equity. Consider two individuals, one who earns $100,000 a year, and another who receives gifts from her parents of $100,000 per year. Is it fair that the earner pays tax on her income each year, and the recipient of the gifts pays nothing? Unless we were to change the income tax to include gifts and inheritances, in the absence of an estate or inheritance tax this is precisely what would happen. And what galls many observers, especially those who are concerned with growing inequality, is that the repeal of the transfer taxes would only benefit the wealthiest individuals who inherit enormous sums of money, and who can best afford to contribute to the country's financial needs.[9] While those on the right side of the aisle view this as an impermissible redistribution of wealth, transfer tax proponents argue that the taxes are necessary simply as a matter of equity.

Interaction with the Income Tax

Another traditional argument made by transfer tax proponents is that the taxes serve to backstop the income tax in two ways. First, they tax amounts that escape income taxation, and second, they add an additional degree of progressivity to a federal tax system that has become increasingly less progressive over the years.[10] In 2014, 34% of federal revenue was generated by payroll taxes, most of which tax income only up to a set amount, and are borne entirely by wage earners. The income tax contributed 46% of revenue, and because of preferences for capital gains and investment income, it too falls most heavily on wage earners. The .6% contributed by the wealthiest decedents through the estate tax adds a small amount of progressivity to a tax system heavily weighted against wage earners.[11]

Opponents of the transfer taxes argue that they actually reduce income tax revenue because they encourage wealthy individuals to make large transfers to charities, who will pay no income tax on the earnings from the transferred amounts. Some also argue that the transfer taxes are unfair because they subject the transferred wealth to double taxation: that

---

[8] For a much more thorough and illuminating discussion of these issues, see Miranda Perry-Fleisher, *Divide and Conquer, Using an Accessions Tax to Combat Dynastic Transfers*, 57 B.C. L. Rev. 913 (2016).

[9] See Graetz, *It's Fair*, supra note 4. Professor Graetz cites Paris Hilton and the heirs of George Steinbrenner as examples.

[10] See generally, Graetz, *It's Fair*, supra note 4.

[11] *Joint Committee Report,* supra note 3.

the assets of the estate of a transferor have already been subject to the income tax and that they should not be subject to yet another tax.

This latter argument is not persuasive. A significant portion of most large estates has never been subject to the income tax for two reasons. First, gifts and inheritances are not included in the income of the beneficiary.[12] Therefore, if substantial amounts of wealth move from one generation to the next, those amounts are never subjected to an income tax. Second, because unrealized gains are not subjected to the income tax upon gift or death, if a wealthy person owns assets that have appreciated in her hands, that gain may be completely exempted from the income tax. If she makes a gift of those assets, the appreciation will possibly be subject to tax if the donee sells them,[13] but if she holds the property until death that gain escapes income taxation entirely, because the basis of the assets is "stepped up" to its date of death value.[14] This factor is quite significant, because unrealized appreciation comprises more than 50% of the typical large estate.[15]

Family Businesses and Entrepreneurship

A long standing argument against the transfer taxes is that they are a threat to family businesses and farms, because the next generation may lack the cash to pay the estate tax liability. This, opponents argue, not only puts the family farm at risk, it discourages entrepreneurship.

In response, transfer tax proponents argue that while some businesses and farms do face liquidity issues, Congress has enacted several provisions designed to mitigate the problem of lack of liquidity, including special valuation rules and rules that allow the estate tax bill to be paid over time. Further, the data that exists does not seem to indicate that many small businesses or farms are heavily hit by the estate tax, and this becomes increasingly true as the exemption increases.[16] With a five plus million dollar exemption, which is effectively doubled for married couples, most family businesses and farms would seem to be safe from fear of being wiped out by estate taxes.[17] That said, the taxes do necessitate that some family farms and businesses do spend time and energy planning around the taxes

---

[12] § 102.

[13] The donee generally takes a carryover basis. See § 1015(a).

[14] § 1014.

[15] See Chye-Ching Huang and Chloe Cho, *Ten Facts You Should Know About the Federal Estate Tax,* Center on Budget and Policy Priorities May 5, 2017 ("Huang & Cho, *Ten Facts*").

[16] See "Effects of the Federal Estate Tax on Farms and Small Businesses," Congressional Budget Office Report, July 2005.

[17] According to the Tax Policy Center, only 5200 of the country's projected 2.7 million estates in 2017 will owe any estate tax, and of those only 50 (1%) are expected to be family farms or small business. Of those, the TPC estimates that the estate tax burden will be less than 6% of their assets, on average. See Huang & Cho, *Ten Facts,* supra note 15.

and taking steps to ensure liquidity (buying life insurance, for example) in the event there is an estate tax bill on the death of the owner.

Effect on Savings

Transfer tax opponents assert that the estate tax impedes economic growth because it discourages savings and encourages current consumption; the wealthy would prefer to spend their wealth rather than see it consumed by taxes at death.[18]

Proponents point to lack of evidence to support the notion that the transfer taxes push the wealthy to consume more than they otherwise would.[19] There are dueling economic studies arguing for both positions, with little empirical support for the spendthrift argument.

Conclusion

How one feels about the transfer taxes largely depends upon one's philosophical approach to government and taxes in general. As discussed below, the first decade of this century was a taxing (pun intended) time for estate planners and teachers, as the transfer taxes were buffeted by the political winds of the time. Under the current administration and Congress, we may be in store for a return to those times.

Part B. History & Structure of the Transfer Taxes

The history of the transfer taxes can be divided into three significant segments, the period from original enactment to unification in 1976 (which we describe as "Ancient History"), unification in 1976, and the post-Unification period.

Ancient History: Pre-1976

In 1916 Congress enacted the estate tax statute that evolved into the law that is in effect today. That was not, however, Congress' first attempt to tax gratuitous transfers of wealth. Indeed, prior to 1916, Congress enacted wealth transfer taxes three times. The principal purpose for all three was to raise revenue for a conflict or a war, and each was repealed shortly after the hostilities were resolved.

First, in 1797 Congress enacted a stamp duty based upon the value of intestate transfers. The purpose for this tax was to fund the armed conflict with France that occurred between 1798 and 1800, and it was repealed in 1802. Second, in 1862 Congress enacted an inheritance tax to raise revenue for the Civil War. The tax was repealed in 1870. Finally, in 1898, Congress

---

[18] See *Republican Report*, supra note 5.
[19] See Repetti, supra note 6.

enacted the first estate tax to help fund the Spanish American War (1898–1900). It was repealed in 1902.

The origin of the modern estate tax is similar to that of its predecessors. It was enacted in 1916 in an effort to make up for the reduction in tariffs caused by World War I, although unlike its predecessors it was *not* repealed following the end of the war. The tax was intended only to apply to large estates; it therefore "exempted" a certain amount (originally $50,000) so that decedents dying with assets valued below that amount were not subject to the tax. This principle of limiting the reach of the tax by exempting transfers below some amount continues to this day.

An obvious way to avoid the early estate tax was to give the assets away during life. This was largely possible until 1932, when Congress permanently enacted a gift tax to backstop the estate tax.[20] From 1932 until 1976, the estate and gift taxes operated independently: each had a separate exemption, and a separate progressive rate structure. These separate regimes made it possible for wealthy transferors to lower their overall transfer tax liability by taking advantage of both exemptions, and of the lower rate brackets in each rate structure. This seemingly incoherent structure was highly criticized and the centerpiece of calls for reform.

Another much-used means of avoiding the estate and gift taxes was to skip a generation of tax. If we assume a certain "natural" movement of wealth through families, a tax is collected at each generation. To illustrate, consider Grandparent, who owns assets substantially in excess of both the estate and gift tax exemptions. If Grandparent either gifts those assets or transfers them at death to her Child, and Child ultimately passes those assets to her child (Grandchild), then this "normal" method of passing family wealth would incur two levels of transfer tax, once on the transfer from Grandparent to Child, and again on the transfer from Child to Grandchild. For individuals with substantial wealth, one of those levels of tax could be avoided by transferring some portion of the assets directly from Grandparent to Grandchild. If Child is sufficiently wealthy in her own right, this causes her no problem. If Child is not sufficiently wealthy, the same result could be achieved by having Grandparent leave the assets in a trust that supports Child during her lifetime, and passes the assets to Grandchild on Child's death. If structured correctly, this trust (sometimes called a dynasty trust) could substantially reduce the family's transfer tax burden. This avoidance opportunity also prompted calls for reform.

Unification: The Tax Reform Act of 1976

The Tax Reform Act of 1976 was a seminal piece of legislation, which enacted comprehensive reform of the transfer taxes and related income tax

---

[20] There was a gift tax in effect for a two year period from 1924 to 1926.

provisions. Most notably, it responded to the two planning opportunities described above and implemented two major reforms:

> **First** and foremost, the 1976 Act "unified" the estate and gift taxes. The separate exemptions for each tax were eliminated, and instead each individual became entitled to a "unified credit" against estate and gift tax liability. This essentially created a single "exclusion amount," against which both intervivos gifts and transfers at death were measured.[21] In addition, the Act created one unified rate structure, which applied to both intervivos and at death transfers. No longer were transferors entitled to get the benefit of two separate exemptions, and the lower rates in both rate tables. The 1976 Act set the original unified credit at $47,000, an amount that exempted wealth transfers of $175,625, and it set the maximum rate on transfers at 70%. As illustrated below, in the years since Congress has drastically changed the exclusion amount and the maximum tax rate under the rate schedule. Nevertheless, the basic "unified" structure created in 1976 remains intact today.

> **Second**, the Act created the first tax on "Generation Skipping Transfers." While seriously flawed (and ultimately retroactively repealed) the legislation was Congress' first attempt to impose a transfer tax on wealth as it moved through each generation. Even though it was not successful, it laid the groundwork for the current version of the GST tax that was enacted in 1986.

Political Football: Post-1976

Although the 1976 Act had bipartisan support (it was enacted under the Ford administration, during a time that the Democrats controlled both the House and the Senate), it wasn't long before the compromises reached began to unravel. The election of Ronald Reagan in 1980 began the gradual dismantling of the transfer taxes, which has continued to this day.[22]

Since 1976, Congress has dramatically changed the transfer tax system by varying (i) the amount of the unified credit, and hence the exclusion amount, and (ii) the maximum rate under the rate tables. The table below summarizes those changes. While Congress made changes in other years, by far the most significant occurred in 1981, 2001, 2010 and 2012, which are discussed below.

---

[21] The term "exclusion amount" has gradually replaced the term "exemption," though the latter term is still used occasionally. We may be guilty of using them interchangeably. As we illustrate below, providing a credit against a set amount of tax has the effect of exempting or excluding the amount of transfers that would trigger that amount of tax.

[22] For a thorough recounting of how the estate tax became a political football, see Michael J. Graetz and Ian Shapiro, DEATH BY A THOUSAND CUTS (Princeton 2005).

Year	Exclusion Amount	Maximum Rate
1976	$175,625	70%
1982–86	$600,000[23]	50%
1998–2001	$625,000–675,000[24]	55%
2002/03	$1,000,000	50/49%
2004/05	$1,500,000[25]	48/47%
2006–08	$2,000,000	46/45%
2009	$3,500,000	45%
2010	no tax	
2011	$5,000,000	35%
2012	$5,120,000[26]	35%
2013	$5,250,000	40%
2014	$5,340,000	40%
2015	$5,430,000	40%
2016	$5,450,000	40%
2017	$5,490,000	40%

1981 Changes

The Economic Recovery Tax Act of 1981 (ERTA), championed by the Reagan administration, made two fundamental changes to the transfer taxes. First, as illustrated above, it dramatically increased the exclusion amount from $175,625 to $600,000 and slashed the maximum tax rate from 70% to 50%. This had the effect of reducing the number of estates subject to the tax from approximately 5% to less than 1%. Second, the Act introduced the "unlimited marital deduction." The marital deduction is discussed in detail in *Chapter Seven*, but suffice to say for the moment that this change essentially treats a married couple as the taxable unit for purposes of the transfer taxes. The taxes are triggered only if wealth is transferred outside the marital unit, which often does not occur until the death of the second spouse.[27] To illustrate, consider a couple with $20,000,000 in assets, held jointly, whose wills provide: "I leave my estate to my spouse if s/he survives me, and if not then to my children in equal

---

[23] The Economic Recovery Tax Act of 1981 increased the exclusion amount to $600,000 and reduced the maximum rate to 50%. These changes were phased in gradually over the period 1982–1986.

[24] The Taxpayer Relief Act of 1997 increased the exemption to $1,000,000, phased in over the period 1998–2006. Congress acted again in 2001, however, before the phase in was complete.

[25] The gift tax exemption remained at $1,000,000 between 2004 and 2010.

[26] The amounts for 2012 and thereafter are the inflation adjusted amounts as required by the 2010 Act discussed below.

[27] There is also an unlimited gift tax marital deduction. § 2523.

shares." Because of the unlimited marital deduction, when the first spouse dies, his or her taxable estate will be zero. When the surviving spouse dies and leaves the property to the children, only then will those assets be subject to tax.

2001 Changes

In 2001 the Republicans gained control of the White House and the House of Representatives, and it was a banner year for tax cutting. Congress enacted the Economic Growth and Tax Relief Reconciliation Act of 2001 ("the 2001 Act"), which made huge cuts (which came to be known as the "Bush Tax Cuts") in income tax rates, and sought to put an end to the transfer taxes. The changes made in 2001 were designed to eventually repeal the estate tax and generation-skipping tax. This repeal was to be done in increments, by gradually increasing the exclusion amount and reducing the maximum rate through 2009, ending with total repeal in 2010.[28] However, the income tax and estate tax cuts in the 2001 Act were inherently temporary, because of the "sunset" provisions in the Act.[29] The result of the sunset provisions was that, unless Congress acted again to make the changes permanent, the transfer taxes would spring back to life in 2011, in the form in which they existed at the time of the 2001 Act, i.e., a $1,000,000 exemption and maximum rate of 55%. During the balance of the Bush administration Congress did not make the cuts permanent.

The political landscape changed dramatically with implosion of the American economy and the election of Barack Obama in 2008. Given the enormous deficits of the decade, and Democratic control of the White House and Congress following the 2008 election, most commentators expected that Congress would intervene prior to 2010 and provide a permanent extension of the transfer taxes. Nevertheless, Congress did not act, and the estate tax and GST tax were repealed in 2010. As a result, it appeared that estates like those of George Steinbrenner would pass entirely free of estate taxes. Both Democrats and Republicans were under tremendous pressure to act, though, because the sunset provisions were looming. If Congress did nothing then the transfer taxes would be back in 2011 at their 2001 levels.

---

[28] The gift tax was to continue, with a $1,000,000 exclusion amount, in lieu of the estate tax there was a modified "carry over basis" rule, which limited the availability of the step-up basis rules for beneficiaries of estates. The rationale for continuation of the gift tax was an income tax one. As a result, the estate and gift taxes were "de-unified" from 2004, when the estate tax exemption rose to $1,500,000, until 2010. The two taxes were "re-unified" with the 2010 Act.

[29] The 2001 Act was passed under the "reconciliation process" as part of a budget resolution. Under this process, legislation is not subject to filibuster in the Senate, which makes passage easier. Legislation passed under this process, however, cannot increase the deficit beyond the term of the budget. This is the reason that the tax reductions in the bill were to end, or "sunset" in 2010.

2010 Changes

Finally, in late 2010 Congress agreed to a temporary compromise. It retroactively reinstated the transfer taxes as of January 1, 2010, and extended them for two years, 2011 and 2012, with two significant modifications. First, the exclusion amount was raised to $5 million (the amount to be annually adjusted for inflation) and the maximum rate dropped to a historic low of 35%.[30] In addition, Congress also introduced the concept of "portability" of the exclusion amount.

Portability represented a significant change for many estate planners. Prior to this innovation, if most assets were held in one spouse's name, married couples were able to make use of the exclusion amount for both spouses only if they engaged in some well accepted but slightly complicated estate planning techniques. If they did not, and had simple wills leaving the entire estate to the surviving spouse, then no tax would be due on the death of the first spouse because of the marital deduction, and the exclusion amount of the predeceased spouse would essentially expire, unused, at that time. With portability, the exclusion amount of the predeceased spouse survives, and is available for use by the surviving spouse's estate at his or her later death. Section § 2010(c) provides that a surviving spouse is expressly permitted to make use of the unutilized exclusion of the predeceased spouse. The effect of this is to essentially allow an exclusion amount of $10,000,000 (adjusted for inflation) for married couples.

To illustrate, reconsider our married couple above, who had $20,000,000 in combined assets. As noted above, if the husband predeceased the wife in 2011 with a gross estate of $10,000,000, all of which was left to his wife by will, his taxable estate would be zero, because the entire amount qualified for the marital deduction. Assume (unrealistically) that there are no changes in asset value nor any inflation adjustment, and the wife then died in 2012 and left her $20,000,000 in assets to her children. Absent "portability", the wife's unified credit would exempt $5,000,000[31] in her estate, subjecting the remaining $15,000,000 to tax at the rate of 35%. This is unfortunate, because the couple made no use of the husband's $5,000,000 exclusion amount. Prior to the 2010 Act this result could only be avoided by some not too complicated estate planning, but planning was required. The 2010 Act made the husband's exclusion amount "portable," i.e., available to the surviving spouse. Under § 2010(c)(2) the wife's estate is not only entitled to her "basic exclusion amount" of $5,000,000, but she is also entitled to a "deceased spousal unused exclusion amount," which is

---

[30] Executors of the estates of decedents dying in 2010 were offered a choice, they could either could pay the estate tax as reinstated, or choose to pay no estate tax and follow the carryover basis rules in the 2001 Act.

[31] The actual inflation adjusted exclusion for 2012 is $5,120,000.

essentially the amount of her husband's exclusion amount that went unused.

Portability is trickier than it sounds, although its main selling point is simplicity. Treasury has issued regulations dealing with some of the thornier issues.[32] One particular trap for the unwary is the requirement in § 2010(c)(5) that portability is only available to the estate of the surviving spouse if the executor of the estate of the first spouse to die files an estate tax return that elects portability. Thus, even if the gross estate of the first spouse to die is below the exclusion amount, so that a return would not be required,[33] the executor must timely file a return in order to preserve the possibility of portability when the second spouse dies. The regulations allow for a simplified return in these situations, but nevertheless the return must be filed.[34]

2012 Changes: Permanent Legislation at Last

As noted above, the 2010 legislation imposing the $5,000,000 exclusion amount and 35% maximum rate was subject to sunset at the end of 2012, which meant that the exemption would drop back down to $1,000,000, and the maximum rate would revert to the 2001 level of 55%. In the face of this possibility, Congress permanently extended the transfer taxes in the early hours of 2013, setting the exemption (for all three taxes) at $5,000,000, adjusted for inflation, and setting the maximum rate at 40% beginning in 2013. The 2012 Act also made portability of the exemption amount permanent.

Part C. Structure: The Calculation of the Gift Tax, the Estate Tax, and the Operation of the Unified Credit

A word of caution: many of the calculations done in the following few pages are largely unnecessary under current law, as will be explained below. Nevertheless, to fully appreciate the transfer taxes, it is necessary to have a basic understanding of the statutory structure. So do not be discouraged by the statutory complexity, do not get lost in the trees, because by the end of this section, the forest should be clear.

The Role of the Unified Credit

As you work through the Examples below, keep in mind that the estate and gift taxes are designed to impose a tax on lifetime and at death transfers if and only if, in the aggregate, they exceed the exclusion amount. Each transferor is permitted to make tax-free transfers (during life and at

---

[32] § 20.2010–2.
[33] Ordinarily no return is required unless the gross estate exceeds the exclusion amount. § 6018.
[34] § 20.2010–2(a)(7).

death) up to the applicable exclusion amount. This is accomplished by giving each individual a "unified credit," defined in § 2010, that will offset any gift tax incurred during life, and any estate tax bill due at death. Only if the aggregate gift and estate tax liability exceeds the credit will any tax be due.

Under § 2010, the credit is computed with reference to something called the "applicable exclusion amount," and the dollar amount of the credit is the amount of tax that would be due on a transfer of that exclusion amount, applying the rate tables in § 2001(c).[35] For example, in 2011 the exclusion amount was $5,000,000 and the maximum estate tax rate was 35%. If we calculate the tax due on a $5,000,000 transfer in 2011, we get the amount of $1,730,800.[36] That is the amount of the unified credit for an individual making transfers, either by gift or at death, during 2011. The credit is first applied to offset any gift tax liability on transfers made during life, and to the extent a balance remains unused at death, it is available to offset any estate tax liability following the individual's death. Thus, an individual dying in 2011 could have made transfers during life and at death aggregating up to $5,000,000 without incurring any gift or estate tax liability. If she transferred more than $5,000,000 then some tax will be due, because the credit would be exhausted.

The recent legislation introduced a new level of complexity to these calculations, by indexing the exclusion amount, and by increasing the maximum rate. The rate of tax influences the amount of the credit, and because the exclusion amount is adjusted for inflation, the unified credit must be adjusted as well, so that each year the credit will shelter the amount of tax on the exclusion amount. The actual inflation-adjusted amounts of the credit for years since 2010 are as follows:

---

[35] The statute uses the term "tentative tax." For our present purposes, disregard the term "tentative."

[36] Applying the rate tables in effect in 2011, on the last line of the table in § 2001(c) the tax is the sum of the tax on the first $500,000, ($155,800), plus 35% of the excess $5,000,000 over $500,000. 35% of $4,500,000 is $1,575,000. The total tax is therefore $1,730,800.

Year	Exclusion Amount	Max Rate	Unified Credit
2011	$5,000,000	35%	$1,730,800
2012	5,120,000	35%	1,772,800
2013	5,250,000	40%	2,045,800
2014	5,340,000	40%	2,081,800
2015	5,430,000	40%	2,117,800
2016	5,450,000	40%	2,125,800
2017	5,490,000	40%	2,141,800

For estate planning purposes the most important number to focus on in this table (aside from rates) is the exclusion amount, though planners frequently speak in terms of the credit. In order to illustrate the operation of the credit, in the examples that follow we will make the simplifying assumption that for years after 2016 the exclusion amount is fixed at its 2017 amount of $5,490,000, and the unified credit is fixed at $2,141,800.

Calculating the Gift Tax

Section 2501 imposes a tax for each calendar year on all taxable gifts made during that year as computed under § 2502. Under § 2502(a), the amount of gift tax is equal to difference between:

(1) the tentative tax on all taxable gifts made in the current year and in all previous years, and

(2) the tentative tax on all gifts made in previous years.

Both tentative taxes are determined under the table found in § 2001(c)— the same table that is used to determine the estate tax. It can be confusing to some that we must first add up current and prior gifts, and then subtract the tax on the prior gifts. This is necessary because, technically, the rates imposed by the statute are progressive; they increase as the amount of transfers increase. The rate table reaches the maximum rate of 40% when transfers exceed $1,000,000, and transfers below that amount are subject to lower rates (review § 2001(c)). The purpose of adding in prior transfers is simply to place the current transfer in the correct rate bracket, and once that has been accomplished we must subtract the tax on those prior transfers to avoid double taxing them. Under current law, this step is purely mechanical, because the exclusion amount is far more than $1,000,000, so all tax due transfers will be taxed at the 40% rate.

Example #1: **D made no taxable gifts prior to 2017. Beginning in 2017 she made the following taxable gifts (disregard the annual exclusion, and assume a fixed exclusion amount of $5,490,000, and unified credit of $2,141,800):**

Year	Taxable Gifts
2017	$500,000
2018	$500,000
2019	$6,490,000

2017 consequences

In 2017, the gift tax on D's $500,000 gift is $155,800, determined under § 2502(a) as follows:

(1) the tentative tax on $500,000, or $155,800, less

(2) the tentative tax on all prior gifts, here $0.

Note, however, that there will be no gift tax due in 2017 because D is entitled to her unified credit under § 2505(a). Under this provision, D is entitled to the "applicable credit amount" determined under § 2010(c), reduced by any amounts allowable as credits in earlier years. Since D made no prior gifts, the credit allowable in 2017 is the full $2,141,800. D must file a gift tax return, and utilizes $155,800 of her unified credit, so no gift tax is due. The balance of her credit ($1,986,000) is available for future transfers.

2018 consequences

In 2018, the gift tax under § 2502 on D's $500,000 gift is $190,000, determined as follows:

(1) the tentative tax on all current and prior taxable gifts ($1,000,000), or $345,800, less

(2) the tentative tax on all prior taxable gifts ($500,000) or $155,800,

= $190,000[37]

Note once again that D will not actually have to pay any taxes because of the remaining balance of her unified credit. Under § 2505(a), her credit for 2018 is:

(1) the full amount of the credit, $2,141,800, less

(2) the amount of credit previously allowed, $155,800

= $1,986,000.

---

[37] This is an excellent illustration of the effect of the graduated rate tables in § 2001(c), and the reason for adding back prior gifts before computing the tax. Both transfers were of the same amount, but the resulting tax is different. That is because the first transfer was taxed at the 34% rate, while the second was pushed into the 39% rate bracket because of the addition of the prior gift.

This is sufficient to offset her gift tax of $190,000, so again she must file a gift tax return, but will owe no tax. She uses an additional $190,000 of her credit, leaving her with a balance of $1,796,000.

2019 consequences

In 2019, the gift tax under § 2502 on D's $6,490,000 gift is $2,596,000 determined as follows:

(1) the tentative tax on all taxable gifts ($7,490,000), or $2,941,800, less

(2) the tentative tax on all prior taxable gifts ($1,000,000) or $345,800,

= $2,596,000

Under § 2505(a), D is entitled to the balance of her unused credit of $1,796,000 determined as follows:

(1) the full amount of the credit, $2,141,800 less

(2) the amount of credit previously allowed, $345,800

= $1,796,000.

The credit will reduce D's gift tax liability down to $800,000, which she must pay with her gift tax return for 2019. She has now exhausted her entire credit, so that (ignoring inflation adjustments) all future transfers by her will bear a 40% tax.

Notice that if we take a step back, it should come as no surprise that D owes $800,000 in tax. She made total wealth transfers of $7,490,000. D's unified credit protected her from having to pay tax on the first $5,490,000 of those transfers, but the remaining $2,000,000 is not protected by the credit. If we apply the maximum rate of 40% to that amount, we get $800,000 in gift taxes owed.

This example illustrates two important concepts. First, the role of the unified credit is to protect from taxation transfers below the exclusion amount. It does so by offsetting any gift (or estate) tax due. Second, once transfers exceed the exclusion amount, tax will be due, at a rate of 40%. Indeed this example illustrates that it is possible to view the estate and gift tax as imposed at a flat rate of 40% on all wealth transfers in excess of the exclusion amount.

Calculating the Estate Tax

The estate tax is calculated under § 2001(b), which invokes a four-step process:

1. The first step is to determine the total of all taxable wealth transfers made by the decedent during life and at death, and is sometimes referred to as the "unified transfer tax base", or

"UTTB."[38] The UTTB is the sum of the decedent's "taxable estate" plus the amount of any "adjusted taxable gifts" that she may have made during life. Exactly what constitutes a decedent's taxable estate is the subject of much of this book. Suffice it to say for present purposes that it is the decedent's gross estate less certain permitted deductions.[39] "Adjusted taxable gifts" is a term of art that is defined as the amount of taxable gifts made by the decedent during her life that are not otherwise included in her taxable estate.[40]

2.   The second step is to determine the "tentative tax" on the UTTB. The tentative tax is the total amount of tax that the decedent would owe on all of her taxable wealth transfers in the absence of the unified credit if they all had been made in the year of her death.

3.   Section 2001(b)(2) then instructs us to reduce the tentative tax by the amount of gift tax "payable" with respect to any taxable gifts that the decedent made during her life-time.[41] This is the amount of gift tax that the decedent would have been required to pay on those prior gifts determined using the rate schedule under § 2001(c) on the date of the decedent's death.[42] Because it is limited to gift taxes "payable" the amount of gift tax is reduced by the unified credit. The function of this step is similar to that involved in calculating gift taxes. There we subtracted the gift taxes on prior gifts, after we added those gifts to the base, avoiding double taxation. Essentially that is the function of this step as well.

4.   Finally, the estate tax liability determined under § 2001(b) is offset by the unified credit under § 2010(a), resulting in the amount of tax actually due.

The examples below illustrate how the estate tax is computed. For purpose of these examples, assume once again that D is an individual who has never been married, that the applicable exclusion amount for years after 2017 is $5,490,000 and the unified credit is $2,141,800. In addition, ignore the gift tax annual exclusion.

---

[38]   Credit for this terminology goes to Professor Emeritus Leo Schmolka of NYU School of Law School. We adopt it here because we find it very useful. Thanks Len!

[39]   § 2051.

[40]   As we shall see, it is possible for a taxable gift to be included in the donor's estate. See, e.g., §§ 2036–2038.

[41]   The statute actually includes only gifts made after 1976.

[42]   § 2001(g).

Example #2:   **D dies in 2017 with a taxable estate of $5,490,000 having made no taxable gifts during her lifetime.**

Under § 2001(b) we are directed to determine the tentative tax under § 2001(c) on her taxable estate ($5,490,000) plus her adjustable taxable gifts ($0), which is $2,141,800.[43] D's estate however is entitled to a credit under § 2010(c) of $2,141,800 which offsets the tax bill entirely, so no tax would be due.

Variation: **Assume instead that D made a $1,000,000 taxable gift in 2013 and died in 2017 with a taxable estate of $4,490,000.**

While the computation is more complicated, the result is the same: because aggregate lifetime and death transfers do not exceed the exclusion amount, no tax is due. The computation is done as follows:

Step #1: Under § 2001(b)(1), D's UTTB is $5,490,000 determined as follows:

(A)	D's taxable estate	$4,490,000
(B)	adjustable taxable gifts	$1,000,000
		$5,490,000

Step #2: Under § 2001(c), the tentative tax on $5,490,000 is $2,141,800.[44]

Step #3: The tentative tax must be reduced by the amount of tax that would have been *payable* on all of D's taxable gifts, determined using the rates under § 2001(c) in effect for 2017. The amount of gift taxes payable is zero, because the unified credit exceeded the $345,800 tax on the gift.

Step #4: Finally, D's tentative tax of $2,141,800 is reduced by her unified credit, also $2,141,800, and there will be no estate tax due.

Example #3:   **D made a $10,490,000 taxable gift in 2017, and died in 2021 with a taxable estate of $10,000,000.**

In contrast with *Example #2*, here D's earlier gift would result in gift tax liability. The 2017 gift of $10,490,000 would have resulted in a gift tax bill of $2,000,000.[45]

To calculate D's estate tax liability we go through the four step process:

---

[43]   For those who want to review, the tax is $345,800 plus 40% of the excess over $1,000,000. That amounts to $345,800 plus 40% of $4,490,000 [$1,796,000] for a total of $2,141,800.

[44]   The calculation is the same as in note 43.

[45]   Again the calculation would be $345,800 plus 40% of the excess over $1,000,000. That amounts to $345,800 plus 40% of $9,490,000 [$3,796,000] for a total of $4,141,800. This would be offset by the unified credit of $2,141,800, leaving $2,000,000 in tax due.

Step #1: Under § 2001(b), D's UTTB is $20,490,000 determined as follows:

(A)	D's taxable estate	$10,000,000
(B)	adjustable taxable gifts	$10,490,000
		$20,490,000

Step #2: Under § 2001(c), the tentative tax on $20,490,000 is $8,141,800.[46]

Step #3: The tax that would have been payable on D's taxable gifts using 2021 rates would have been $2,000,000 determined as follows:

Tentative Gift Tax on $10,490,000	$4,141,800, less
adjustable taxable gifts	$2,141,800
	$2,000,000

Therefore the tentative tax is reduced by this amount to $6,141,800.

Step #4: Finally, to determine the actual tax due, the tentative tax is further reduced by the unified credit:

$6,141,800

$2,141,800

$4,000,000

Thus, D's executor must pay $4,000,000 with the estate tax return for D's estate. Once again, if we take a step back, this result is not surprising. Before D died, she had already used up her entire unified credit, therefore we would anticipate that her entire taxable estate of $10,000,000 would be taxed at the rate of 40%. This is exactly what happened! Again, one can view the unified estate and gift regime to be a flat tax on all taxable transfers in excess of the applicable exclusion.

As the examples illustrate, the unified credit has the effect of exempting a dollar amount of wealth transfers for each transferor, whether those transfers are made during life or at death. Only after a transferor transfers wealth in excess of that exempted by the credit, will there be gift or estate tax due. Also, the rate tables applicable to all transfers are the same. Thus, unification has narrowed the ability of taxpayers to lower their

---

[46] Calculated as $345,800 plus 40% of the excess over $1,000,000. That amounts to $345,800 plus 40% of $19,490,000 [$7,796,000] for a total of $8,141,800.

transfer taxes through the use of lifetime gifts, in contrast with pre-1976 law. It has, however, not completed eliminated that possibility.

Continued Benefits of Lifetime Giving

Even though the 1976 Act's unification limited the ability of taxpayers to lower their tax liability through the separate rate schedules and exemptions, after unification there are still ways in which a decedent's estate tax bill can be lowered through the making of lifetime gifts. Think about our decedent in *Example #2*. We assumed that the decedent either (1) died owning assets of $5,490,000, or (2) made a gift of $1,000,000 of those assets during life, and then died with and estate of $4,490,000. But that is not the whole story. What we (purposely) ignored was the fact that the $1,000,000 in assets gifted during life may well have increased in value between the time of the gift and the decedent's death in 2017. The same is true of our decedent in *Example #3*, who transferred $10,490,000 during life. We calculated her transfer tax liability on that transfer at the time of the gift, in 2017. Any increase in value between the time of the gift and D's death in 2021 is not touched by the gift or the estate tax. As a result, through making lifetime gifts an individual can essentially "freeze" the value of a particular asset for transfer tax purposes; once a gift is reached by the gift tax any increase in the value of the gift belongs to the donee, and is not included in the donor's estate.[47]

Another way to reduce transfer tax liability by making lifetime gifts is to take advantage of the "tax exclusive" nature of the gift tax. Consider the decedent in *Example #3*. Had that decedent not made her lifetime gift, the $10,490,000 in gifted assets, together with any appreciation in those assets, would have been included in her estate at death. What else would have been included in her estate? Note that the $2,000,000 in gift taxes paid with respect to the 2017 gift was also removed from her estate, together with any growth in those funds. That check went to the government, and it was *not subject to tax*. Had D not made the gift, those funds (and any growth on those funds) would have been in her estate at death, and would have been subjected to the estate tax. This illustrates what is often referred to as the "tax exclusive" nature of the gift tax. In contrast with the estate tax, where the funds used to pay the tax are part of the tax base ("tax inclusive"), funds used to pay gift taxes are not part of the measure of the gift, hence the term "tax exclusive." While the benefit is offset somewhat by the fact that the taxpayer is paying the tax dollars earlier than he otherwise would, giving the government the use of the money in the interim, the benefit remains.[48]

---

[47] In fact, there are certain types of lifetime transfers that will be brought back into the estate, but we will reserve that discussion until later.

[48] As we will learn later in the course, if the gift is made within three years of death, the gift taxes paid are brought back into the estate, in order to mitigate this effect. So, in our example, had

Finally, there is another important method of reducing transfer taxes through lifetime gifts that is commonly availed of: the annual exclusion. As we will discuss in more detail in **Chapter Two**, amounts sheltered from the gift tax by the annual exclusion are completely removed from the transfer tax base.

The Estate and Gift Taxes Are Now a "Flat Tax" on Amounts over the Exclusion Amount

We stated above that the complicated calculations under §§ 2001 and 2502 are no longer necessary, and that is largely true, certainly in the planning context. That is because under the current rate schedules, the maximum rate of 40% is achieved at $1,000,000, which is well below the current exclusion amount of $5,000,000, as adjusted for inflation. As a result, calculating the tax is much simpler: it is essentially a flat tax of 40% on transfers over the exclusion amount. Thus, in many cases the complicated calculations that we performed above are no longer necessary once a taxpayer transfers assets in excess of the exclusion amount.

To illustrate, assume single taxpayer D dies in 2017 with a taxable estate of $8,490,000, having made no prior gifts.

The long way: Using the mechanism of the statute used above, the tax on $8,490,000 under the rate tables is $345,800 plus 40% of $7,490,000, or $2,996,000, for a total of $3,341,800. The unified credit is the amount of tax due of an estate of $5,490,000, which is $2,141,800. Thus, the tax due by the estate is $1,200,000.

The short cut: D's estate exceeds the exclusion amount by $3,000,000. Thus, the tax will be 40% of that amount, or $1,200,000.

So now that we have fought our way through the trees, you can comfortably rely on the shortcut for purposes of estimating tax liability. This is certainly what estate planning practitioners do.

Part D. Introduction to Generation-Skipping Transfers

As noted at the beginning of this chapter, historically if a family was wealthy enough they could bypass the transfer tax at one or more generations by "skipping" generations. As we saw in the example above, historically if Grandparent placed assets in trust for Child's benefit, rather than leaving them outright to Child, they could pass to Grandchild on Child's death without imposition of an estate tax. Similarly, if Grandparent left the assets directly to Grandchild, skipping Child entirely, the family could again eliminate tax on one generation.

D made the gift within three years of her death, the $2,000,000 of gift taxes paid would have been included in her gross estate. See § 2035(b).

Congress' first attempt to address the generation skipping problem was in 1976. The tax enacted was fatally flawed, and was repealed before it ever became effective. In 1986, however, Congress enacted a new and improved Tax on Generation Skipping Transfers ("GST tax"), found in Chapter 13 of the Code, beginning with Section 2601. The GST tax is quite complicated and is discussed in detail in *Chapter Nine*. In general, the GST tax may apply whenever a gratuitous transfer is deemed to skip a generation. To illustrate, in the example above if Grandparent leaves assets directly to Grandchild, that would constitute a generation skipping transfer. Similarly, if Grandparent created a trust providing income to Child for life, remainder to Grandchild, the death of Child would also constitute a generation skipping transfer. There is a GST tax exemption applicable to all transferors, which is tied to the exclusion amount under § 2010, so that in 2017 the exemption is $5,490,000. When it does apply the GST hits hard: it imposes a tax at the maximum estate tax rate of 40%, and the tax will apply *in addition to* estate or gift taxes. For example, in the case where Grandparent left her assets directly to Grandchild, if Grandparent's estate was sufficiently large then the assets going to Grandchild would be subject not only the estate tax, but to the GST tax as well.

Because of the complexity of the statute, we will delay further discussion of the details of the GST tax until *Chapter Nine*.

Part E. Related Income Tax Issues

Intertwined with the policy issues surrounding the transfer taxes are various income tax issues, most importantly the rules determining the basis of property transferred by gift or at death. For those students who have not studied income tax, this will provide a quick overview.

For income tax purposes, gains that accrue on assets go untaxed until they are "realized," which normally means the asset is sold or exchanged. At the time property is sold or exchanged, gain is realized to the extent that the "amount realized" (i.e., the sales price) exceeds the "adjusted basis" (at its simplest, its cost). For example, if I purchase stock for $100, hold it for ten years and sell it for $500, I will pay tax on the $400 gain at the time I sell it. Under current law, this gain is taxed as long term capital gain, at a preferential rate, currently no more than 23.8%[49] in most circumstances.

The question relevant here is what happens if instead of selling the stock when it is worth $500, I make an intervivos gift of the stock to my child, or I die and leave it to my child by will. Neither the gift nor my death will trigger recognition of the gain for income tax purposes. In the case of

---

[49] Under § 1(h), this gain would be subject to a maximum tax rate of 20%. However, under § 1411(a) an additional 3.8% tax is imposed on "net investment income", which includes capital gains.

an intervivos gift, the donee takes a basis in the property equal to that of the donor.[50] Thus, if I gift the stock in the above example to my child, she will take a basis in the stock equal to mine, or $100, and if and when *she* sells the stock, she will report as gain the difference between her amount realized and that basis.

However, a very different rule applies if property is transferred at death. Under § 1014(a), the basis of property received from a decedent is equal to the fair market value of the property at death. Thus, the basis is essentially "stepped-up" or "stepped down" to its date of death value. The effect of this rule is to eliminate any accrued gains (and losses) from income taxation at death. So, for example, if I die when the stock has a value of $500, and leave it to my child in my will, my child will take a basis in the stock equal to $500, and if she subsequently sells it she will only report gains or losses that accrue during the time that she owns the stock.

Moving Forward

Now that we have gained a little perspective on the transfer tax system as a whole, we will turn to a detailed study of the three transfer taxes. Teachers differ on where best to begin; what we have chosen to do here is begin with an introduction to the gift tax, which we believe will give you a helpful foundation before we move to the estate tax. So in *Chapter Two* we will undertake to introduce important gift tax principles that we will encounter throughout the course.

---

[50] § 1015(a). There is a different rule that applies if the transferred property has depreciated in the hands of the donor that effectively prevents the shifting of that loss to the donee.

CHAPTER TWO

GIFT TAX FUNDAMENTALS

■ ■ ■

As noted in **Chapter One**, the primary role of the gift tax is to backstop the estate tax, to prevent depletion of an estate by lifetime transfers.[1] Since unification of the estate & gift taxes in 1976, the unified credit allows an individual to pass a certain amount of wealth ("the exclusion amount") tax free, during life and at death. Thus, to the extent that an individual's unified credit is not used to offset the tax on gifts made during life, it available to offset estate tax at death. As also noted in **Chapter One**, however, unification is not complete: there are still opportunities for tax savings through the making of lifetime gifts.

Part A. Transfers Subject to the Tax

Section 2501 of the Code imposes a gift tax on a completed "transfer of property by gift". The statute does not define either the term "property" or "gift." In this section we will explore the meaning of those terms, and in Part B we address the question of when a gift is complete.

What Is a Gift?"

Donative Intent

Although the statute does not define the term "gift," § 2512(b) provides some assistance. It states that "where property is transferred for less than full and adequate consideration in money or money's worth, then the amount by which the value of the property exceeded the value of the consideration shall be deemed a gift."

Those students who have studied basic income tax will no doubt remember *Commissioner v. Duberstein,*[2] in which the Supreme Court defined the term "gift" for purposes of the income tax as one made from "detached and disinterested generosity." This definition requires an inquiry into the donor's intention in making a transfer, whether it was motivated by "affection, respect, admiration, charity or like impulses." Only

---

[1] It is worth noting that the 2001 Act de-coupled the estate and gift taxes, to some extent. The exclusion for gift taxes was fixed at $1,000,000, while the estate tax exclusion increased eventually to $3,500,000. This was apparently a result of concerns about income tax avoidance through gifts. Since the 2010 Act the two taxes have been re-unified, and are subject to the same exclusion amount.

[2] 363 U.S. 278 (1960).

transfers so motivated are eligible for exclusion from the donee's income under § 102 of the Code.

The inquiry is not the same under the gift tax, and the reason lies in the role of the gift tax in backstopping the estate tax: its function is to prevent taxpayers from depleting their taxable estates by making lifetime transfers. Section 2512(b) therefore directs the inquiry into whether a transfer was made for adequate and full consideration in money or money's worth. If it was not, then a gift will exist, because if a transfer of property has not been replaced with property of equal value, the donor has depleted his estate. Consider D, who owns a painting worth $1,000,000. If D sells the painting, it will no longer be in her estate at death, but the $1,000,000 proceeds will be.[3] Her estate is not depleted by the sale. However, if she makes a gift of the painting to her daughter, neither the painting nor any sale proceeds will be in her estate at death; her estate has been depleted by the gift.

The leading case in this area is *Commissioner v. Wemyss*,[4] in which the Supreme Court needed to decide whether a taxpayer made a taxable gift when he transferred stock to his future wife in exchange for her agreement to marry him. The bride-to-be was the income beneficiary of a trust created by her deceased husband's will, and her interest would terminate in the event of her remarriage. The couple agreed that if the taxpayer transferred stock to her, she would marry him, and suffer the loss of trust income. The Court of Appeals found that the existence of the arm's length bargaining that took place negated any "donative intent," and hence there was no gift. The Supreme Court reversed, holding that the language of the statute (the predecessor of § 2512(b)) makes inquiry into the existence or lack of donative intent unnecessary: the sole inquiry is whether the value of the asset in the estate is replaced with consideration of equal value in money or money's worth.[5] In Wemyss, the taxpayer transferred stock, and nothing replaced it. In *Merrill v. Fahs*,[6] a case decided the same day as *Weymss*, the court similarly found for the government where the transfer in anticipation of marriage was made not in exchange for a promise to marry, but for release of the bride-to-be's marital property rights under a pre-nuptial agreement. The regulations

---

[3] Unless, of course, she consumes the proceeds.

[4] 324 U.S. 303 (1945).

[5] Income tax students may also remember the *Farid-es-Sultaneh* case, in which the Second Circuit Court of Appeals, just three years after *Weymss*, found that a transfer of stock in contemplation of marriage was *not* at a gift for purposes of calculating the basis of the transferee: in that case the bride to be was given a cost basis because she received the stock in exchange for release of valuable marital rights. The Commissioner argued that *Weymss* should control. Noting the different purposes of the income tax and the transfer taxes, the court stated "in our opinion the income tax provisions are not to be construed as though they were in pari material with either the estate tax law or the gift tax statutes." The court held that the surrender of marital rights was valuable consideration for purposes of the income tax, even though it would not be for gift tax purposes. Farid-Es-Sultaneh v. Commissioner, 160 F.2d 812 (2nd Cir. 1947).

[6] 324 U.S. 308 (1945).

now expressly provide that: "A consideration not reducible to a value in money or money's worth, as love and affection, promise of marriage, etc., is to be wholly disregarded. . . . Similarly, a relinquishment of a dower or curtesy . . . or of other marital property rights in the spouse's property or estate, shall not be considered to any extent a consideration "in money or money's worth."[7] Again, the taxpayer parted with property and nothing replaced it.

Ordinary Business Transactions

While it is tempting to say that donative intent is entirely irrelevant for gift tax purposes, it does play a role to some extent. Under the regulations at § 25.2512–8, "a sale, exchange or other transfer of property made in the ordinary course of business (a transfer which is bona fide, at arm's length, and free from any donative intent), will be considered as made for adequate and full consideration" within the meaning of the statute. This provision makes it unnecessary to examine ordinary business transactions, or more broadly market transactions, to determine if full consideration was truly paid, an inquiry that would be impossible for the government in any event. Under the regulations, so long as a transaction takes place in the ordinary course of business, the consideration requirement is deemed satisfied. The question of donative intent comes in when deciding whether the transaction is in the ordinary course.

To illustrate, assume T owns a piece of property appraised at $1,000,000. She sells it to X for $900,000. Should this be treated as a gift of $100,000? The regulations tell us it will not if it was made in the ordinary course of T's business. So we need to know more, including the identity of X. If T and X are unrelated, and bargained at arms' length for the sale price, then we will deem the consideration to be adequate. If, however, there is some relationship between X and T and the facts indicate a lack of bargaining and an intent on T's part to make a gift to X, then the bargain element of the sale will represent a gift subject to the tax.

Support Obligations

Does a parent make a gift when she purchases food and clothing for her child, or pays her child's private school tuition? While clearly there has been a transfer for no consideration, the transfer is not necessarily a gift. Who is the beneficiary of that transfer? If the transfer discharges the transferor's obligation under local law to support the child, then there is no gift.

Perhaps the best justification for this rule is that when the parent is simply meeting her obligation to support her child, she is not making a gift. In a very real sense, she is consuming the property for her own benefit by

---

[7] § 25.2512–8.

discharging her own obligation, and one's own consumption is never treated as a gift. Determining just what comes within the support obligation can be tricky: the age of majority for this purpose will vary from state to state, and the level of support provided will vary from family to family. For this reason, the American Law Institute in 1969 proposed excluding any "transfers for consumption" to the transferor's child or any other member of the transferor's household.[8] Consistent with this study, in 1981 Congress enacted § 2503(e), which excludes certain transfers to health providers and educational institutions from the gift tax base that might otherwise be considered taxable gifts. In addition, in the case of many other transfers, the basic annual exclusion might very well obviate the issue. Both of these exclusions are discussed in Part D of this chapter.

What Is Property?

Cash & Non-Cash Assets

The other essential element of a gift under § 2501 is a transfer of "property." The term "property" clearly encompasses transfers of cash and non-cash assets alike. Valuing cash and publicly traded stock poses no serious problem, but valuing more complex assets, like closely held business interests, real property, personal property, art and antiques, can be much more difficult. In **Chapter Ten** we discuss the methods used for valuing these "hard to value" assets.

Interests in Trust

In construing the term "property," the courts have taken an expansive view and have included various property interests, including vested and contingent interests in trusts. For now we put aside the issue of how to value such interests, which we will discuss in Part C, below.

> **Vested interests.** Assume D transfer his residence into trust, providing that he will have the use and benefit of the property for life, and that it will be distributed to his daughter, or her estate, on his death.[9] D has transferred a vested remainder interest in the trust to his daughter, and its value will be taxed as a gift. It will be valued in accordance with the rules discussed in Part C of this chapter.

> **Contingent Interests.** Assume D transfers stock into a trust that provides for income to his mother for life, remainder to D if he survives his mother, and if not then to his daughter. D has clearly made a gift of the income interest. But what about the interest to his daughter? She has a remainder interest in the

---

[8] American Law Institute, Federal Estate and Gift Taxation 19–21(1969).

[9] This is essentially the same as transferring a remainder interest in the house to his daughter, reserving a legal life estate, and the same rules apply to such transfers.

trust, but unlike the above example it is not vested. It is contingent upon D *not* surviving his mother, a contingency that is obviously difficult to evaluate. Does that mean D has not made a gifts of the remainder? In *Smith v. Shaughnessy*[10] the Supreme Court's rejected the taxpayer's argument under similar facts that he had not made a gift of the remainder. That case and the method of valuing such interests is discussed further in Part C.

Services

A gift of services is not a transfer of property, and hence not subject to the tax. This is in contrast with the income tax regulations, which include "income realized in any form, whether in money, property, or services."[11] Thus, if I enter into a barter transaction with my doctor, and exchange legal services for medical services, I will have income subject to the income tax. If I render legal services without charge to my daughter I have not made a taxable gift. The basis for the distinction is a little unclear, although it probably makes sense for several reasons. In the income tax context, the rule is necessary to avoid a shift to a barter economy that could erode the tax base in a meaningful way. In the gift tax context, the chances of me seriously depleting my estate by rendering services to my daughter instead of a paying client are probably pretty low, and unlikely to justify the valuation complications. There is always the question of taxpayer tolerance, as well, which would be tested by a rule taxing gratuitous services to one's family members.

If my services ripen into a property right, which I transfer to my daughter, that is another story. If I perform legal services to a paying client and then transfer the right to be paid to my daughter, I have at this point made a transfer of property within the meaning of the statute. The issue has arisen in the context of executor's commissions, which are often waived when one family member acts as administrator of an estate. Rulings in the area respect the waiver if it is made shortly after the executor begins rendering services (gift of services, not property) but disregard the waiver if made after the services are performed (gift of property, not services).[12]

Use of Property, Below Market Loans

If a donor lends money to a child, under an enforceable promissory note, no gift of the principal has been made. However, if that loan bears no interest (or interest at a steeply discounted rate), then the loan provides a significant economic benefit. The question is, should that economic benefit be subject to the gift tax? Early cases, in both the income and gift tax contexts, rejected the Commissioner's attempts to tax these transactions

---

[10]　*Smith v. Shaughnessy*, 318 U.S. 176 (1943).

[11]　§ 1.61–1(a).

[12]　Rev. Rul. 64–225, 1964–2 CB 15, and Rev. Rul. 66–167, 1966–1 CB 20.

for both income and gift tax purposes.[13] As a result, interest-free loans became a popular tool for avoidance of income and gift taxes. Consider for example, a wealthy parent who prior to 1984 makes a demand loan of $1,000,000 to her son at a zero percent interest rate. Assume that the parent's other cash is invested in CD's that earn 4% per year. What income and transfer tax benefits accrue from the loan?

Income Tax: If the parent had invested the funds, she would have earned $40,000 per year, fully taxable at the parent's rate. If instead the child invests the funds, the child will report the interest on the investment at perhaps a lower tax rate. Thus, interest free loans allowed for shifting of investment income from the lender to the borrower, and in the years when interest rates were significantly higher and income tax rates were steeply graduated, the benefit could be substantial.

Transfer Taxes: If the parent invested the funds, earned $40,000 on the investment, and transferred those earnings to the child, she would have made a taxable gift. But if instead the parent lends the $1,000,000 to the child, who makes the same investment, the child ends up with $40,000 but there has been no gift. Additionally, if the child invests the loaned funds, any growth in the value of the assets would also accrue to the child's benefit at no gift tax cost. So, for example, assume the child invested the $1 million loan proceeds in stock that grew to $2,000,000 by the time the loan is repaid. The child would repay the $1,000,000 in principal, but the $1,000,000 in appreciation would escape the gift tax.

Because of the government's lack of success in the courts, below market loans were widely used as income and estate planning tools until 1984. In that year the Supreme Court decided *Dickman v. Commissioner*,[14] and accepted the government's argument that an interest-free loan is economically equivalent to an interest-bearing loan, coupled with a gift in which the lender funds the borrower's interest costs. As we will see in **Chapter Three**, in the estate tax context the Court has taken a narrow approach to defining what constitutes a property interest for purposes of the basic estate tax inclusion section, § 2033. The majority in *Dickman* caught many by surprise when it took a much broader view when considering what constitutes a "transfer of property" for purposes of § 2501, stating "we have little difficulty accepting the theory that the use of valuable property—in this case money—is itself a legally protectable property interest." In dissent, Justice Powell criticized the majority's role in overturning the "long-standing principle" that interest-free loans were not subject to the gift tax, arguing instead that the Court should have left the issue to Congress. Further, Justice Powell noted that the majority's

---

[13]	*J. Simpson Dean v. Commissioner,* 35 T.C. 1083 (1961) (income tax), *Crown v. Commissioner,* 67 T.C. 1060, aff'd 585 F.2d 234 (7th Cir. 1978) (gift tax).

[14]	465 U.S. 330 (1984).

expansive reading of § 2501, and the language quoted above, could extend well beyond the interest-free loan situation, stating:

> Under this theory, potential tax liability may arise in a wide range of situations involving the unrecompensed use of property. Examples could include the rent-free use of a home by a child over the age of minority who lives with his parent, or by a parent who lives with her child. Taken to its logical extreme, this theory would make the loan of a car for a brief period a potentially taxable event.

The majority acknowledged these possibilities, but dismissed their significance on the assumption that the IRS would not pursue them.

In the same year as the *Dickman* case, Congress enacted § 7872, which provides specific rules for taxing below market loans, including loans in the nature of gifts, both for income and gift tax purposes.[15] The statute follows the government's argument in *Dickman* by imputing payments that don't actually take place: the interest foregone on the loan is treated as transferred from the lender to the borrower, and repaid to the lender as interest. These imputed transfers have gift and income tax consequences: the lender has made a gift of the foregone interest, and has income equal to the interest payment deemed received. Arguably Congress' failure to provide rules for taxing other "use of property" situations indicates its desire not to pursue those possibilities, although the potential reach of *Dickman* remains unclear.

In order to tax below market loans, Congress needed to identify some rate of interest to use as a benchmark. It chose the "applicable federal rate," or "AFR," in effect under § 1274(d), which is published monthly.[16] A gift loan[17] is a below market loan subject to § 7872 if it bears interest at a rate lower than the AFR. The treatment of a gift loan under § 7872 depends on whether it is a demand loan or a term loan.[18] For income tax purposes, *all* below market gift loans are governed by § 7872(a), which treats the amount of foregone interest[19] as transferred from the lender to the borrower as a gift, and then retransferred back to the lender as interest. For gift tax purposes, while demand loans are also governed by § 7872(a), term loans

---

[15] The statute applies to loans made in other contexts as well, including corporation-shareholder loans and employer-employee loans.

[16] This is, essentially, the government's rate of borrowing, expressed as a short-term, mid-term or long-term rate. If the loan in question is for a set term, the rate will be that on U.S. bonds with a similar term. If the loan is a demand loan, the rate used is the federal short-term rate. § 7872(f)(2). The AFR is substantially below commercial loan rates, which means that in a world of high interest rates there remain opportunities for planning using below market loans.

[17] Defined as any below-market loan where the foregoing of interest is in the nature of a gift. § 7872(f)(3).

[18] A demand loan is one that is repayable on the lender's demand. A term loan entitles the borrower to use the money for a set term.

[19] § 7872(e)(2).

are governed by § 7872(b).[20] Under this provision, the excess of the amount loaned over the present value of all payments due under the loan (discounted by the AFR) will be treated as a gift in the year that the loan was made. A de minimis exception makes § 7872 inapplicable to gift loans between individuals if the aggregate amount of loans outstanding between those individuals is $10,000 or less, although the exception does not apply if the borrower uses the loan funds for investment purposes.[21]

To illustrate these rules, consider the following example and variation. In both cases, assume the **AFR is 4% compounded annually**, and ignore the annual exclusion (discussed in Part C below).

Example #1: **Parent lends Child $1,000,000 on January 1, 2017, repayable on demand, at zero percent interest, and the loan is outstanding throughout the year.**

Because it bears an interest rate below the AFR, this is a below market loan. For both income and gift tax purposes, this gift loan is treated under § 7872(a). The forgone interest is $40,000.[22] On December 31, 2017 Parent is treated as transferring that amount to Child, and Child is treated as transferring the same amount back to Parent as interest. For income tax purposes, Parent has $40,000 of interest income and Child has interest expense of $40,000. For gift tax purposes, Parent has made a taxable gift to the child of $40,000. The income and gift tax consequences will recur each year the loan is outstanding.

Variation: **On January 1, 2017, Parent lends Child $1,000,000 at zero percent interest. The loan is repayable in 5 years.**

For income tax purposes, this loan is treated under § 7872(a) and the income tax consequences are exactly the same as in *Example #1*.[23] For gift tax purposes, however, this loan is treated under § 7872(b). Under § 7872(b) the foregone interest is equal to the excess of the amount loaned ($1,000,000), over the present value of all required payments on the loan. The present value of $1,000,000 payable in 5 years discounted by 4% is roughly $822,000. Therefore the foregone interest of $178,000 is treated as a gift from Parent to Child on the date the loan was made. While the income consequences will recur each year, there will be no further gift tax consequences from the loan.

---

[20] § 7872(d)(2).

[21] § 7872(c)(2).

[22] $1,000,000 times 4% = $40,000.

[23] § 7872(d)(5) taxes gift term loans as demand loans for income tax purposes only.

Part B. The Concept of "Completed Gift"

Section 2501(a) imposes a tax on the "transfer of property by gift." Until the gift is completed, the tax will not be triggered. The timing of a gift can be important for a number of reasons. The issue rarely comes up in the case of outright transfers of property.[24] It arises most frequently when a transfer is made in trust, and the donor retains some level of control over the property after the transfer, either in her individual capacity or as trustee of the trust. Essential to completion of a gift is the surrender by the donor of "dominion and control" over the transferred property.

The issue of when a gift in trust is complete arose early in the history of the gift tax, when donors had an incentive to argue that a transfer in trust made prior to the effective date should escape the tax. In *Burnet v. Guggenheim*[25] the taxpayer created two trusts for the benefit of his children in 1917, when there was no gift tax. The taxpayer retained broad powers over the trusts, including the right to revoke them. The Tax Act of 1924 enacted the first gift tax. In July of 1925 the taxpayer surrendered his retained powers over the trust, including the right to revoke. At that time, the trust assets were worth approximately $13,000,000. The taxpayer argued that the gift took place 1917, well before the effective date of the taxing statute, and the government argued that the gift was not complete until he surrendered his power to revoke in 1925, resulting in a gift tax bill of almost $2,500,000. In holding for the government, the court found that the power of revocation retained by the taxpayer rendered the gifts "inchoate and imperfect." No gift took place until that power was surrendered, and when it was, the gift tax should apply.

The Court turned to the issue again in *Sanford v. Commissioner,*[26] where the trust in issue, created in 1913, gave the grantor the right to revoke, and allowed him to change the identity of the beneficiaries. In 1917 he gave up the right to revoke, but retained the power to change the trust beneficiaries, excluding himself as a potential recipient. In August 1924, after the effective date of the gift tax, Sanford surrendered his remaining powers over the trust. He died in 1928. The Court rejected the estate's argument that the gift was complete in 1917, when Sanford gave up the right to revoke. It held that the gift was not completed until August 1924, when he surrendered his remaining powers over the trust, and it was not until then that he "fully parted with his interest in the property given."

The question of when a gift is complete remains important today for a number of reasons. First, for those gifts resulting in tax due, the timing of

---

[24] One issue that does come up is when a gift by check is made. If a donor writes a check in one year, but it is not deposited or cashed by the donee until the following year, the gift does not take place until the following year. In the interim the donor could revoke the gift. See, e.g., Rev. Rul. 96–56, 1996–2 CB 162.

[25] 288 U.S. 280 (1933).

[26] 308 U.S. 39 (1939).

the gift will determine when the liability for the tax arises; gift tax returns must be filed annually. Second, if the gift would qualify for the annual exclusion, the timing of the gift will determine the year in which the exclusion will be utilized. Third, and perhaps most importantly, the making of a gift has the effect of "freezing" the value of the gifted asset for transfer tax purposes, even if no gift tax is currently due because of the exclusion amount. This often creates an incentive by a donor to transfer property as early as possible. Yet the donor may not be fully prepared to part with control over the asset. This attempt to transfer the property yet retain strings may result in the inclusion of the property in the donor's estate under one of the "transfer" sections discussed in ***Chapter Four***. But even if it does not, the date for fixing value of the transferred asset may be delayed if the donor has not parted with dominion and control.

The regulations at § 25.2511–2 incorporate the principles of the early cases, and provide guidance on when a donor has made a completed gift. The basic proposition is that a gift is complete when "the donor has so parted with dominion and control as to leave in him no power to change its disposition, whether for his own benefit or for the benefit of another."[27] A transfer in trust can create multiple interests, and the regulations make clear that a single transfer can result in a gift of one interest that is complete, and a gift of another that is not. Thus, each interest created must be examined separately to determine if the transferor has parted with dominion and control.[28]

Under the regulations, the power to revoke a transfer will render a gift incomplete. So too will a power to change the identities or shares of the beneficiaries, unless it is a fiduciary power constrained by an "ascertainable standard,"[29] discussed in more detail below.

The treatment of jointly held powers depends on the identity of the co-holder of the power. If the co-holder of the power has an interest that is substantially adverse to its exercise, the donor will not be considered to have retained dominion and control over the interest.[30]

The following examples illustrate the rules of the regulations.

Example #2: **Grantor transfers property in trust to T as Trustee. The trust provides for income to A for life, remainder to B, or his estate. Grantor reserves the power to direct the Trustee to distribute principal to B during A's life.**

The gift of the income interest to A is not complete. Notice that the Grantor's power to distribute the principal to B allows the Grantor to

---

[27] § 25.2511–2(b).

[28] Id.

[29] § 25.2511–2(c).

[30] § 25.2511–2(e).

reduce A's interest by diverting the property (and its future income) to B. The gift of the remainder interest to B, however, is complete. The Grantor's power over the principal cannot reduce B's interest. Her power over the principal allows the Grantor to decide when, not to whom, the principal will be distributed. As further discussed in *Example #6*, below, such powers that merely affect the time and manner of enjoyment of the property will not prevent completion of a gift.[31].

Variation 2(a): The trust requires that T consent to any distribution to B.

T, as Trustee, does not have an interest in the property that will be negatively affected by the exercise of the power (i.e., no "adverse interest"), and as a result the gift of the income interest is not complete.[32]

Variation 2(b): The trust requires that A must consent to any distribution to B.

A clearly has an interest that is substantially adverse to exercise of the Grantor's power. Any distribution to B would deprive A of the income from that portion of the trust. As a result, the gift of both the income interest and the remainder are complete.

Example #3: In year one Grantor transfers property in trust, naming herself as Trustee. The trust directs the Trustee to distribute the income to Grantor's daughter D for life, remainder to Grantor's son S, or his estate.

In this case, even though Grantor acts as Trustee of the trust, the Trustee has no power to determine who will receive the income or the remainder, so she has made a completed gift of the entire property. Although Grantor's role as Trustee puts her in control of the trust investment decisions, which could certainly impact the amount of income generated by the trust, the regulations hold that fiduciary powers that do not allow the donor to change the beneficiaries will not render the gift incomplete.[33]

Example #4: In year one Grantor transfers property in trust, naming herself as Trustee. The trust directs the Trustee to divide the income between D and S in such shares as the Trustee deems appropriate. On the death of the survivor of D and S, the trust is to be distributed to Grantor's issue, by representation.

---

[31] § 25.2511–2(d).

[32] Id. One might argue that T is adverse, because T's right to trustee compensation would be adversely affected if trust principal was distributed to B. Nevertheless, the cited regulation makes it clear that a Trustee, as such, lacks an interest adverse to disposition of the property or its income.

[33] § 25.2511–2(g).

Now, by naming herself as Trustee, Grantor has retained the unconstrained power to determine how to divide the trust's income between D and S. Therefore the gift of the income interest is incomplete.[34] Because the Grantor has retained no power over the remainder, the gift of the remainder is complete.

Variation 4(a): **The Grantor distributes the first year's income ($200,000) entirely to D.**

The income interest was incomplete when it was created. But when the first year's income is distributed to D, Grantor has parted with control of that amount. Grantor has made a gift of $200,000 to D at the time she makes the distribution.[35]

Variation 4(b): **In year three Grantor irrevocably resigns as Trustee, naming her attorney as successor Trustee.**

Once Grantor resigns as Trustee, she no longer has control over the income, so at that time the gift of the income interest becomes complete.[36] Note that in this case the gift of the remainder is complete in year one, while the gift of the income interest is not complete until year three.

Example #5: **In year one Grantor transfers property in trust, naming herself as Trustee. The trust directs the Trustee to distribute the income under the variations described below. On the death of D, the trust is to be distributed to S, or his estate. For the reasons we have discussed above, the gift of the remainder is complete. In this example we want to focus solely on the income interest.**

Variation 5(a): **The trust directs the Trustee to divide the income between D and S in such shares as the Trustee deems appropriate.**

This variation is a repeat of *Example #4*, above. Grantor's unconstrained power will render the gift of the income interest incomplete.

Variation 5(b): **The Trustee is to distribute $50,000 of income each year to D for her life, with the balance going to S, or his estate.**

In this case, because the amounts passing to D are fixed, the Grantor has parted with dominion and control on creation of the trust, and the gift of the income interest is complete at that time.

---

[34] Id.

[35] See § 25.2511–2(f), which provides that the receipt of income by the beneficiary frees the income from the power, and constitutes a gift of the income.

[36] Similarly, § 25.2511–2(f) provides that termination or relinquishment of a power is the event that completes the gift.

Variation 5(c): The trust provides that the Trustee shall distribute income to D as needed for her health, education, maintenance and support in her accustomed standard of living. The balance of the income is payable to S or his estate.

Variations 5(a) and 5(b) create a spectrum: at one end is *Variation 5(a)*, the incomplete gift, where the Grantor as Trustee retains full discretion over the amounts of income to be distributed to D and S. At the opposite end of the spectrum is *Variation 5(b)*, the completed gift, where the Trustee is directed to distribute a fixed dollar amount of income to D. The question is where to place the power described in *Variation 5(c)* on the spectrum; because the amounts are to some extent within the Trustee's (Grantor's) discretion, we could say the gift is incomplete. But the Trustee's discretion is not unlimited. The trust provides a standard for the exercise of that discretion: health, education, maintenance and support. This standard may sufficiently limit the Grantor's discretion as Trustee so that the power will end up on the completed gift end of the spectrum.

The concept of "ascertainable standard" is one we will encounter frequently in this course. It is particularly important when we discuss the estate taxation of powers of appointment. In the current context, § 25.2511–1(g)(2) provides guidance on the issue: it seeks to identify what is a "clearly measurable standard under which the holder of a power is legally accountable." In our example, if D were in need of income to pay her living expenses, and the Trustee refused to distribute the income to her, she could request a court to determine the amounts to which she is entitled. By considering her standard of living, and her rent, food, medical and other expenses, a court could come up with a number that the Trustee should distribute to her. In fact, these magic words "health, education, maintenance and support" are the classic ascertainable standard. Contrast that language with a trust in which the Trustee is to distribute income as needed for the beneficiary's "happiness." That is not a measurable standard, and hence the gift would be incomplete.

Example #6: **Grantor transfers assets to a trust, naming herself as Trustee. The terms of the trust provide that for 10 years the net income of the trust shall be distributed to Grantor's daughter D in such amounts as the Trustee deems appropriate. Any income not distributed shall be accumulated and added to principal. After ten years the trust shall terminate and be distributed to D, or her estate.**

In this case, because the Trustee's power is limited to deciding *when* D will receive the income, the gift of the income interest is complete, even if Grantor is Trustee. The regulations at § 25.2511–2(d) provides that a gift is not incomplete "merely because the donor reserves the power to change the manner or time of enjoyment."[37]

Part C. Introduction to Valuation

Among the most important issues in the transfer taxes is the question of valuation. The gift tax is imposed upon the donor's "total amount of gifts," defined in the regulations as "the sum of the values of the gifts made. . ." The estate tax computation begins with the "gross estate," which is based on "the value at the time of death." The taxable amount under the GST tax is based on the value of property involved in the taxable transaction. So in each case it is necessary to calculate the "value" of property.

Basic Valuation Principles

The regulations are the starting point in determining value. For gift tax purposes, § 25.2512–1 begins with the proposition that "the value of the property is the price at which such property would change hands between a willing buyer and a willing seller, neither being under any compulsion to buy or to sell, and both having reasonable knowledge of relevant facts." The estate tax regulations contain identical language at § 20.2031–1(b). The value used in a transaction for gift or estate tax purposes is used in applying the GST to the same property. § 2642(b). Thus, the starting point for determining value is this theoretical transaction.

In practice, the task of arriving at an accurate measure of the value of property is very straightforward with respect to some assets, and terribly difficult with respect to others. Consider the assets that are transferred in gratuitous transfers, either intervivos or at death. Cash is obviously the easiest to value. Next in line come publicly traded securities, which in most if not all cases the value can be easily valued by calculating the mean between the highest and lowest quoted selling prices on the relevant date.[38] These essentially liquid assets fall into the "easy to value" category. Then come the "difficult to value" assets, where it becomes necessary to invoke the theoretical transaction because there are not actual transactions in the same asset on the same date. Values determined under that method are necessarily subjective, and the fodder for disputes, because the interests of the taxpayer in finding a low value and that of the government in arriving at a high value are squarely in conflict. Real estate, antiques, and artwork can certainly be appraised with reference to sales of similar property, but

---

[37] As we will learn in *Chapter Four*, this is one area in which the gift tax and estate tax rules diverge. Even though powers over time and manner of enjoyment will not prevent completion of a gift, in this example the power retained by Grantor would be sufficient to bring the property back into the donor's estate under §§ 2036 and 2038.

[38] § 20.2031–2(b)(1). The regulations contain more rules where there are no trades on the relevant date, or if the trading information is unavailable.

no two appraisers will likely come up with the same number. Particularly difficult to value are interests in non-publicly traded businesses. What was a share of Facebook worth in the year leading up to its IPO? What is the local mom and pop grocery store worth? While the regulations offer some guidance,[39] resort must be made to appraisals, and the chances are high that the government's appraiser will disagree with the taxpayer's, and it is left to the parties to work out a compromise.

In *Chapter Ten* we will address the rules and strategies involved in valuing assets in more detail. At this point we want to address the rules for dividing the value of assets transferred in trust among the various property interests created.

Valuing Interests in Trusts

There are various reasons that we need to value trust interests. First, intervivos transfers of interests in trusts are subject to the gift tax. Second, some interests held in a trust by a decedent are property interests subject to the estate tax that must be included in the gross estate at their fair market value.

General Principles

Consider the following example:

Example #7: **Grantor (G) makes an intervivos transfer of $1,000,000 in cash to a trust that provides as follows:**

1. **Income to G's friend, F, for life,**

2. **On the death of F, the property is to pass to F's son S, or his estate.**

At the time the trust is created, G is 70 years old, F is 60 years old, and S is 30 years old, and the federal mid-term rate is 5%.

G has made a gift of two interests in property: an income interest to F and a remainder interest to S. What is the value of each at the time of transfer? If S dies 5 years after creation of the trust, what is the value of his remainder interest? We will see that there are several reasons that we may need to value these property interests, and the question is how to accomplish that task.

First, we know that at the time of transfer the total value of the trust is $1,000,000. For perfectly understandable reasons, the tax law presumes that the sum of the values of F's income interest and S's remainder interest is also equal to $1,000,000. Therefore, if we can determine the value of one of these interests, we can easily determine the value of the other. So let's start with F's income interest. Essentially F has been given an annuity for

---

[39] § 20.2031–3.

her life, the value of which is dependent on her life expectancy and the appropriate rate of interest. Section 7520 authorizes Treasury to prescribe tables based upon these two factors to determine the value of both income interests for life and remainder interests. It directs that the appropriate interest rate shall be 120% of the federal mid-term rate under § 1274(d)(1).[40] The current tables are found in § 20.2031–7(d)(7). Note the title of the tables, "Single life remainder factors." These tables are designed to value remainder interests that follow an income interest measured by the life of one person. Because we assume the value of the remainder and the income interest will total the value of the property, the tables allow us to indirectly value the income interest.

To calculate the values in our example, because the current federal mid-term rate is 5%, then the § 7520 rate is 120% of that, or 6%. We must locate the table under § 20.2031–7(d) that utilizes that rate (there are different tables for different interest rate ranges). The tables do the present value computation for us, taking into account F's age of 60. Looking across the row for age 60, to the column for the 6% rate, you will see that the appropriate "remainder factor" to use to value S's remainder interest is .33625. This factor could be viewed as a percentage (i.e., 33.625%) and is essentially that portion of the value of the corpus attributable to the remainder. Implicit in this determination is that the balance of the value of the corpus, 66.375%, must be attributable to F's income interest. Therefore, the value of S's remainder interest is $336,250 and that of F's income interest is $663,750.[41] The first number represents the present value to S of receiving the $1,000,000 principal upon the death of F. The second number represents the estimated present value to F of the right to receive a stream of payments from the trust for her lifetime at a rate of 4%. A couple of points are worth emphasizing here. First, these are estimated values; we obviously don't know precisely how long F will live, nor do we know what rate of income the trust will actually earn. Section 7520 makes a "best guess," which is very apt to be wrong. Nevertheless, in order to make the system administrable, we need to make that guess conclusively. Second, note that as time passes, the value of F's interest will gradually decrease, as her life expectancy declines, and the value of S' remainder will increase, and the expected date of distribution gets closer.[42]

Variation 7(a): Let's make the example a little more complicated. Assume instead that the trust created by G provides:

---

[40] We have used the AFR before, see note 16. The rate determined under § 7520 (20% of the AFR) is sometimes referred to as "the § 7520 rate." Therefore, it is important when approaching an example or problem to determine which rate is being offered, the AFR or the § 7520 rate.

[41] We are told under § 20.2031–7(d)(2)(iii) that to determine the appropriate factor to value a life interest one simply subtracts the remainder factor from 1.

[42] You can prove this to yourself by examining the tables, and comparing what F's interest would be worth we she reaches age 70.

1. **Income to F for life.**

2. **On F's death, if G is alive the trust reverts to her.**

3. **If G does not survive F, then remainder to S, or his estate.**

Now what interests has G transferred, and how do we value them? We know that the trust holds $1,000,000, but now less than all of that value has been transferred by G. She has transferred an income interest to F, which we know how to value. She has also transferred a "contingent remainder" to S. And she has retained the possibility of getting the property back, a "contingent reversion." Unlike the basic facts of *Example #7*, where S (or his estate) was sure to receive the property eventually (and hence his remainder was "vested"), in this case S or his estate will receive the principal only if G fails to survive F. If G does survive F the property will revert to her, and S will receive nothing. In order to determine the value of the contingent remainder transferred to S, one must evaluate the chances that G will survive F, a much more complicated actuarial determination than the one above.

In *Smith v. Shaughnessy*,[43] an early gift tax case involving facts similar to ours, the transferor argued that, while it was possible to value the income interest that he created, it was impossible to value the remainder under these facts because of the contingency that the property might revert to the transferor. Put another way, insertion of the difficult to value reversion made valuation of the remainder impossible, limiting the taxable gift to the value of the income interest.

Speaking for the Supreme Court, Justice Black stated: "We cannot accept any suggestion that the complexity of a property interest created by a trust can serve to defeat a tax." The court held that the value of the trust, minus only the value of the reversionary interest, was subject to tax, and it put the onus of establishing the value of the reversion on the taxpayer. Unless that value can be established, the entire transfer is subject to the gift tax.[44] As we see below, under current law § 2702 makes valuing that retained reversion very easy in many cases.

Gift Tax Valuation of Trust Interests Transferred to Family Members: § 2702

An important caveat to the rules discussed above is that they do not apply in *many* situations when a grantor transfers an interest in trust to a family member, and retains an interest in the same trust. That is because of § 2702 of the Code, which was enacted to control some tax planning

---

[43] 318 U.S. 176 (1943).

[44] § 25.2511–1(e). The government issues tables that provide the rules necessary to determine values when two lives must be taken into account, and computer programs are available to do the computation.

techniques considered abusive. Section 2702 responds to the inherent flaws in the assumptions made by § 7520; the assumption that assets will generate a fixed amount of income, and their underlying value will remain fixed. In fact a Trustee has considerable control over the amount of income produced by a trust, and by exercising that control it is possible that trust interests can be under or overvalued by § 7520. The planning techniques involved, generally referred to as "GRITS," or "Grantor retained income interest trusts," are discussed in detail in *Chapter Eight*, but for the moment suffice it to say that when a grantor creates a trust for members of his family (as defined by the statute), then the value of any "interest" retained by the grantor may be zero, and the full value of the assets transferred will be subject to the gift tax. An "interest" for this purpose includes an income interest, a remainder, or a reversion. It also includes a power over a trust, if it is the type of power that would render a gift incomplete.[45] It does not include certain "qualified interests," specifically defined by the statute to include certain types of interests where the value is not susceptible to manipulation. These include annuity interests, unitrust interests, and qualified remainders. We will defer a detailed discussion of § 2702 until *Chapter Eight*.

Part D. Statutory Exclusions from Taxable Gifts

Section 2503 specifically excludes certain transfers from the computation of taxable gifts. It is important at the outset to understand the difference between an exclusion and a deduction. The tax base for the gift tax is "taxable gifts" which is equal to total gifts minus allowable deductions.[46] So if Grantor transfers $100,000 to a charity, her total gifts will be $100,000, but her taxable gifts will be zero, because of the charitable deduction. Exclusions are different. Amounts excluded under the sections we discuss below are not a part of the total gifts, they don't go into the calculation of taxable gifts at all.

Section 2503(b): The Annual Exclusion

Under § 2503(b), each year the first $10,000 of gifts to each donee is *excluded* from the computation of taxable gifts. That $10,000 amount is adjusted for inflation, and in 2017 the amount of the so-called "annual exclusion" is $14,000. Throughout this chapter we will assume an annual exclusion of $14,000.

The annual exclusion originated with the 1932 gift tax statute, and was designed to "obviate the necessity of keeping an account of and reporting numerous small gifts."[47] The amount of the exclusion has

---

[45] § 25.2702–2(a)(4).

[46] The Code allows a deduction, i.e. a subtraction, against total gifts for amounts passed to charity (§ 2522) and to one's spouse (§ 2523). Deductions are the subject of *Chapter Seven*.

[47] S. Rep. No 665, 72d Cong., reprinted in 1939–1 (Part 2) CB 496, 525.

fluctuated widely. In 1932 it was set at $5,000 per donee, a generous amount given the stated purpose. It was reduced to $4000 in 1939, and then to $3000 in 1943, where it remained until the Economic Recovery and Tax Act of 1981 increased the amount to $10,000. In 1997 Congress added § 2503(b)(2), which requires that the amount of the exclusion be adjusted for inflation. In 2017 the inflation-adjusted amount is $14,000.

Basic Rules

The exclusion is allowed each year to each donor, and is available to shelter gifts to any number of donees, regardless of their relationship to the donor. Under § 2513, if one member of a married couple makes a gift, the other can elect to treat that gift as being made one-half by each spouse, thereby doubling the possible exclusion. To illustrate, consider the following example and variations:

Example #8:   In 2017 Donor transfers $14,000 in cash to each of her three adult children.

Donor has made no taxable gifts. Even though she has transferred $42,000, because each 43one received $14,000 each gift will be excluded from her total gifts by § 2503(a). She will be able to do this every calendar year, to as many friends, relatives, and strangers as she chooses.

Variation 8(a): In 2017 Donor transfers $28,000 in cash to each of her three adult children.

Donor's taxable gifts are computed as follows: The first $14,000 going to each recipient is excluded (total of $42,000 excluded). Her total gifts, and taxable gifts, are therefore the balance of $42,000. While the annual exclusion wipes out the first $14,000 going to each child, it does not eliminate the balance.

Gift Splitting

Under § 2513, if one member of a married couple makes a gift, the other may elect to treat that gift as being made by each spouse, thereby doubling the available annual exclusions. The following two variations illustrate this rule.

Variation 8(b): Donor's spouse consents under § 2513 to treat the gifts made in Variation 8(a) as made one-half by him.

Now neither spouse has made any taxable gifts. Each spouse is treated as gifting $14,000 to each child, and all of those transfers are sheltered by the annual exclusion.

Variation 8(c): Donor makes gifts in the same amount in 2018, and again her spouse consents to split the gift under § 2513.

The same result will occur in 2018: no taxable gifts. The annual exclusion is a per year, per donor, per donee exclusion.

Present Interest Rule

The principal limitation on the availability of the annual exclusion is the so-called "present interest rule." The statute specifically provides that gifts of future interests are not eligible for the exclusion. *Chapter Eight* contains a detailed discussion of the rule, but we will give a brief preview here.

Under the regulations, the term future interest includes "reversions, remainders, and other interests or estates, whether vested or contingent."[48] In contrast, "an unrestricted right to the immediate use, possession, or enjoyment of the property or the income from property (such as a life estate or term certain) is a present interest in property." While outright gifts of cash or property will qualify for the exclusion, many gifts in trust will not.

To illustrate, consider the following example.

Example #9: **In 2017 Donor transfers $14,000 in trust for the benefit of her adult child C. The trust provides for income to C (or her estate) for ten years, remainder to the Donor's grandchild GC, or her estate. Assume the § 7520 value of the income interest is $8,000, and the value of the remainder is $6,000. Disregard any issues raised by the GST tax.**

Although the total amount of the gift is within the amount of the annual exclusion, the donor has made two gifts to two different donees, each of which might potentially qualify for the $14,000 exclusion. We must consider each gift separately. In this case, the gift of the income interest will qualify for the annual exclusion, because C has the current right to receive the income from the trust.[49] But the grandchild's remainder will not qualify for the exclusion, because it is a future interest. As a result, of the $14,000 transferred only $8,000, the value of the income interest transferred to C, will qualify for the exclusion. The gift of the remainder to D, valued at $6000, does not qualify for the exclusion and is a taxable gift.[50]

Variation 9(a): **The trust allows the Trustee in any given year to withhold the income, and add it to principal.**

Because C's right to receive the income is subject to the Trustee's discretion, it is not a present interest and not eligible for the annual exclusion.[51] So no part of the transfer will qualify for the exclusion.

---

[48] § 25.2503–3(a).

[49] § 25.2503–3(b).

[50] While the gift must be reported on a gift tax return, tax will be due only if the donor has previously exhausted his exclusion amount.

[51] § 25.2503–3(c) Ex. 1.

Trusts for Minors

The restriction imposed by the present interest rule could make it difficult for donors to shift wealth to minor beneficiaries. Many donors would be unwilling (and understandably so) to transfer significant amounts of wealth outright to young children. The statute provides some relief in § 2503(c), under which certain trusts for the benefit of beneficiaries under age 21 will not be treated as future interests. The statute and regulations establish specific criteria for the trust to meet if it is to qualify. In addition, the government has by ruling allowed the exclusion for transfers made to minors under the Uniform Gifts to Minors Act, and the Uniform Transfers to Minors Act.[52] We will return to a detailed discussion of these issues and other planning possibilities concerning the annual exclusion in *Chapter Eight*.[53]

Section 2503(e): Transfers for Medical Care and Educational Expenses

Section 2503(e) is another exclusion section. It excludes certain "qualified transfers" from the gift tax. The two types of transfers coming within the exclusion are amounts paid as tuition on behalf of an individual (i) to an educational organization, and (ii) to a provider of medical services. The trickiest part of § 2503(e) is that payment must be made *directly* to the provider; reimbursement of expenses made by the donee will not qualify for the exclusion. Once that hurdle has been passed, the exclusion is potentially very generous.

Example #10: **Grandchild enrolls in college. Grandparent pays the child's annual tuition bill of $50,000, making payment directly to the college. He does so for each of the grandchild's four years of college.**

Under § 2503(e) each payment of $50,000 is excluded from the gift tax, and therefore Grandparent has made no taxable gifts. It is also worth noting that payments that qualify for exclusion under § 2503(e) are similarly exempt from the GST tax.[54] Grandparent may also, if he chooses make annual exclusion gifts to the grandchild; the two are mutually exclusive.

Part E. Introduction to Disclaimers

Imagine Lucky Luis, who learns that his rich great-Uncle Ernie, who he never met, has left him $10,000,000 by will. Lucky earned his name

---

[52] Rev. Rul. 59–357, 1959–2 C.B. 212, Rev. Rul. 73–287, 1973–2 C.B. 321.

[53] One of the topics discussed in *Chapter Eight* involves the use of so-called *"Crummey* Trusts," which have been blessed by a series of court decisions and offer planning opportunities for the annual exclusion.

[54] § 2642(c)(3).

because of his extraordinary investment acumen: he is already worth $20,000,000 in his own right. Luis would prefer to see Ernie's $10,000,000 go to his children, Abby and Bobby. Yet if Luis receives Ernie's estate, and then transfers those funds to his children, he will have made a gift of $10,000,000.

Most if not all state laws have historically permitted a will beneficiary to "renounce" or "disclaim" a bequest, and those laws typically dictate that the property disclaimed will be distributed as though the disclaiming beneficiary had predeceased the testator. Thus, if in our example Ernie's will provided that the $10,000,000 bequest should go to Luis' children in the event Luis failed to survive Ernie, then if Luis disclaimed the property it would pass to his children under state law. The federal law question is whether or not we should tax Luis as though he had received the property, then gifted it to his children.

The answer is supplied by § 2518, which provides that if the disclaimer is a "qualified" one, then the property will be taxed as though it never passed through Luis' hands, and therefore Luis will not be treated as having gifted the property to his children.

The requirements for a qualified disclaimer are very specific, and simply satisfying the state law rules will not be sufficient. Because the rules for disclaimers (or renunciations) vary from state to state, Congress intended to create a uniform set of rules to govern the tax treatment of disclaimers. Thus, qualified disclaimers must be in writing, and must be effectuated within 9 months (there are specific rules regarding delivery), the disclaimant cannot accept the interest or any portion of it, and the property has to pass to the ultimate recipient (who, with one exception, cannot be the disclaimant) without any direction by the disclaimant. Disclaimers are discussed in detail in *Chapter Eight*.

Moving Forward

Now that you have a firm foundation in the basic rules of the gift tax, we will change our focus to the estate tax. In the following four chapters we will study the provisions that include various types of property and interests in the gross estate. Then in *Chapters Seven* and *Eight* and *Nine* we will return to issues that directly implicate the gift tax.

CHAPTER THREE

PROPERTY OWNED AT DEATH
(§§ 2033 & 2040)

■ ■ ■

The estate tax and the gift tax are excise taxes on gratuitous transfers of wealth. We've seen that the gift tax applies when a transfer of property to the donee is complete, and in most cases it is not that difficult to determine what to include in the gift tax base, issues of valuation aside. In *Chapter Two* we explored some of the issues that arise under the gift tax, including the question of whether services or the use of property constitute gifts, and when a transfer is complete for gift taxes.

The estate tax is different, though. Instead of focusing on an individual transfer by a donor to a donee, it seeks to identify the aggregate amount of wealth that is transferred as a result of a decedent's death. Section 2001(b) imposes the tax on the "taxable estate," which is defined in § 2051 as the excess of the "gross estate" over the deductions allowed under the statute. Most of this book is devoted to determining what is included in the gross estate (*Chapters Three* through *Six*) and what amounts are allowable as deductions in arriving at the taxable estate (*Chapter Seven*).

In this chapter we address the most basic of the inclusion sections (§ 2033), and the rules applicable to jointly held property (§ 2040).

Part A. Assets Owned at Death: § 2033

As a starting point in determining the gross estate, § 2033 includes "the value of all property to the extent of the interest therein of the decedent at the time of his death." The regulations expand on this a bit, saying § 2033 includes "the value of all property, whether real or personal, tangible or intangible, and wherever situated, beneficially owned by the decedent at the time of his death." Section 2033 will include property interests held in a decedent's name at death, most of which will pass to the beneficiaries of the decedent's will or by intestacy. Therefore real estate, bank accounts, securities, automobiles, and any other assets, tangible or intangible, owned by the decedent will be included in the decedent's gross estate under § 2033. It will also reach amounts owed to the decedent at the time of death, including unpaid salary and dividends declared prior to death, and loans made by the decedent to others, even if cancelled by the will.[1]

Certain assets not necessarily passing under the will or by inheritance may be reached by § 2033 as well. Examples include employee death benefits, pay-on-death accounts,[2] and vested remainder interests that pass to the decedent's heirs or will beneficiaries.

One important rule to note is that § 2033 does *not* reach property interests or rights held by the decedent during life that terminate with his death. For example, assume D holds a legal life estate in a piece of real property. When D dies that interest is extinguished, and the property will pass under the deed to the remainderman. Contrast the situation where D owns a remainder interest in real property, preceded by a legal life estate in another. If D dies before the life tenant, the remainder interest survives D and will pass under the terms of his will. The value of the remainder at D's death is included in D's gross estate under § 2033.

It is tempting to think of § 2033 as the estate tax analog of § 61 under the income tax, which includes in gross income "all income from whatever source derived." Section 61 has long been read very broadly by the Supreme Court, which has established that unless excluded by some specific Code provision, all accessions to wealth that have been realized by a taxpayer are included in gross income.[3] The Court took a different approach in estate tax issues under § 2033 (and its predecessors). In early cases the Supreme Court read § 2033 very narrowly when the government attempted to include non-probate assets under its umbrella.[4] As a result, § 2033, standing alone, would be totally inadequate to effectively measure the wealth transferred by the decedent at death for several reasons. First, there may be wealth transfers at death that do not pass under the decedents will or to his heirs, including property held in joint tenancy. We'll see in this chapter how § 2040 deals with that. Insurance and retirement plans similarly pass outside the will, and because the interest of the decedent in those assets terminates with his death, they elude the reach of § 2033. Yet they often constitute real transfers of wealth by the decedent, and hence should be part of the gross estate. In **Chapter Five** we will study the provisions governing those assets. In addition, the decedent may have transferred property away during life, yet may have retained sufficient interest in or control over those assets that the transfers amount to

---

[1]   § 20.2033–1(b).

[2]   A pay on death account may be held with a bank or a broker. It directs the bank or broker to distribute the account to one or more designated beneficiaries upon the account owner's death, and the owner of the account can change that designation at any time. It is a fairly simple way to avoid probate of amounts in the account.

[3]   *Commissioner v. Glenshaw Glass Co.* 348 U.S. 426 (1955).

[4]   For example, in *Helvering v. Safe Deposit & Trust Co.* 316 U.S. 56 (1942) the Supreme Court held that even though the decedent held powers over property that were substantially the equivalent of outright title, the property was not includible in the decedent's gross estate.

"testamentary substitutes," and the decedent should be treated as owning those assets at death, even though he does not actually own them. The decedent may have powers over property that amount to the equivalent of ownership. As we will learn in subsequent chapters, Congress has enacted additional statutes to bring some of these assets into the gross estate. As a result, instead of the income tax approach, which is that an item is included in income unless specifically exempted by statute, the estate tax approach is that an item is part of the gross estate *only* if specifically *included* by statute.

State, not federal, law determines the existence of property rights. As a result, in transfer tax disputes the federal court must often determine how state law would apply to a particular property interest or transfer. These types of disputes most frequently come up in the estate tax context, where a state probate or surrogates court may be in charge of administering the decedent's estate, and may have ruled on an issue involving the decedent's property rights. One would expect that a state court's determination would be the best information the federal government would have in resolving a property rights dispute. However, probate court practice is different from other typical state litigation. In particular, the parties involved are usually related, and except in unfortunate circumstances the family may actually get along. Even if the estate beneficiaries are not particularly fond of one another, they usually share a common goal of minimizing the federal government's piece of the estate. Thus, an estate might ask for a probate court ruling that would have the effect of decreasing federal transfer tax liability, such as a finding that the decedent was not the owner of property in his possession at death. If the estate and its beneficiaries are all agreeable, the court's ruling may amount to little more than a rubber stamp of their position. If the government disputes that finding for estate tax purposes in in federal court, should the state court ruling be determinative? In *Commissioner v. Estate of Bosch*,[5] the Supreme Court held no. The Court held that, absent a decision by the state's highest court, the federal court must "apply what they find to be the state law after giving 'proper regard' to relevant rulings of other courts of the State."

The following examples explore the scope of § 2033.

Example #1:   At the time of her death the decedent held title to a piece of real property as trustee for the benefit of her sister.

Section 2033 only reaches property that is "beneficially owned" by the decedent. As trustee she held only legal, not beneficial title, so the assets will not be included in her estate under that section.[6]

---

[5]   387 U.S. 456 (1967).

[6]   § 20.2033–1.

Example #2: At the time of her death, D was a beneficiary of a trust created by her parents that contained the following alternate provisions:

Variation 2(a): Income to D for life, remainder to D's surviving children in equal shares.

Because D's interest in the trust terminates with her death, there is no asset to include under § 2033.[7]

Variation 2(b): Income to X for life, remainder to D or her estate. X survives D.

Even though the trust is still in existence at her death, D's interest in this trust is a vested remainder interest and it survives D. Even though D herself won't enjoy the remainder, it will go to her estate, and hence to her heirs or will beneficiaries, when X later dies. The remainder will be included in her gross estate under § 2033 at its actuarial value.[8]

Variation 2(c): Income to X for life, remainder to D if she survives X, and if not then to Y.

Here D's remainder is contingent upon surviving X. If she fails to do so, then the remainder is extinguished by her death, and hence not included under § 2033.

Variation 2(d): Income to X for life, remainder to Y if living, and if not then to D or her estate. X and Y survive D.

Even though she has died, D still holds an interest in this trust, a contingent remainder. Her remainder is contingent upon Y's failure to survive X. When D dies survived by both X and Y, we still don't know if the remainder will become possessory. Nevertheless, this contingent remainder interest will be included in D's gross estate under § 2033. The value of the remainder will reflect the fact that it is subject to a contingency.[9]

Variation 2(e): Income to D for life, remainder as D appoints by will, in default of appointment to X or her estate.

Even though D has substantial rights with respect to the trust, including the right to enjoy it during life and direct where it passes when she dies, at the time of her death she doesn't hold an "interest" in the property within the meaning of § 2033, and the trust assets will not be included in her estate under that section. Her income interest terminates when she dies, and the property bypasses her probate estate, even though her will directs where it goes. Nevertheless, the rules of § 2041 (see

---

[7]   As we will see in *Chapter Nine,* D's death may trigger the GST tax.

[8]   Recall the rules discussed in *Chapter Two* for valuing interests in trust.

[9]   Valuing the remainder will be trickier, but is still possible using actuarial principles.

Chapter Six) will determine if the power of appointment held in this case by D will result in estate tax inclusion of the trust assets under that section.

Example #3: **D was injured badly in an automobile accident caused by a negligent driver. D lived for 3 days and then died. The executor of her estate brought a wrongful death action against the driver. The action was settled for $8,000,000, $1,000,000 of which was for D's pain and suffering.**

The technical legal issue under § 2033 is whether D possessed at the time of death a claim against the negligent driver. Although the Service once argued that recoveries such as these should be includible in the decedent's estate, the courts did not agree.[10] In their view, the interest in property, i.e., the cause of action, was created by, and arose after, D's death. The Service has acquiesced in this view, ***as long as*** the decedent did not possess a claim during her lifetime for damages.[11] On these facts, at the time of D's death, she would have had a claim against the negligent driver for her medical expenses and pain and suffering. For this reason, the estate should include $1,000,000 of the settlement in D's gross estate under § 2033.

Example #4: **D died owning two life insurance policies, one on her own life and one on X's life. X survived D.**

The life insurance policy on X's life is clearly includable in D's gross estate under § 2033. Under the regulations, this policy would be valued at an amount that comparable policies would cost: essentially its replacement value.[12]

The life insurance policy on D's own life is also theoretically includible in her gross estate under § 2033. As owner of the policy, D had the right to choose, and to change, the designated beneficiary. Yet the interest held by D the moment prior to death was worth no more than the value of the policy, while that ripened into the death benefit on D's death. Current law resolves the issue by resorting to § 2042, which provides for specific rules for taxing insurance on the decedent's life. In this case, where D was the owner of the policy, § 2042 would include the entire death benefit payable. We will study § 2042 in detail in ***Chapter Five.***

Example #5: **D, a cash method taxpayer, died on August 31 of the current year. On that date, D's employer owed D $20,000 for**

---

[10] *See Connecticut Bank & Trust Co. v. U.S.,* 465 F.2d 760 (2d. Cir. 1972).

[11] Rev. Rul. 75–127, 1975–1 C.B. 297.

[12] § 20.2031–8(a)(1). The regulations recognize that this method may not be suitable for all policies, especially for whole life policies that have been in place for a substantial period of time and have accumulated a substantial cash surrender value. In such a case, the policy may be valued by using the "interpolated terminal reserve" as of the decedent's death, adjusted for a portion of the last premium paid. The interpolated terminal reserve is essentially the cash surrender value of a life insurance policy on a particular date. For an illustration of how it is computed, see § 20.2031–8(a)(3) Ex. 3.

work she had performed during August. After D's death the amount is paid to D's estate.

The estate tax consequences are straightforward. Because D had a claim to the $20,000 on the date of her death, that amount must be includible in her estate under § 2033.

The income tax consequences are less obvious. Even though D earned $20,000 during August, it will not be included on her final income tax return (which ends with the date of her death) because she is a cash method taxpayer and she did not receive the amount during life. This is an example of what is known as "income with respect of a decedent," or IRD. Items of IRD are not entitled to a step-up in basis under § 1014(a).[13] The income tax rules for taxing IRD are found in § 691. Under that provision, IRD is included in the income of the person entitled to receive it, in this case D's estate.[14] In calculating its income taxes, D's estate will be entitled to deduct the amount of any estate tax that is allocable to the $20,000.[15] The purpose of this deduction is to ensure that the total income and estate tax liability attributable to the salary will be approximately the same as it would have been had D received the salary check on the day before she died. To illustrate, suppose both D and D's estate are in the 35% income tax bracket, and that D's estate is in the 40% bracket for estate tax purposes.

If D had actually received the $20,000 before death, she would have owed $7,000 of income tax,[16] and the remaining $13,000 would have been in her estate. D's estate tax bill on that amount would have been $5,200,[17] leaving a net amount to her beneficiaries of $7,800.[18] Under this scenario, there would have been a total of $12,200 paid in combined income and estate taxes.

On the other hand, if D did *not* receive the $20,000 before death, the entire $20,000 would be in her estate, and subject to the 40% estate tax, resulting in tax of $8,000. In addition, when D's estate receives the $20,000 payment, it must include in income the entire amount. This would seem to double tax the salary. Section 691 solves this by giving the estate an income tax deduction of $8,000, the estate tax attributable to the inclusion. So the amount included in income by the estate will be $20,000 less $8,000, or $12,000, resulting in income tax due of $4,200. Once again, the combined income and estate taxes paid are $12,200, leaving $7,800 for the beneficiaries.

---

[13] § 1014(c).

[14] § 691(a).

[15] § 691(c).

[16] 35% of $20,000 = $7,000.

[17] 40% of $13,000 = $5,200.

[18] $13,000 − 5,200 = $7,800.

Part B. Jointly Held Property

The estate tax treatment of jointly held property varies with the method of holding title. We explore those differences here.

Tenancy in Common

Section 2033 includes an interest in property "to the extent of the interest therein of the decedent at the time of his death." If the decedent is sole owner of property, its full value will be included under § 2033. If a decedent owns an undivided partial interest in the property as a co-tenant, then only the decedent's proportionate share of the property will pass under his will or to his heirs, and only that portion will be included in the gross estate by § 2033.

Joint Tenancy: § 2040

Another common method of jointly holding title is the joint tenancy. A defining feature of the joint tenancy is that, upon the death of one tenant, the entire property vests by operation of law in the surviving tenant(s). To illustrate, suppose D his brother B equally contribute to the $1,000,000 purchase price of a piece of real property, and take title as joint tenants with right of survivorship. D dies first, when the property is worth $2,000,000, and title to the property vests in B by operation of law.

Has D made a transfer of wealth that should be subject to the estate tax? Up until the moment that he died, D had the ability to sever the tenancy, and take sole title to his half. By not doing so, he has effectively transferred his one-half interest to B. And if he had severed, then his half of the value would have been included in his estate under § 2033. Yet because D did not sever, his interest in the property ceased at death, and there is nothing to include under § 2033. So we have to figure out what to do about D's half interest that went to B.

Let's complicate the example further. Assume that D supplied the entire $1,000,000 purchase price for the property. As we saw in *Chapter Two*, creation of the tenancy resulted in a gift to B of an undivided one half interest in the property,[19] because of his right to sever and walk away with his half. So it appears that the transfer taxes have effectively dealt with B's half, and maybe we don't need to worry about that. But what if B had died first? By creating this joint tenancy, D reserved the possibility that the whole property would come back to him one day, and maybe that "string" held on the transferred property should be taken into account.

Section 2040 steps into the void left by § 2033 here, and will include in D's gross estate the value of the property *to the extent* that consideration for the property was supplied by D. So in the case of the joint purchase,

---

[19] § 25.2511–1(h)(5).

where B and D each contributed equally to the purchase price, if D predeceases B then one half of the value will be included in D's estate under § 2040. In the case where D supplied the full consideration for the property, § 2040 will include the full value of the property in his estate, at its value as of D's date of death.[20]

It can be tricky to determine what portion of the property will be included in the decedent's gross estate under § 2040. The statutory language is somewhat cumbersome, but the regulations state the rule more clearly.[21] In essence, joint tenancy property held by the decedent and another person will be included under the following rules:

(1) The entire value of the property is included, except for any portion of the value attributable to consideration supplied by the other owners. Thus, if D dies with a joint tenancy interest in property that he and B purchased together, each supplying half of the consideration, then only the one-half of the property attributable to D's contribution will be included in his gross estate. BUT if B's contribution to the purchase can be traced to a gift from D, then that contribution is disregarded. So if D makes a gift of $500,000 to B, and then D and B jointly purchase property for $1,000,000, the full value of the property will be included in D's gross estate if he dies before B.[22]

(2) If D and the other co-owner(s) acquired title to the property by gift or inheritance, then only D's fractional share of the property is included. Thus, if D and B inherited the property from their parents, then only D's one half share will be included in his gross estate.

(3) Because of the difficulty of tracing contributions to spousal joint tenancies, § 2040(b) adopts a simplifying rule: It conclusively presumes that each spouse contributed one-half of the consideration.[23] Thus if D owns the property, and transfers title to himself and his spouse S as joint tenants, then even though he supplied the entire consideration, only one-half of the property will be included in D's gross estate.[24] Similarly, if S predeceases D then one-half of the property

---

[20] § 2040(a).

[21] § 20.2040–1(a)(2).

[22] Id.

[23] The rules of § 2040(b) also apply to tenancies by the entirety between spouses. Tenancies by the entirety are similar to joint tenancies, but there is usually no right to sever.

[24] The unlimited marital deduction makes this issue largely academic, because any portion of a spousal joint tenancy included in D's estate would be offset by the marital deduction, discussed in *Chapter Seven*.

will be included in her gross estate, even though she actually provided none of the consideration.

The following examples illustrate these rules.

Example #6: **Father (F) and Son (S) own Blackacre as joint tenants with right of survivorship. In the current year F dies when Blackacre is worth $2,000,000. They acquired the property under the following alternative methods:**

Variation 6(a): **They purchased the property several years ago for $500,000; F contributed $400,000 and S contributed $100,000 towards the purchase price.**

Because title to the property will pass to S by operation of law, no part of Blackacre will be includible in F's gross estate under § 2033. Under 2040(a), however, 80% of the value of Blackacre ($1,600,000) must be included in F's gross estate because F paid 80% of the purchase price.

Variation 6(b): **Same as *Variation 6(a),* except that, shortly before the acquisition of Blackacre, F made a gift to S of $100,000 cash.**

On these facts, it would seem that the $100,000 that S paid for Blackacre came from F, so that the entire value of Blackacre will be included in F's gross estate.

Variation 6(c): **F and S acquired Blackacre as joint tenants through a bequest in the will of F's mother.**

In this case, § 2040 will only include F's fractional share of Blackacre, or 50%.

Example #7: **At the time of her death the decedent owned a piece of investment real property as tenants by the entirety with her spouse. The property was owned by decedent prior to the marriage.**

Section 2040(b) conclusively presumes that each spouse contributes equally to the property, and so one-half is included in the decedent's estate.

Variation: **The decedent and her husband live in a community property state, and held title to the property as community property (not joint tenancy).**

Because each spouse in a community property state owns an undivided one-half interest in the community assets, half of the property is owned by the decedent at death and will be included in her gross estate under § 2033.[25]

---

[25] Due to what can best be described as a quirk in the income tax, property held as community property receives significantly better treatment than joint tenancy property when determining the

Moving Forward

As the examples illustrate, the reach of § 2033 is fairly narrow, and it does not pretend to encompass the full value of wealth transferred by a decedent. Section 2040 partially fills the gap, by including property held as joint tenants with right of survivorship. Congress has enacted a series of other statutes that attempt to do refine the measure of the decedent's wealth, and we will turn to those in the following chapters. Those statutes will address retirement plans and insurance, and certain powers that the decedent holds over property. In addition, as we will now see in *Chapter Four*, the statute includes in the gross estate certain "testamentary substitutes" that Congress has deemed equivalent to ownership of property at death.

---

basis of the surviving spouse. See § 1014(a)(6). For this reason, residents of community property estate are usually ill-advised to take title to property as joint tenants.

CHAPTER FOUR

PROPERTY TRANSFERRED DURING DECEDENT'S LIFETIME (§§ 2035, 2036, 2037 & 2038)

■ ■ ■

Part A. Introduction

In *Chapter Three* we studied the initial inclusion section, § 2033, which includes in a decedent's gross estate property owned by the decedent at his death. Those assets largely (but not entirely) consist of assets that will pass through probate under the terms of the decedent's will, or to his heirs, at death. Transfers such as these are sometimes referred to as "testamentary transfers," because they do not take effect until death, and are governed by the decedent's will or the intestacy statute. We also learned that § 2040 captures one common type of non-probate asset, the joint tenancy. In *Chapter Five* we will study two statutory provisions that capture other potential wealth transfers not subject to § 2033, specifically annuities and retirement plans (§ 2039), and life insurance (§ 2042). *Chapter Six* deals with powers of appointment, which are another means of transferring wealth at death. All of these sections, working with § 2033, seek to include in the gross estate all transfers of wealth made by a decedent at death.

In this chapter we consider a group of statutes (§§ 2035, 2036, 2037 and 2038) that are designed to refine the measure of wealth transferred by a decedent by bringing into the gross estate certain property that the decedent *transferred away during life*. These Code sections have their origin in the 1916 estate tax statute, and understanding them requires a brief review of the history of the estate and gift tax.

As you will recall, when Congress enacted the 1916 estate tax it did not enact a gift tax. The permanent gift tax statute was not enacted until 1932.[1] During the years that there was no gift tax in effect, the simplest way to avoid the estate tax was to transfer assets prior to death.[2] While it was true that the estate tax could be avoided by lifetime gifts, in the estate tax statute Congress imposed a couple of limitations. First, it provided that

---

[1]   There was a short-lived gift tax in effect from 1924 to 1926.

[2]   We've seen that it was during this era that the "completed gift" rules, discussed in *Chapter Two*, were first developed.

gifts made "in contemplation of death" should be brought back into the gross estate, which was aimed at near death transfers made with the purpose of avoiding the estate tax. Second, the law provided for inclusion of property "to the extent of any interest therein of which the decedent has at any time made a transfer intended to take effect in possession or enjoyment at or after his death." This latter provision was aimed at "testamentary substitutes," i.e., transfers made during life that were functionally equivalent to holding the property until death and then leaving it by will.

Even after enactment of the gift tax, it remained advantageous for taxpayers to make life-time gifts. That was because of the structure of the law at the time, when there were separate exemption amounts and rate tables applicable to the gift and the estate tax. In addition, when property is taxed as a gift, the amount subject to the transfer taxes is set at the date of gift value. Any subsequent appreciation is removed from the donor's estate. Finally, to the extent that a donor pays gift tax, the tax itself is never subject to the transfer tax. Taxpayers could take advantage of these structural "defects" in the system, and reduce their overall transfer tax liability by making life-time gifts.[3] The contemplation of death and testamentary substitute provisions were continued to put limits on that type of planning.

Gifts Within Three Years of Death: § 2035

The contemplation of death rule was problematic from the outset. Although there were statutory presumptions, those were rebuttable, and for the government to prevail it had to determine the state of mind of a decedent at the time of the gift.[4] The modern version of the statute is § 2035, and in 1976 Congress amended it to eliminate the subjective "contemplation" rule, and provide that all gifts made within three years of death were included in the gross estate. The 1976 Act also added a provision, found now in § 2035(b), which includes in the estate any gift tax paid on gifts made within three years of death.

But remember what else Congress did in 1976: it unified the gift and estate taxes, eliminating the ability to use the separate rate structures and exemptions (which was one of the main benefits of life-time giving). Life-time gifts could still result in transfer tax savings by eliminating post-gift appreciation from the estate, and by removing any gift tax paid by the donor from the estate. The 1976 Act eliminated these benefits for any gift made within three years of death. So after 1976, the increase in the gross estate caused by § 2035 with respect to *outright gifts* was limited to at most

---

[3]   These rules are further discussed in ***Chapter One***.

[4]   At one point early on, Congress created a conclusive presumption that gifts made within two years of death were made in contemplation of death, but that was held unconstitutional. *Heiner v. Donnan*, 285 U.S. 312 (1932).

three years' worth of post-gift appreciation in gifted assets, and inclusion of gift tax paid. In 1981 Congress amended the statute again, in a way that substantially reduced its scope. After several revisions, the current basic rule is found in § 2035(a). Under current law, *outright gifts* made within three years of death are *not* included in the gross estate, although under § 2035(b) any gift tax paid on those gifts is still included.

Instead, under current law, the only lifetime transfers that will trigger inclusion of assets under § 2035(a) are those of *powers or rights* over property that would have resulted in inclusion under §§ 2036–2038 and § 2042 had decedent held them at death. Because we have yet to study those provisions, we will delay a more detailed discussion of § 2035 until we've covered §§ 2036–2038, and we will review it again when we study life insurance in *Chapter Five*.

Transfers with Retained Interests and Powers (The "String Provisions")

History

Sections 2036 through 2038 are the modern version of the rule in the 1916 estate tax law that included property in the estate "to the extent of any interest therein of which the decedent has at any time made a transfer intended to take effect in possession or enjoyment at or after his death." As we noted above, the rule was aimed at "testamentary substitutes," i.e., transfers made during life that were functionally equivalent to holding the property until death and then transferring it by will.

While arguably any transfer that postponed the donee's enjoyment of the property until the decedent's death could have come within the statute, early cases held that simply delaying the enjoyment of the transferred property until the decedent's death was not enough. They held that the decedent must also have had some sort of continuing interest in or control over the property in order to have it brought back into her estate.[5] Thus, the original statute applied when the decedent transferred property during life, if the donee had to survive the decedent to receive full enjoyment of the property, *and* if the decedent retained a sufficient power over or interest in the property. If so, the property would be brought back into the decedent's estate for estate tax purposes as though never given away.

Current Law: The "String Provisions"

Sections 2036, 2037 and 2038 are the modern versions of that early statute, and each acts to include in the gross estate property that the

---

[5] *Reinecke v. Northern Trust Co.,* 278 U.S. 339 (1929); *Shukert v. Allen,* 273 U.S. 545 (1972). Thus, if D transfers property in trust with income to X for D's life, remainder to Y, the gift to Y is delayed until D's death, but absent more he has retained no interest in the property that would cause it to be brought back into his estate.

decedent transferred during his lifetime, but with respect to which he retained some interest in the property for his life, or held some *power* over the property at death (i.e., held onto some "strings" with respect to the property). Section 2036 addresses situations where the decedent retained powers over or interests in the income from the property, § 2037 addresses situations where enjoyment of a property interest is delayed until after the decedent's death AND the decedent reserved a right to get the property back (i.e., a reversion), and § 2038 deals with powers over any interest in the underlying property, i.e., not just the income or a reversion. Unlike its siblings, § 2038 does not require that the power be "retained," just that the decedent has previously transferred the property, and then holds a power over it at death. Because § 2038 powers are typically "retained," we include our discussion of § 2038 here even though we commonly refer to these three sections as covering "transfers with retained interests." We will also see that, because of their common parentage, the sections frequently overlap, and you can be assured that the government will pursue the theory that yields the greatest inclusion.

There are two common elements to each of the three sections:

(i) The decedent must have made a transfer of property during life. Absent such a transfer, none of the sections will apply.

(ii) That transfer was not made in exchange for full and adequate consideration. If the decedent received full value for the property transferred, none of the three sections will apply. However, be wary of transfers for partial consideration: in such a case §§ 2036–2038 might still apply, and only the amount of the consideration received will be backed out (see § 2043).

We will begin with § 2036, which, consistent with its title ("Transfers with retained life estate") applies when the decedent transferred property during life, but retained certain rights with respect to the *income from or use of* the property during his life. Take a close look at § 2036(a). It has two prongs. Section 2036(a)(1) applies when the decedent retained the right to possess or enjoy the property, or its income, and § 2036(a)(2) applies when the decedent didn't retain the right to enjoy the income herself, but retained the right to exert control over the beneficial enjoyment of the income or the property by others. We'll then turn to § 2038 ("Revocable Transfers"), which applies when the decedent has previously transferred the property and at death holds the right to exert control over any interest in the property, not just the income interest. Finally we will turn to § 2037 ("Transfers Taking Effect at Death"), which under certain circumstances will bring back into the gross estate property interests that have been postponed until the decedent's death, if the decedent retained a reversionary interest in the property. Section 2037 can be tricky; it is similar to § 2036(a)(1), because it applies when the decedent retained an interest in the property for his own benefit, but like § 2038 it focuses on rights over the property itself, not just the income. Finally, we will return to § 2035 and explore how it interacts with the string provisions.

Part B. Section 2036

In General

Sections 2036(a)(1) and (a)(2) describe the types of "strings" that the decedent must retain over the income from transferred property in order for it to be brought back into her estate under that section. The Congressional rationale for both is that if the decedent held onto any of those rights with respect to the property's income, that decedent should be treated as if she never gave the property away. Consider the "bundle of sticks" approach to property ownership. One of the most significant sticks in the bundle is the right to receive and dispose of the income that the property generates. Another is the right to use the property. Under § 2036 if a decedent gives the property away but holds onto those sticks, then the statute treats the decedent for estate tax purposes as if she still owned the property at death. The statute has two separate prongs:

> *First:* Section 2036(a)(1) provides that if the decedent retained the right to receive the income from the property for the requisite period, the property is brought back into her estate. Not all property produces a regular income stream (consider personal residences, antiques, artwork).[6] In such a case the statute will also apply if the decedent retained the "possession or enjoyment" of the property. Use of the income to satisfy a legal obligation of the decedent, including the obligation to support a minor child, is treated as retention of the right to receive the income by the decedent.[7]

> *Second:* Even if the decedent does not retain the right to the income or the use of the property for her own benefit, if she retains the power "to designate the persons who shall possess or enjoy the property or the income therefrom," then under § 2036(a)(2) the property is swept back into the estate. Again the retention of this attribute of ownership, the right to determine who gets to enjoy the property, whether in the form of income or use, is considered sufficient to treat the decedent as if she never gave the property away.

---

[6]   Enjoyment of the use and possession of such property does have value, as you learned in your basic income tax class: we refer to that as "imputed income." While we do not tax imputed income for income tax purposes, § 2036 does recognize its value, and treats it similarly to actual income.

[7]   Reg. § 20.2036–1(b)(2).

Because of its focus on powers over property, § 2036(a)(2) is very similar in its operation to § 2038. We will discuss those similarities below, and identify some of the differences. We have said that § 2036 is aimed at retained interests and powers over *income*, yet the statute actually appears to go beyond that. Section 2036(a)(2) refers to powers over "the property or the income." The regulations, however, specify that § 2036 does not apply if the power affects only the underlying property and not the income, leaving those powers to § 2038.[8] As a result, although there is often an overlap between § 2036(a)(2) and 2038, the two are not identical.

As discussed above, § 2036 is aimed at testamentary substitutes, i.e., transfers in which the decedent does not completely part with the property until death. The statute implements this notion by providing that the requisite right or power over income must have been retained by the decedent "for his life or for any period not ascertainable without reference to his death or for any period which does not in fact end before his death. . ." At the risk of using too many stick metaphors, § 2036 will only apply if the decedent's life is used as the measuring stick for determining when she entirely surrenders control of the property. We'll explore this aspect of the statute, as well as other aspects of § 2036, in the following examples.

Section 2036(a)(1): Retained Rights to Income or Enjoyment

In each of the following examples, assume that all parties are unrelated, and that D appoints an independent Trustee, unless the facts explicitly state otherwise.

Example #1: **During her lifetime D transfers $3,000,000 in publicly traded stock to a bank as Trustee under an irrevocable trust that provides as follows:**

> **The Trustee shall pay to D the entire net income from the trust, in annual installments, and on D's death the Trustee shall distribute the trust principal to D's friend F, or to his estate.**

When D dies five years later, the trust has a value of $6,000,000.

When D creates the trust she has made a completed gift of the remainder interest, which will be valued under actuarial principles, so that some portion of the initial trust principal will be taxed as a gift.[9] Nevertheless, on D's death the full date of death value of the trust ($6,000,000) will be included in her estate under § 2036(a)(1), because D has retained the right to the income from the property for her life. Why should this be true? Although D parted with title to the property during

---

[8]   Reg. § 20.2036–1(b)(3)(iii).

[9]   If D and F were related within the meaning of § 2702, D's retained income interest would be valued at zero, so the full $3,000,000 would be taxed as a gift. Depending on her prior gifts, the gift may or may not result in payment of gift tax.

her life, she held onto one of the most significant attributes of ownership of property: the right to receive the income. From F's perspective, his right to enjoy in the property is delayed until after D's death, just as if D had never made the transfer. As a result, D will be treated as if she never gave the property away, i.e., the same way she would have been treated had she held onto the property until death and left it to F in her will: the FULL DATE OF DEATH fair market value will be included in the estate.[10]

This, indeed, is the main rub of the retention statutes. As discussed in **Chapter One**, one of the estate planning benefits of making life-time gifts is that the value of the gifted property is essentially "frozen" for transfer tax purposes at its date of gift value. If the property appreciates between the date of gift and date of death, that appreciation is not part of the estate. When § 2036 applies to bring the property back into the estate, it captures all of the post-gift appreciation. We will see that, of the retention sections, § 2036 usually hits hardest by often causing inclusion of the entire value of the property at death. In contrast, §§ 2037 & 2038 are more targeted, and often bring in less than the entire value of the property.

Consider the following variations on **Example #1:**

Variation 1(a): Same as **Example #1** except that under the terms of the trust D is entitled to only one-half of the trust's net income.

Under § 20.2036–1(a) of the regulations, where the decedent retains an interest with respect to only a part of the income from the property transferred, the "corresponding proportion" of the property is included in the estate. Thus, one half of the date of death value of the stock ($3,000,000) is included in the gross estate.

Variation 1(b): Same as **Example #1** except that the terms of the trust provide that D is entitled to all of the net income from the trust except for the income earned during the year of her death.

Here we see the application of the "period not ascertainable without reference to his death" language of the statute. Because it would be impossible to calculate the end date of D's income interest without taking into account her date of death, the interest has been retained for the proscribed time, and § 2036(a)(1) will apply.[11] Whenever the end date for D's income interest depends on her date of death, the statute will apply.

---

[10] As we saw in **Chapter One**, we avoid taxing the gift twice by reducing the tentative tax on D's estate by the amount of any gift tax that would have been payable on the original gift using the rates in effect for the year of D's death. § 2001(b)(2).

[11] § 20.2036–1(b)(1)(i).

Variation 1(c): **The trust provides income to D or her estate for 10 years, at which time the trust terminates and the corpus is to be distributed to F. D dies after 5 years.**

Now the term of D's income interest makes no reference to her life, indeed it does not terminate on D's death and will be enjoyed by her estate until the end of the trust term. Nevertheless, because D's income interest does not in fact end before her death, § 2036(a)(1) will reach the value of the interest that is postponed until after her death: F's remainder. Note under our facts the full value of the property will be included in D's estate, and that value will include the remaining 5 years of income payments to be made to D's estate as well as F's remainder.[12] If, however, D survives the ten year trust term, the property will vest in F, and nothing will be included in D's estate.

Variation 1(d): **The trust provides for income to X for life, then to D for life, remainder to F, or her estate. X predeceases D, so at the time of D's death she is the income beneficiary.**

Here D's life is used as the measuring stick for enjoyment of F's remainder, so we are within the statute. In this case the regulations describe the retention as either for D's life or for a period which does not in fact end before her death, and the full date of death value will be included in her estate under § 2036.[13] Note that once D dies, the entire value of the property is represented by F's remainder.

What if D died while X was still alive, so that D's income interest never commenced? Nevertheless, D's income interest is measured by her life, so should we include the full value of the property under § 2036? In answering these questions it is useful to focus on the statute's target of "testamentary substitutes." There are two interests in the trust at issue, X's income interest, and F's remainder. Only F must wait until after D's death to enjoy his interest, X's was in existence during D's life, and D did not retain any strings with respect to it. As a result, the value of F's remainder, which in this case will be the fair market value of the property *minus* the value of X's income interest, will be included in the estate.[14]

Example #2: **D transfers assets to a bank as Trustee under an irrevocable trust for the benefit of her Son (S), age 6. The trust provides that until S reaches age 21, the Trustee shall distribute income and principal to him in such amounts as the Trustee deems necessary for S's support and maintenance. When S reaches age 21 the principal of the trust is to be distributed to S. If S dies before**

---

[12] § 20.2036–1(c)(1)(i).

[13] § 20.2036–1(b)(1)(ii).

[14] Id.

reaching the age of 21, the principal of the trust is to be distributed to S's estate.

At first blush it would appear that D has parted with all of her interests in the assets transferred to the trust, and has retained no interest. However, state laws impose on parents a legal obligation to support their minor children, and to the extent that the trust income can be used to defray that obligation, D has retained the right to the income from the property within the meaning of § 2036(a)(1).[15] Defining a parent's support obligation under state law can be difficult, as it can vary with the means of the family. Presumably the § 2036(a)(1) problem could be avoided in this case if the trust instrument specifically directed the Trustee to make distribution only in excess of D's legal obligation to support the child. A better drafted trust might allow the Trustee unfettered discretion to make income and principal distributions, rather than couching them in terms of S's support and maintenance[16]

Example #3: On February 1 of the current year, Brother (B) transfers $1,000,000 to the B Trust which provides as follows: Income to Sister (S) for life, remainder to S's children or their estates.

If the form of this transaction is respected, B has simply made a taxable gift of $1,000,000. Since B has apparently not retained any interest in the trust, when B dies no part of the trust will be included in his estate.

Variation: Same facts as ***Example #3,*** except that, in addition, on May 1 of the current year S transfers $800,000 to the S Trust, which provides as follows: Income to B for life, remainder to B's children or their estates.

The issue raised by the additional facts in this variation is whether the creation of the two trusts will be seen as independent transactions, or as "reciprocal trusts." The Supreme Court in *U.S. v. Estate of Grace*[17] held that in making that determination the key factor is whether the two trusts were interrelated. The subjective intent of the settlors does not matter. What does matter is "whether the trusts created by the settlors placed each other in approximately the same objective economic position as they would have been in had each created his own trust with himself, rather than the other, as the life beneficiary." If the trusts are determined to be reciprocal, then "to the extent of mutual value" the settlors will be treated as if they created a trust naming themselves as beneficiaries.

The two trusts in the ***Variation*** fall squarely within *Estate of Grace* and will be treated as reciprocal trusts to the extent of $800,000. Therefore

---

[15] § 20.2036–1(b)(2).

[16] Indeed, as we will see in ***Chapter Eight***, if D wants the contributions to the trust to be eligible for the annual exclusion, that sort of unfettered discretion is necessary.

[17] 395 U.S. 316 (1969).

B will be treated as if he were the sole settlor of the **S Trust**, and S will be treated as being the settlor of 80% of the value of the **B Trust** (B having contributed the balance). On B's death, the entire value of the **S Trust** would be includible in his estate; and on S's death, 80% of the value the **B Trust** would be includible in her estate.

Example #4: **D gave to her friend, F, a painting worth $1,000,000, and memorialized the gift in writing. The painting remained hanging on D's wall until she died several years later. At D's death the painting was worth $2,000,000.**

Here, although the painting does not generate current income, D may have retained the "possession or enjoyment" of the property, the other leg of § 2036(a)(1). The reasoning should be clear: F may be in the same position she would have been had she owned the painting until she died, and left it to F by will. The trickier question is whether the necessary "retention" has taken place: as part of the transfer to F did D reserve the right to continued possession of the painting? If the deed of gift expressly recited that D would hold onto the painting until she died, then the "retention" element of the statute would be easy to satisfy. But if it did not, then we don't know why the painting never moved; maybe F could have taken the painting at any time, but never got around to picking it up. Or maybe there was an unwritten agreement that D would keep the painting. The regulations take the position that "an interest or right is treated as having been retained or reserved if at the time of the transfer there was an understanding, express, or implied, that the interest or right would later be conferred."[18]

Litigation in this area has mostly involved residences, and the courts have been willing to find the implied understanding where exclusive possession is in the decedent's hands until death.[19] It would seem likely that the same principle would apply to the painting.

Retention of Voting Rights in a Controlled Corporation: § 2036(b)

Section 2036(b) treats the retention of the right to vote shares of stock in a controlled corporation as the retention of the enjoyment of those shares for purposes of § 2036(a)(1). The threshold for control is not majority ownership. Under § 2036(b)(2) a controlled corporation is one in which,

---

[18] § 20.2036–1(a).

[19] If the decedent gives the family residence to a family member but continues to live in it by herself rent-free until she dies, § 2036(a)(1) almost surely will apply. Rev. Rul. 70–155, 1970–1 C.B. 189. The harder cases are where the decedent gives the residence to a family member and continues to live in the residence with the donee. In Rev. Rul. 78–409, 1978–2 C.B. 234, the Service ruled that where the decedent gave his son the family residence but continued to live there until his death, § 2036(a)(1) applied even though the son paid all the expenses and lived there with his wife. Even though there was no explicit agreement, the Service assumed an understanding among the parties. But see, Estate of *Spruill v. Comm'r*, 89 TC 1197 (1987) (on similar facts, no inclusion).

after the transfer and during the three years prior to the decedent's death, the decedent either (1) owned, or (2) had the right to vote, 20% or more of all shares of voting stock. In determining stock ownership (not voting power), the statute refers the attribution rules of § 318 of the Code.

Section 2036(b) was enacted in 1976 to overrule the Supreme Court's decision in *U.S. v. Byrum*.[20] In *Byrum*, the decedent had irrevocably transferred stock in a family owned corporation to a trust, retaining the right to vote the stock. The government's principal argument was that the value of the stock should be brought back into his gross estate under § 2036(a)(2).[21] It argued that by retaining voting control, the decedent had control over corporate dividend policy and therefore controlled the flow of income to the trust. The Supreme Court, however, thought this was a stretch and rejected the government's argument, holding that ". . . Byrum did not have an unconstrained *de facto* power to regulate the flow of dividends to the trust, much less the 'right' to designate who was to enjoy the income from the trust property . . ."[22]

Following the loss in *Byrum* the Treasury successfully made the argument to the Congress, which responded by enacting § 2036(b). To more fully understand § 2036(b), consider the following example.

Example #5: **Family Corp. is entirely owned by D and her family. It has only one class of stock, and of its 100 shares outstanding D owns 15 shares and her husband, H, owns 10 shares. The remaining 75 shares are owned by D's siblings. D transfers 10 shares of Family Corp. stock to a trust for the benefit of her children, naming herself as Trustee. At the time of D's death, D was acting as Trustee, and no shares of stock in Family Corp. had changed hands since D created the trust.**

In order for § 2036(b) to apply, two conditions must be met. First, D must have retained the right to vote the transferred shares, either directly or indirectly. Second, the shares transferred must be those of a "controlled corporation," as defined by § 2036(b)(2).

Retention of Voting Rights: Because D transferred the stock to a trust of which she is Trustee, she will continue to have power to vote that stock, so the necessary "retention" has occurred.

Controlled Corporation: Because we have the necessary retention, we must then decide whether Family Corp. is a controlled corporation within the meaning of the statute. If D either owns, or has the right to vote, at least 20% of Family Corp.'s voting shares, the corporation will be controlled. In determining the number of shares that D is deemed to own,

---

[20] 408 U.S. 125 (1972).

[21] It also argued that the stock should be brought back under § 2036(a)(1) because the retention gave him job security and protected his compensation. Id. at 145–50.

[22] Id. at 143.

we apply to stock attribution rules of § 318. Note that the attribution rules of § 318 apply *only* for purposes of determining stock ownership, not voting power.

Here D has the right to vote 15 shares (5 owned individually and 10 as Trustee), so she lacks the necessary voting power to reach control. We must therefore determine how many shares she owns within the meaning of the statute, and to do so we must refer to § 318. Section 318(a)(1) treats stock owned by the members of an individual's family as if they were owned by the individual (ownership of the stock is "attributed to" the individual). The statute defines "members of family" to include one's spouse, children, grandchildren and parents. It does not attribute stock owned by one's brothers and sisters. On these facts, therefore, in addition to the 5 shares D actually owns, she is considered to own the 10 shares owned by H and any shares owned by her children. D's children do not own any shares outright. They are, however, the beneficiaries of the trust that owns the 10 shares that D transferred. Section 318(a)(2)(B) attributes stock owned by a trust to the trust beneficiaries, in proportion to their interests. As a result, the 10 shares owned by the trust will be attributed to the children under § 318(a)(2), and then further attributed to D under § 318(a)(1).[23] After all the dust settles, D is considered to own the 5 shares she owns outright, the 10 that are owned by her husband, and the 10 that are owned by the trust. These 25 shares represent 25% of the stock of Family Corp. and as a result the corporation is "controlled" within the meaning of the statute. As a consequence, § 2036(a)(1) will apply, and the stock that D transferred to the trust will be included in her gross estate at its fair market value as of the date of her death.

To the extent that Congress' goal in enacting § 2036(b) was to include in the gross estate stock over which the grantor retains voting control, it does a poor job. Indeed, § 2036(b) could be aptly described as a trap for the unwary. As long as one is aware of it, it is easy to avoid. For example, in **Example #5**, above, if D appointed her husband H, as Trustee, she would not retain the right to vote the transferred stock and § 2036(b) would not apply. This is true because while we apply the attribution rules for purposes of calculating how many shares she owns, they do not apply in determining the shares she has the power to vote.

To illustrate the statute's limitations, consider D who owns 100% of the shares in her closely-held corporation. She would like to transfer half the value of the corporation to a trust for her children, but does not want to share control of the corporation. One way to accomplish her goals without running afoul of § 2036(b) would simply be to engage in a tax-free recapitalization, creating a new class of stock that has no voting rights. She could then transfer the non-voting stock to a trust, and if she wanted to,

---

[23] This is sometimes referred to as "double attribution." Section 318(a)(5) contains operating rules that prevent double attribution in some situations, but not this one.

name herself as Trustee. Although D has maintained absolute control over the corporation, since she did not retain the vote of the shares she transferred, § 2036(b) does not apply.

Section 2036(a)(2): Retained Powers over Income

We now turn to the second prong of § 2036. As discussed above, § 2036(a)(2) applies when the decedent has not retained the right to personally enjoy the income from the property, but has retained the power to determine who will enjoy it. Transfers subject to § 2036(a)(2) may also be picked up by § 2038, discussed below.

Section 2036(a)(2) is structured similarly to § 2036(a)(1). The difference is that while § 2036(a)(1) is triggered by retaining a *beneficial interest* in the income from the property, § 2036(a)(2) is triggered by the decedent retaining "the right, either alone or in conjunction with any person, to *designate the persons* who shall possess or enjoy the property, or the income therefrom."

As noted above, even though § 2036(a)(2) seems to apply to powers over either the income *or* the underlying property, the regulations limit its application to powers that affect the enjoyment of the *income* of the property, leaving to § 2038 powers that only affect the remainder.[24]

The following example illustrates the application of § 2036(a)(2).

Example #6: **D transfers stock worth $1,000,000 into an irrevocable trust, and the trust instrument provides as follows:**

> **So long as D is alive the Trustee shall distribute the net income of the trust between F and G in such shares as the Trustee determines in its sole discretion. On D's death the Trustee shall distribute the trust corpus to F or her estate.**

Consider the consequences under § 2036(a)(2) in each of the following variations:

> *Variation 6(a):* **D names herself as Trustee, and is acting in that capacity until her death five years later, when the trust assets are worth $2,000,000.**

Here D has not retained any right to receive the income herself, so § 2036(a)(1) is inapplicable. Nevertheless, D's retained power, as Trustee, to designate the amounts of income to be distributed between F and G is sufficient to bring the property into her estate under § 2036(a)(2). The date of death value of $2,000,000 will be included in her estate.

> *Variation 6(b):* **D names a bank as Trustee, but under the terms of the trust instrument she has the right to remove**

---

[24] § 20.2036–1(b)(3).

the Trustee and appoint a successor Trustee, including herself. The bank is still acting as Trustee when D dies.

The power over enjoyment of the income is held by the Trustee in this variation, and that is not D. Nevertheless, D's right to remove the Trustee and take the reins into her own hands will result in inclusion under § 2036(a)(2).[25] Essentially the powers of the Trustee are attributed to D because of the right of removal. Note that if D wants to retain the right to remove the Trustee, the eligible successors should explicitly exclude D.

There is nothing in the regulations that considers the relationship between the decedent and the Trustee; the inquiry is limited to whether D is the Trustee or has the power to remove the Trustee and appoint herself. Indeed, there is substantial case law support for the proposition that D can appoint a friend, relative or spouse as initial Trustee.[26] Nevertheless, the government's position in the context of removal powers is that the eligible successors must be individual or corporate successor trustees that are not related or subordinate to the decedent (within the meaning of § 672(c) of the Code).[27] This position seems to us to be highly questionable. It is hard to explain why it is permissible to name certain individuals as initial trustees but not name them as eligible successor trustees.

Variation 6(c): **D names herself as Trustee. The trust gives the Trustee the discretion to divide the income between F and G, but F and G need to consent if the distribution is other than equal. D acting as Trustee at the time of her death.**

Here it would seem that D's retained power is subject to a substantial restriction: neither F nor G would readily agree to reduce their share of the trust income. Indeed, the adversity of F and G's interests would be sufficient to render the gift of the income interest complete under § 25.2511–2(e). Nevertheless, § 2036(a)(2) will apply, and bring the entire property into D's estate.[28] The regulations provide that it is immaterial whether the power is exercisable alone, or in conjunction with another person, whether or not that person has an adverse interest.

Variation 6(d): **D names herself as Trustee. The trust provides for income to F for 10 years, remainder to G or his estate. In any given year the Trustee can withhold income from F and add it to the trust principal (referred to as**

---

[25] § 20.2036–1(b)(3). If, however, she has the ability to "trustee shop" by retaining the right to remove one corporate trustee and appoint another corporate trustee § 2036 will not apply. *Estate of Wall v. Comm'r*, 101 T.C.300 (1993).

[26] *Comm'r v. Irving Trust Co.*, 147 F.2d 946 (2d Cir 1945).

[27] Rev. Rul. 95–58, 1995-2 C.B. 191.

[28] § 20.2036–1(b)(3).

"accumulating" the income). D dies while acting as Trustee.

Here D's power to withhold income from F in any given year, and shift it to G via the remainder, is clearly sufficient to result in inclusion under § 2036(a)(2).

Variation 6(e): **D names herself as Trustee. The trust provides for income to F for 10 years, remainder to F or his estate. The Trustee has the power to accumulate the income during any given year. D dies while acting as Trustee.**

Here it would seem that the statute should not apply, given that D seems to have not retained "the right . . . to designate the persons who shall possess or enjoy the property or the income therefrom". F (or his estate, if he fails to survive D) will receive the income either way; it is only a question of when he will receive it. Yet the Tax Court[29] and several Circuit Courts of Appeal[30] have found that inclusion will result under these facts. Section 2036(a)(2) applies when the decedent has retained a power to "designate the persons who shall possess or enjoy the property or the income therefrom." In this case, D's power is limited to deciding between current receipt of the income by F, or later distribution to F or his estate. We typically view F and his estate as one person, nevertheless the cases cited consider the possibility that the accumulation decision will place the income in the hands of F's heirs and assigns, which they deem a sufficient power to trigger the statute. Although we believe this is a very strained interpretation of the statute, it appears to be settled law.

Again note the contrast between the result here and the gift tax result. Under § 25.2511–2(d), a gift is not rendered incomplete "merely because the donor reserves the power to change the manner or time of enjoyment." So while the donor does relinquish dominion and control for gift tax purposes, it is not a sufficient relinquishment to avoid application of § 2036(a)(2).

Variation 6(f): **D names herself as Trustee. The trust provides for income to X for life in amounts as needed for X's health and support, any excess income is accumulated and added to principal. On X's death the principal is distributed to Y, or his estate. D dies while acting as Trustee capacity.**

Here it would seem that the trust should be included in D's estate under § 2036(a)(2), because D retained the power to choose to distribute the income between X and Y. But that power is not unconstrained; the

---

[29] *Estate of O'Connor v. Comm'r,* 54 TC 969 (1970).

[30] *Joy v. U.S.,* 404 F.2d 419 (6th Cir. 1968).

Trustee is subject to an ascertainable standard, i.e., "health and support," and the courts have held that powers so constrained are outside the scope of § 2036(a)(2).[31] If, however, the trust used a standard such as "comfort and happiness," the statute would apply.

Part C. Section 2038

Section 2038, entitled "Revocable Transfers," brings back into the gross estate property that the decedent transferred during life

> "where the enjoyment thereof was subject at the date of his death to any change through the exercise of a power (in whatever capacity exercisable) by the decedent alone or in conjunction with any other person . . . to alter, amend, revoke, or terminate. . ."

This language is quite broad and sweeping, and has the ability to reach many interests. It often will apply to income interests that are also governed by § 2036(a)(2). There is one important distinction between the two sections, however. When § 2036(a)(2) applies it will usually cause inclusion of the entire property, income interest and remainder alike. Section 2038 is more targeted. It focuses on each separate interest, and only those that are subject to the proscribed power will be brought back into the estate.

The classic example of a transaction subject to § 2038 is a revocable living trust, a popular probate avoidance device. The grantor of a revocable living trust transfers the bulk of his assets to the trust during life, and retains the right to revoke the trust. The trust essentially functions as a surrogate for the grantor during his life, and as a will substitute at death. The grantor is often the Trustee, is entitled to all of the income of the trust during his lifetime, and as much of the principal as he chooses. The grantor's interest terminates at death, and the trust directs where the property goes at that time, just like a will. Because the grantor's interest terminates at death, the trust is beyond the reach of § 2033. But it represents a quintessential "testamentary substitute," and will be included in the grantor's estate. The only question is which section will apply. The grantor's rights and powers over income and principal would be sufficient to bring the property into the grantor's estate under either § 2036(a)(1), (a)(2) or 2038. Section 2038 gets there most directly, because of the power of revocation.

Despite its title ("Revocable Transfers") § 2038 reaches well beyond express powers to revoke, like those in the revocable living trust situation. Like § 2036(a)(2), its focus is on powers held by the decedent at death which allow him to "alter, amend, or revoke," i.e., to control the enjoyment of

---

[31] The case most often cited for this proposition is *Jennings v. Smith*, 161 F.2d 74 (2d Cir. 1947). That case found the same result for purposes of § 2038. The rule has not found its way into the regulations, but has been relied upon by the IRS in various rulings.

others in the trust, and frequently those powers are held in the capacity of trustee. So revocable trusts clearly come with § 2038, and irrevocable trusts can if the decedent holds powers over a trust created by him. As was true under § 2036(a)(2), if the decedent retains the right to remove a trustee and appoint himself instead, the trustee powers will be attributed to him.[32]

One item of note is that, in contrast with § 2036(a)(2), § 2038 does not require that the decedent "retain" the prohibited power at the time of the initial transfer, just that he hold it at death. Assume, for example, the decedent created a trust with an independent trustee, who subsequently resigned. If an eligible successor wasn't available, and a court were to appoint the decedent as successor trustee, if he were acting in that capacity at death then § 2038 would apply.

The following examples illustrate the more complex applications of § 2038, and compare its reach to that of § 2036(a)(2).

Example #7:   **G transfers $1,000,000 in assets to an irrevocable trust that provides for income to A for life, remainder to A's issue. G dies survived by A. Consider the consequences under §§ 2038 and 2036(a)(2) in each of the following variations.**

Variation 7(a): G retains the power to allocate the remainder among A's issue.

In this case G does not retain the right to retake the property for her own benefit. Nevertheless, she has retained a "power" over the property; she has reserved the right to decide which of A's issue will receive the property when A dies. The enjoyment of the remainder is subject to G's power, and hence the value of the remainder at G's death will be included in her estate under § 2038.

Note that § 2038 will not sweep the entire property into G's estate; it only acts to bring in the interest over which the decedent held the power. In this case G's power is limited to controlling the remainder, and only the actuarial value of the remainder will be included in her estate; the value of A's remaining income interest will not be included. Contrast this result with the consequences of invoking § 2036. Under that section if a decedent retains control over the income from property, typically the entire value of the property is swept into his estate. Section 2038 operates in a much more targeted fashion.

By its terms it would seem that § 2036(a)(2) could apply in this instance, because the statute requires inclusion if the decedent retained the right "to designate the persons who shall possess or enjoy *the property* or the income therefrom." Yet, as noted above, the regulations limit the

---

[32] § 20.2038–1(a)(3).

reach of § 2036(a)(2) to powers over income.[33] As we will see below, there are many instances in which both sections will apply, and the government will argue for the theory that requires the largest measure of inclusion, which is usually § 2036. To that end, after you have read this Part and worked through the examples, we suggest that you review the examples in Part B dealing with § 2036(a)(2) to try to determine whether and how § 2038 would apply in those situations.

The bottom line in this variation is that the actuarial value of the remainder will be included in G's estate under § 2038.

Variation 7(b): **The trust instrument authorizes the Trustee to distribute principal to A during her lifetime in the Trustee's sole discretion.**

(i)   G is acting as Trustee at the time of her death.

Through exercise of this power G has the ability to eliminate the interests of the remaindermen, A's issue, thus the value of the remainder will be included in G's estate at death under § 2038. Exercise of the power will not reduce A's income interest, she will receive the income in any event, either by virtue of her income interest in the trust or as outright owner of the property. As a result, the income interest is beyond the reach of both § 2038 and § 2036(a)(2). Thus, the actuarial value of the remainder interest will be included in G's estate under § 2038, the income interest will not.

(ii) G is not the Trustee of the trust, nor is she an eligible successor Trustee.

In this case § 2038 will not apply, because the power to change the interests of the remaindermen is not held by G. Since G did not retain any power over the income interest, § 2036(a)(2) cannot apply. So neither the income nor the remainder will be included in G's estate.

Variation 7(c): **The trust instrument authorizes the Trustee to distribute principal to A during her lifetime in such amounts as the Trustee deems necessary for A's health and education. G is acting as Trustee at the time of her death.**

As was the case under § 2036(a)(2), the courts have long held that powers constrained by judicially enforceable ascertainable standards, which are generally agreed to include health and education, are not subject to § 2038.[34] So neither § 2036(a)(2) nor § 2038 will apply.

Example #8: **G transfers $1,000,000 in an irrevocable trust for the benefit of her 25 year old son S. The Trustee is directed to distribute the entire net income to S in annual installments, and to**

---

[33] § 20.2036–1(b)(3)(iii).

[34] *Jennings v. Smith*, supra note 31.

distribute the principal to S when he reaches age 40. The Trustee is also authorized to distribute the principal to S at an earlier age if the Trustee decides S is sufficiently responsible. If S dies prior to reaching age 40 the trust is to be distributed to his estate. G is acting as Trustee of the trust at the time of her death, when S is 35 years old.

In this case it appears that G does not have the power to decide *who* will receive the property, the income and the remainder will pass to S (or his estate) regardless. What G has retained is the power to determine *when* S will received the principal; she has the ability to accelerate the receipt by S of the principal by terminating the trust early. We saw in ***Chapter Three*** that this type of power to alter the "time and manner of enjoyment" of property will not render a gift of the property incomplete; in this case G has made a completed gift of the entire trust at the time she creates it.

Nevertheless, such powers ***are*** sufficient to trigger § 2038. The Supreme Court held so in *Lober v. U.S.*,[35] and the rule of *Lober* is now contained in the regulations at § 20.2038–1(a), which states:

> Section 2038 is applicable to any power affecting the time or manner of enjoyment of property or its income, even though the identity of the beneficiary is not affected.

Because it applies in a targeted fashion, we have to examine how § 2038 will apply to each separate interest in the trust. Here G's power to accelerate the time when S will receive the principal will cause inclusion of the remainder in her estate under § 2038. Although the amount of income generated by the trust will be reduced if G distributes principal to S, as the fee owner of that principal amount S will continue to receive that income in his individual capacity. Thus G does not have any power over the income interest that would invoke either § 2038 or § 2036(a)(2). Therefore, the actuarial value of the remainder, but not the income interest, at the time G dies will be included in G's gross estate. Put another way, the value of the trust, minus the value of the income interest, will be included in her gross estate.

Part D. Section 2037

Section 2037 is probably the most elusive of the "string" provisions. Like §§ 2036 and 2038, it will only apply when the decedent made a transfer during life for less than full and adequate consideration. It is important to remember that all three sections had their genesis in the 1916 "testamentary substitutes" rule. As we noted at the beginning of this chapter, inclusion under that rule required not only that enjoyment of an interest was postponed until the decedent died, but also that the decedent

---

[35] 346 U.S. 335 (1953).

has retained or held some "string" with respect to the property. We have seen that the necessary strings for §§ 2036 and 2038 have to do with enjoyment of or powers over income or the property, the "string" that will invoke § 2037 is the possibility reserved by the decedent when he created the trust that he might get the property back (a "reversion), so long as the value of that reversion is more than a de minimis amount. When the decedent has retained that reversion IT IS NOT just the reversion that is brought back into the estate. The reversion is just the necessary string. Instead, as we'll see in the examples, if the decedent did retain a reversion, all other interests in the trust that can only be enjoyed after the decedent dies are included in the estate under § 2037.

Section 2037 has four distinct requirements, which, if met, will cause a property interest to be brought back into the estate:

1. First, the decedent must have transferred the property interest during life for less than full and adequate consideration.

2. Second, the property interest can be enjoyed ONLY following the death of the decedent. If the interest can be enjoyed while the decedent is living, then it is not a testamentary substitute, and § 2037 does not apply to that interest.

3. The decedent must have retained a right to reacquire the property (i.e., a reversionary interest). This can be done expressly, or it may exist by operation of law.

4. The value of that reversionary interest, as of the time of decedent's death, must be more than 5% of the value of the entire property.

Thus, in considering transactions that might come within § 2037, focus on each interest that the Grantor has transferred, and ask yourself whether each of the four requirements are met *with respect to that interest*. If they aren't, then § 2037 is inapplicable. If they are, then the value of that particular interest will be brought into the estate.

The following example and its variations illustrate the application of § 2037.

Example #9: **Daughter (D) creates an irrevocable trust that provides for income to D's mother (M) for M's life, remainder to D, if she is then living, and if not then to D's son (S), or his estate. D dies during M's life.**

Remember that we are looking for a testamentary substitute. In this case, where is the testamentary substitute? In other words, what interests created by D can only be enjoyed after D dies? M has been enjoying her interest during D's life. But S (or his heirs) cannot possibly enjoy the remainder during D's life. If D is alive when M dies then D will get the property back, and S or his estate will receive nothing under the trust. For S's interest to become possessory, D must die before M. It is this interest, S's remainder, that is the testamentary substitute: It cannot be enjoyed while D is alive.

Now apply the four requirements described above:

1. D transferred the assets into the trust during her life for no consideration.

2. M is enjoying her income interest during D's life, so it won't be reached by § 2037. But S, or his estate, cannot possibly enjoy the remainder if D is alive. We focus on the "interest" held by S or his estate, and if it can't be enjoyed during D's life, then § 2037 will reach it.

3. D retained a reversionary interest in the property. If D is alive when M dies she will receive the property back.

4. If the value of the reversionary interest is more than 5% of the total value of the property, then § 2037 will apply. How would you value the reversionary interest? An actuary would value it as of the moment *before* D dies (it would obviously become worthless at D's death), taking into account the relative ages of D and M. Because M is D's mother, the actuarial chances of D surviving her mother are quite large, so we'll assume that the value of the reversion is greater than 5%.[36]

So long as the 5% test is met, § 2037 will apply. What will it bring into the estate? The answer is only the remainder interest, the "testamentary substitute." Thus, the full value of the property, minus the value of M's income interest, will be included in D's estate.

Variation 9(a): The trust provides for income to M for M's life, remainder to S or his estate.

Will § 2037 apply here? Clearly not, because D did not retain a reversion, and both M's and S's interests can be enjoyed during D's life. Even if D is alive at M's death, S will receive the remainder.

Variation 9(b): The trust provides for income to M or her estate for D's life, remainder to S or his estate.

Will § 2037 apply here? Now S's interest is dependent upon surviving D; there is no way he will receive his remainder until after D dies, because D's life is the measuring stick for M's income interest. So this is to some extent a testamentary substitute. But what is lacking are any "strings"

---

[36] Consider an example where M was 50 and D was 80: now the chances of D surviving M are quite small, and the reversionary interest is worth much less.

held by D with respect to the property. Under § 2036 the required string is some interest in or power over the income. Under § 2038 the required string is some power to alter the enjoyment of the property. And under § 2037 the required string is a chance that the property will revert to the transferor. D has retained no strings, and none of the sections will apply.

Variation 9(c): **The trust provides for income to M or her estate for D's life, remainder to S.**

The difference between this case and **Variation 9(b)** is that the trust fails to designate what happens to the property if S dies during D's life; there is no alternate taker, as was the case in **Variation 9(b)**. When D dies, the income interest will cease, and the principal has to go somewhere. Local law will dictate the result, which in most cases means that the property will revert to D's estate. This is referred to as a "reversion by operation of law," and such interests are included in the term "reversionary interest" for purposes of § 2037. Depending on the ages of the various beneficiaries, that interest could have substantial value, or its value could be trivial.

This problem illustrates the role of the 5% rule. That rule functions as a "de minimis" rule. If the chances of the property reverting to the decedent are remote, so that the value of the reversionary interest equals only 5% or less of the total property's value, then § 2037 won't apply. The rule has its source in a 1949 Supreme Court case, *Estate of Spiegel.*[37] In that case, a decedent's estate was held to include a trust worth more than $1,000,000. Decedent created the trust during his life; it provided for income to the decedent's children so long as he was alive, and at his death the principal was to be distributed to his children (he had three). The share of any deceased child would go to his descendants. The trust did not explicitly state what would happen if the decedent was survived by none of his children or their descendants. Under state law, if that were to happen, the trust would revert to the decedent's estate. In fact, when the decedent died his three children were alive, as were a number of grandchildren, so that the value of this reversionary interest (i.e., the chance that the property would ultimately return to the decedent's estate) was about $70. This resulted in inclusion of the full $1,000,000 trust because at that time the statute contained no de minimis rule. The court's decision was notable for two reasons: first, it made clear that reversions by operation of law were within the ambit of the statute. Second, the statute as then written did not allow for exceptions where the value of the reversion was trivial in relation to the property's value. Congress responded by adding the 5% rule to the statute.

---

[37]   335 U.S. 701 (1949).

Part E. Section 2035

As we discussed in Part A, § 2035 originally included in the gross estate transfers made "in contemplation of death," a subjective rule that was very difficult to administer; how do you determine what the (now deceased) decedent was contemplating when he made a transfer? In 1976 Congress changed the statute to establish an objective rule: gratuitous transfers were brought back into the estate if they were made within three years of death, regardless of the decedent's subjective intent. The statute was also amended to require that gift taxes paid on gifts made within three years of death should be included in the estate. In 1981 Congress narrowed the inclusion rule substantially. No longer are outright gifts made prior to death included in the estate, whenever made. The current statute (§ 2035(a)) is triggered only when the decedent—within three years of death—relinquishes an interest in, or powers over, property that would otherwise cause inclusion under §§ 2036, 2037, 2038 or 2042. Put another way, if those sections would have applied but for the decedent giving up an interest or power within three years of death, § 2035(a) will apply. In addition § 2035(b) includes the gift tax paid on *any* gift made within three years of death.

To illustrate, consider the following examples:

Example #10: **In 2007 D creates a trust that provides for income to D for life, remainder to D's son, S, or his estate. The trust had a value of $1,000,000 in 2007, and in 2017 has a value of $5,000,000.**

Variation 10(a): **D dies in 2017 while enjoying the income interest.**

This is a classic example of the application of § 2036(a)(1). The full date of death value of the trust will be included in D's estate.

Variation 10(b): **In 2015 D transfers the income interest by gift to S, when its actuarial value is $500,000. She dies in 2017.**

Now we are in the territory of § 2035(a). D transferred an interest in property (the income interest) within three years of her death, and had she not transferred it the entire trust would have been included in her estate under § 2036. As a result, the full date of death value of the trust will be included in her estate under § 2035(a). If she paid any gift tax with respect to the gift of the income interest, then it would also be included under § 2035(b). The same result would occur if D had retained a reversion that would invoke § 2037, or a power over the property that would violate § 2038, and surrendered that reversion or power within three years of death.

As noted in the Introduction to this *Chapter Four*, in 1976 Congress added to the statute a rule now found in § 2035(b). That rule includes in the gross estate the amount of any gift tax paid by the decedent (or his estate) on gifts made by the decedent or his spouse within three years of death. This rule is sometimes referred to as the "gift tax gross-up" and is designed to reduce the opportunities for transfer tax savings through lifetime gifts. To illustrate, consider the following:

Example #11: In 2014 D makes an outright lifetime gift to her daughter of $5,000,000 worth of publicly traded stock. She has previously used all of her exemption amount, so has a resulting gift tax bill of $2,000,000. She dies in 2018 with a gross estate of $20,000,000, exclusive of any possible inclusion under § 2035. The stock that she gave to her daughter is worth $7,000,000 when D dies.

In this case § 2035 will not operate, because the gift made by D was made more than three years prior to her death. The gifted securities will not be included in her gross estate, nor will any of the appreciation on those securities between the date of the gift and the date of D's death ($2,000,000 in this case). In addition, the $2,000,000 in gift tax paid by D will not be included in her estate. That $2,000,000 was not taxed as part of the gift, it is not "grossed up" under § 2035 because of the three year rule, so that amount, plus any appreciation on that amount, has been removed from D's estate at zero transfer tax cost. At a 40% estate tax rate that reduces her estate tax bill by at least $1,600,000.

Variation: Same as *Example #11* but D dies in 2016.

Now, because the gift was made within three years of her death, § 2035 will play a role. It will not operate to include the transferred securities in her estate. As we discussed above, § 2035 only brings lifetime gifts into the estate if they are of interests or powers that would have resulted in inclusion under §§ 2036–2038. However, § 2035(b) will apply, and will bring back into her estate the $2,000,000 in gift taxes that are paid on the gift. The estate is "grossed up" to include that amount.

Part F. Exception for Transfers Made for Adequate and Full Consideration

None of the sections that we have studied in this chapter will apply if the decedent's transfer in question was made for "adequate and full consideration." Sections 2036, 2037 and 2038 each contain a parenthetical excepting transfers "(in case of a bona fide sale for an adequate and full consideration in money or money's worth)." Section 2035(d) contains a similar exception for transfers made within three years of death. These exceptions can raise some interesting issues that we will explore in the following examples.

As a threshold matter, we know that a sale of property for its full fair market value does not result in a gift for gift tax purposes. If D sells $1,000,000 worth of stock to his son for cash of $1,000,000, there is no gift. Think about why that is the case. The stock is no longer in D's estate, but the consideration of equivalent value replaces it. The gift tax is aimed at transactions that reduce the amount of the estate, and when an asset is transferred for its full value, then there is no reduction in the estate. This basic principle of taxing transactions that reduce the estate can guide us as we apply the rules to §§ 2035–2038.

Example #12: **In year one D transfers $1,000,000 in stock to a trust that provides income to D for life, remainder to D's nephew N, or his estate. At D's death in year six, the stock has a value of $3,000,000.**

Variation 12(a): **D dies in year six, having made no changes to the trust.**

D has clearly made a transfer that will result in inclusion of the full $3,000,000 value of the trust under § 2036.

Variation 12(b): **In year four, D makes a gift of his retained income interest to his brother. He then dies in year six.**

Now when D dies, he no longer holds the offending income interest, so he has avoided application of § 2036. But has he avoided taxation of the trust altogether? He has not, this is an example of the application of § 2035: because D transferred the income interest within three years of his death, and because § 2036 would have included the trust had he not made the transfer, the trust will be brought back into his estate by § 2035. So his gross estate will include the $3,000,000 date of death value of the stock. Note that if D had shed the income interest more than three years prior to death, the transfer would successfully avoid this result.

Variation 12(c): **In year four, D sells the retained income interest to his brother for its fair market value of $200,000. D dies in year six.**

Now D may have been successful in removing the property from his estate. Simply gifting the income interest didn't work if D died with three years of the transfer (***Variation 12(b)***), but there is an exception in § 2035(d) that says § 2035(a) won't apply to any "bona fide sale for an adequate consideration in money or money's worth." If indeed the fair market value of the income interest, determined under § 7520, is $200,000, then it seems D has been successful in avoiding § 2035.

Is there anything troubling about that result? Going back to the basic proposition that sales for full value do not deplete the estate, how does this transfer fit within that construct? Had D continued to hold the income interest until death, $3,000,000 would have been included in his estate. Is that amount replaced by the consideration paid for the income interest? We think not. So it would seem we have a problem!

This is precisely what the taxpayer tried to accomplish in *U.S. v. Allen*.[38] In that case the decedent created a trust in 1932. She transferred assets to it, and reserved the right to 60% of the income. The remaining 40% of the income and all the remainder went to her children. Roughly 30 years later, when she was 78, she learned that her retained income interest would result in inclusion of 60% of the trust in her estate. So she was advised to get rid of it. Had she made a gift of it, § 2035 would capture the trust if she died within three years. So her advisers decided she should sell the income interest for its fair market value. A willing buyer was found in her son, who paid her $140,000 for the 60% income interest, an amount slightly in excess of its actuarial value. Even though she was apparently in excellent health when she sold the interest, she died very shortly thereafter.

The estate took the position that none of the trust should be included in her estate; because she no longer held the income interest at death, the predecessor of § 2036 did not apply. And even though she disposed the interest shortly before death, the predecessor of § 2035 should not apply,[39] because the income interest was transferred for full and adequate consideration. The government argued that, in order to come within the consideration exception, the sale had to be made for the *entire value* of her share of the trust, not just the value of the income interest. Because she received only the latter, her estate should include the full fair market value of her 60% share of the trust, minus the amount of partial consideration received. The government's position included roughly $900,000, less the $140,000 in consideration she received for the income interest, or a total of roughly $760,000.

As the court framed it, the issue was "must the consideration be paid for the interest transferred, or for the interest which would otherwise be included in the gross estate?" Remember we said that if a $1,000,000 asset is sold for $1,000,000, then the estate is not depleted. Does that rationale save the estate in *Allen*? The court held no. It compared the amount that would have been in Mrs. Allen's estate had she not sold the income interest ($900,000) to the amount of consideration that replaced it ($140,000) and noted that Congress could not possibly have intended to give her that easy an out. The court ultimately held that in order to come with the adequate and full consideration exception under § 2035, the sale must be for the full

---

[38]   293 F.2d 916 (10th Cir. 1961).

[39]   Because she died prior to enactment of the 1954 Code, the court applied the 1939 Code. For our purposes, there is not an important distinction between the old code and the new. We will reference the current code numbers.

value of the property that *would have been included* in the estate under
§ 2036. Later courts have followed *Allen*.[40]

As applied to **Variation 12(c)**, § 2035 will include in D's estate
$3,000,000, equal to the date of death value of the property, less the
$200,000 consideration received.[41]

Variation 12(d): In year one, when D creates the trust, he
sells the remainder interest to his nephew N, for its fair
market value of $600,000. D dies in year 6.

In this case we are not worried about § 2035, but are dealing with the
exception for adequate and full consideration in § 2036. [42] The question is
whether the parenthetical exception in § 2036(a) will apply if D receives
the full actuarial value of the *remainder interest* that he transferred, worth
$400,000. If the exception does not apply, then D has received only partial
consideration for the property transferred (not "full and adequate"
consideration), and 100% of the trust's date of death value would be
included in his estate, less the $400,000 in consideration received (§ 2043).
Although the answer to this question is not entirely free from doubt, we
believe that D should be treated as if he received adequate consideration
for the remainder, and that § 2036 should not apply.

Several early cases held that the parenthetical exception in § 2036(a)
required consideration for the full value of the entire property, not just the
portion transferred.[43] The courts reasoned that to rule otherwise would be
to permit taxpayers to deplete their estates, although it was not clear how
this would occur.

More recent cases have taken issue with the reasoning of the earlier
cases, and have held that it is sufficient if the transferor receives
consideration equal to the fair market value of only the remainder interest
that she transferred.[44] If she has received that, then § 2036 should not
apply.

Think about what happened in our current variation. Before she made
any transfer D owned property worth $1,000,000. After making that
transfer, D owned an income interest worth $400,000 and the $600,000
that he received in exchange for the remainder. His estate has not been
depleted! As time passes, his income interest will be worth less, but the
consideration of $600,000 will grow in his bank account, or brokerage
account. If it grows at the § 7520 rate, then by the time D dies the

---

[40] See e.g., *Estate of D'Ambrosio v. Comm'r,* 101 F.3rd 309 (3rd Cir. 1996).

[41] § 2043(a).

[42] We are not concerned with § 2035, because there has been no transfer within three years
of death.

[43] See, e.g., *Gradow v. U.S.,* 11 Cl.Ct. 808 (1987) (relying on cases decided in the early 1960s),
aff'd 897 F.2d. 516 (Fed. Cir. 1990).

[44] The leading case for this proposition is *Estate of D'Ambrosio v. Comm'r,* supra note 40.

consideration will have grown in value to $1,000,000. If we accept the actuarial assumptions used in valuing the remainder, the government should be made whole.

We know what you're thinking, what about *Allen*?

Allen involved very different facts that were clearly designed to result in tax avoidance. Mrs. Allen was purposely trying to get rid of her income interest in order to reduce the value of her estate, even though she had been enjoying the interest for roughly 30 years. If her last minute attempt to avoid § 2036 by selling just her income interest would render § 2036 (and §§ 2037 and 2038) meaningless. The same in not true in this variation. If we respect the actuarial assumptions made in § 7520, there has been no depletion of the estate.

Moving Forward

The sections discussed in this chapter expand the gross estate well beyond the basic inclusion or property owned at death under § 2033. In the next chapter we will study statutes that include other transfers of wealth that a decedent might make that would not be reached by that basic section, in particular non-probate transfers.

CHAPTER FIVE

ANNUITIES, RETIREMENT PLANS AND INSURANCE (§§ 2039 & 2042)

■ ■ ■

As we learned in **Chapter Three**, the reach of § 2033 is largely limited to assets owned by the decedent at death, which consists mainly of assets in the decedent's probate estate. We also learned that § 2040 includes in the estate joint tenancy property, which passes to the surviving joint tenant outside of probate. In **Chapter Four**, we saw that certain lifetime transfers of property may be brought back into the gross estate under §§ 2035–2038. There remain a number of other types of wealth transfers that fall outside of the rules we have discussed so far, for which Congress has created special rules. These include annuity contracts and retirement benefits (§ 2039), and life insurance (§ 2042). These topics are the subject of this chapter.

Part A. Section 2039: Annuities & Retirement Plans

Congress added § 2039 to the Code in 1954 in an attempt to clarify the tax treatment of two types of potential wealth transmission. The first is standard annuity contracts, which may or may not involve a transfer of wealth that should be subjected to the estate tax. The second is retirement plans, which in many cases do involve transfers of significant wealth.

Section 2039(a) imposes four requirements which, if met, will result in inclusion in the estate.

1. There must be an annuity or other payment payable to a beneficiary by virtue of surviving the decedent;

2. The amount is payable pursuant to any form of contract or agreement;

3. Prior to death the decedent was receiving payments, or had the right to receive payments (either alone or in conjunction with another) under the contract or agreement; and

4. The payments to decedent were payable for the decedents life, or for any period not ascertainable without reference to his

death, or for any period that does not in fact end before his death.[1]

If § 2039 applies, then the value of the amount payable to the beneficiary will be included in the decedent's estate, to the extent that the decedent contributed to the purchase price of the agreement. Contributions by a decedent's employer are treated as though made by the decedent.[2]

Annuity Contracts

A basic annuity is a contractual arrangement between a purchaser (the annuitant) and a counter party (who could be an individual, but who usually is an insurance company or other financial institution) that promises to pay to the annuitant a series of payments. For example, assume D transfers $1,000,000 to Insurance Co, in exchange for the company's promise to pay to D $100,000 per year for the balance of his life. Neither D nor his estate is entitled to any refund, regardless of how long D actually lives.

When D dies the annuity payments cease, and D will not have made a transfer of wealth subject to the tax. But what if the contract contained a refund feature that guaranteed D that he would receive no less than $600,000 in total payments? Assume D dies after receiving 5 payments, and the company pays $100,000 to D's estate. In this case, the estate's right to the payment would be an asset of his estate under § 2033, and we have effectively captured the transfer of wealth by D.

What if, instead, the annuity contract was a "self and survivor" contract, providing for payments to D for life, then to D's spouse S for life. In this case, D's death involves a transfer of wealth to S, in the amount of the value of her right to receive the continuing payments. Section 2033 will not capture the transfer, however, because D's right to receive payments ceased at death, and no amount is payable to his estate.

Although one could probably stretch § 2036 to cover this transfer (and indeed the courts did prior to 1954), § 2039 eliminates any doubt by including in D's gross estate the value of the annuity payable to S, to the extent that D provided the consideration for the annuity contract.[3]

Retirement Plans

While annuity contracts may no longer be a common form of wealth transfer, much of the wealth of many individuals is accumulated in

---

[1] Hopefully this language rings a bell, because it is the same used in § 2036, which we studied in *Chapter Four*.

[2] § 2039(b).

[3] As we will see in *Chapter Seven*, in the case of spousal joint and survivor annuities the estate of the predeceased spouse will be allowed a marital deduction for the value of the amount passing to the surviving spouse. As a result, the net inclusion will be zero.

employer-sponsored retirement plans, and Individual Retirement Accounts. Under those arrangements, an employee may be entitled to receive annuity payments or lump sum payments following retirement, with any unpaid balance remaining at death payable to an employee's designated beneficiary. Unless that beneficiary is the decedent's estate, the amounts will pass outside of probate, and § 2033 will not apply.

This is where § 2039 has its greatest impact. It will bring into the gross estate the amount of any annuity or other payment receivable by the employee's beneficiary if the employee was either receiving payments, or had the right to receive payments, prior to death. While § 2039(b) limits the inclusion to the decedent's contribution to the purchase of the contract, it attributes to the employee contributions made by the employer.

As originally enacted, § 2039(c) contained an extremely generous (and difficult to justify) exclusion for qualified pension and profit-sharing plans. The exclusion was eliminated in 1984, and those plans are now within the ambit of § 2039.

To illustrate the operation of § 2039, consider the following example and its variations:

Example #1: **D purchases a self and survivor annuity for $5,000,000 from an insurance company.[4] Under the terms of the annuity the insurance company agrees to pay $200,000 per year to D for life and then to D's brother, B, for his life. Ten years later D dies, and payments commence to B.**

This is a clear application of § 2039 and the value of the annuity B receives must be included in D's gross estate. B is receiving this annuity by reason of surviving D under an agreement that paid D an annuity for her life. The amount included would be the value of B's annuity on D's date of death, determined under § 7520.[5]

Variation 1(a): **Same as *Example #1* except that B paid half of the $5,000,000 premium.**

This would have the effect of reducing the amount that would be includible in D's gross estate by half. Under § 2039(b), when there is a joint purchase of an annuity, only a proportionate part of the value is includable.

---

[4] Annuities are governed by § 72 for income tax purposes. Under that provision, the annuitant is entitled to exclude a portion of each payment she receives equal to the ratio of her "investment in the contract" (i.e., her cost, here $5,000,000) over her expected return. § 72(c). On these facts the expected return would be $200,000 times the actuarial joint life expectancy of D and B. So if D and B's joint life expectancy were 40 years, the expected return on the annuity would be $8,000,000 ($200,000 times 40), and D and B would be entitled to exclude 5/8 of each annuity payment, and the remaining 3/8 would be included in gross income. It is worth noting that if B survives D, B will not be entitled to a step-up in basis. § 1014(b)(9)(A).

[5] See § 20.7520–1.

Since D contributed one half of the purchase price, one half of the annuity's value is includible in her gross estate.

Variation 1(b): **Same as *Example #1* except that D's employer purchased the annuity as part of her compensation package.**

The entire value of the annuity is includible in D's estate because under § 2039(b) all contributions by D's employer by reason of her employment will be treated as though made by D.

Example #2: **D's employer maintains a qualified retirement plan for its employees. The employer contributes a percentage of each employee's salary to the plan each year.[6] Employees are entitled to the amount in their accounts on retirement, either in the form of annual payments or in a lump sum. Amounts remaining in their account at death are payable to their designated beneficiary, and if none, then to their estate.**

Variation 2(a): **D retires, and elects to take his $3,000,000 retirement account in 9 annual installments. After three years D dies, and the $2,000,000 balance in the account is paid to his spouse as designated beneficiary.**

Section 2039's requirements are met here, and the $2,000,000 paid to the spouse will be included in his gross estate.[7] D's spouse is receiving a payment on D's death and D was receiving payments prior to his death. Even though D made no actual contributions to the plan, the amounts contributed by his employer are attributed to him.

Variation 2(b): **D dies prior to retiring, and the $3,000,000 balance in his account is paid to his spouse as designated beneficiary.**

Again § 2039 will include the entire amount in D's gross estate. Even though D wasn't receiving payments from the plan prior to death, he had the right to receive those payments. Again all employer contributions are attributed to D.

---

[6]   For income tax purposes, contributions to qualified plans are deductible by the employer, but not taxed to the employee until they are withdrawn. A discussion of what constitutes a "qualified plan" is beyond the scope of this book.

[7]   As with spousal joint and survivor annuities, when retirement plan benefits are paid to a spouse any inclusion under § 2039 will be offset by the marital deduction under § 2056, to be discussed in *Chapter Seven*.

Part B. Section 2042: Life Insurance

General Principles

Consider D, age 60 and healthy, who purchases a $1,000,000 10-year term life insurance policy on her own life. The policy calls for fixed annual premiums of $5,000. D's children are the beneficiaries of the policy. D pays four years of premiums, then at age 64 is diagnosed with a terminal disease, and dies. The insurance company pays the death benefit of $1,000,000 to D's children. Has D made a transfer of wealth that should be subject to the transfer taxes? Of what amount?

This is obviously not an easy question. One could argue that the most wealth that D has transferred is the $20,000 in premium payments that she made. But because D made the payments that gave rise to the death benefit, and had the ability to direct where the proceeds would go by changing the beneficiary, maybe she has transferred wealth of $1,000,000.

Largely because of the difficulty of deciding these questions, the estate taxation of life insurance is, for all intents and purposes, voluntary. That is because the inclusion of life insurance proceeds depends entirely on form, and a carefully planned estate can normally very easily avoid taxation of proceeds of insurance on the decedent's life.

Section 2042 will include in the gross estate the proceeds of life insurance on a decedent's life only if:

1. The decedent's estate is the designated beneficiary of the policy, or

2. Someone other than the decedent's estate is named beneficiary, and the decedent held at death one or more "incidents of ownership" with respect to the policy.

Thus, by naming a beneficiary other than her own estate, a decedent can avoid inclusion by ensuring that she owns no incidents of ownership over a policy.[8] Incidents of ownership include a multitude of possible rights with respect to the policy, such as a right to change the beneficiary, to surrender or cancel the policy, to assign the policy, to pledge it as security for a loan, or to borrow against it.[9] Powers held as a trustee can result in inclusion.[10] Payment of premiums by the decedent is not an incident of ownership.[11]

---

[8] Note, however, that even if the estate is not the beneficiary of the policy, if the proceeds must be used to pay expenses or debts of the estate, including taxes, then the amounts used for that purpose are treated as payable to the estate. § 20.2042–1(b).

[9] § 20.2042–1(c)(2).

[10] § 20.2042–1(c)(4).

[11] Prior to 1954 payment of premiums was used in determining incidents of ownership. The legislative history to § 2042 explicitly stated that the statute was intended to change that rule. See *First Nat'l Bank v. U.S.*, 488 F.2d 575 (9th Cir. 1973).

Inclusion of Life Insurance Under § 2035

If a decedent holds an incident of ownership with respect to an insurance policy on her own life, and parts with that incident within three of death, § 2035(a) will bring the proceeds of that policy into the gross estate. However, merely paying premiums does not constitute the transfer of an "incident of ownership." So if D owns a policy on her own life, and transfers ownership to her children more than three years prior to death, the fact that she may continue to fund the premiums on the policy until her date of death will not result in inclusion under § 2035.[12]

Because inclusion in the estate under § 2042 depends entirely on these formal distinctions, the key to estate planning with life insurance is to ensure the estate is not the beneficiary, and that the decedent holds no incident of ownership in the policy. The question then becomes how best to structure ownership of life insurance policies.

Example #3: D purchases a single premium life insurance policy on her own life in the amount of $10,000,000, naming her son S as the beneficiary. As the owner of the policy D has the right to change the beneficiary. D dies during the term of the policy, and the $10,000,000 death benefit is paid to S.

At her death, D owned the policy, holding all incidents of ownership, including the right to change the beneficiary. Therefore, the full $10,000,000 proceeds of the policy will be included in D's gross estate under § 2042.

Variation: Same as Example #3 except that two years before she dies D assigns the policy to S, retaining no incidents of ownership in the policy.

On these facts, when D assigns the policy to S, D has made a completed gift of the policy in an amount equal to its replacement value at that time.[13] Nevertheless, when D dies, the entire $10,000,000 that S receives will be pulled back into D's gross estate under § 2035(a). Since D relinquished all incidents of ownership over the policy within 3 years of her death when she assigned the policy to S, and because the policy would have been included in her estate under § 2042 had she not made the transfer, § 2035 clearly applies. Note, however, that if D had survived for more than 3 years after the assignment, no portion of the proceeds would have been included.

---

[12] Under the pre-1981 version of § 2035, which brought into the estate any property *transferred* within three years of death (or in contemplation of death pre-1976), the government successfully argued that payment of the premiums constituted a "constructive transfer" of the underlying policy. See, e.g., *Bel v. United States,* 452 F.2d 683 (5th Cir. 1971). The current language of § 2035(a)(2), however, which specifically refers to inclusion under § 2042, does not leave room for the constructive transfer argument, because payment of premiums is not a trigger under § 2042. See, e.g., *Estate of Leder v. U.S.,* 893 F.2d 237 (10th Cir. 1989). The government has conceded this result. See AOD 1991–012.

[13] § 25.2512–6. The gift will qualify for the annual exclusion. See § 25.2503–3(a).

Example #4: D purchases a $10,000,000 whole life policy on her own life. The policy calls for annual premiums of $140,000. D immediately assigns the policy to a trust that provides that, after D's death, the net income of the trust will be distributed to D's son S, and her husband H, for life, remainder to their three children or their estates. D names herself co-Trustee with a commercial bank. The Trustees have the normal fiduciary powers over the management of the trust's assets, including the ability to exercise the incidents of ownership over the policy. Each year for next four years, D makes an additional contribution to the Trust of $140,000 to fund the premiums. At the end of the 4th year, while still a co-Trustee, D dies.

When D dies, the full amount of the insurance proceeds will be includible in D's gross estate under § 2042. Since D possessed the incidents of ownership in her capacity as co-Trustee on the date of her death, § 2042(2) applies. Section 2042 expressly applies when the incidents are held alone, or with any other person. The bottom line is that the insured should never be the Trustee or co-Trustee of a trust that holds an insurance policy on her life.

Variation: Same as *Example #4* except D names her spouse, H, as the sole Trustee.

As long as D lives at least 3 years after transferring the policy to the trust (she lived 4), the proceeds of the policy will not be included in her estate.

Note that if D had created the trust with a transfer of cash, and had the trust been the initial owner of the policy, exclusion from the estate would result no matter when D dies, including within three years of the transfer. So as a planning matter, when possible, the trust should apply for and purchase the policy, and the insured should never hold any incidents of ownership.[14]

Special Case: Policy Owned by Controlled Corporation

Suppose a life insurance policy is purchased by a corporation on the life of its sole or controlling shareholder (i.e., a shareholder who owns stock that possesses more than 50% of the combined voting power of the corporation). There is little doubt that the shareholder would have a great deal of control over the life insurance policy. Should such a shareholder be considered to hold incidents of ownership of the policy within the meaning of § 2042? The regulations address this issue and conclude that to the extent that the proceeds of the policy are payable to the corporation (or to a third party for the benefit of the corporation, such as paying a corporate

---

[14] This may not always be possible, for example in some cases the insured may no longer be insurable, and an existing policy owned by the insured must be used.

debt), then the incidents of ownership will not be attributable to the shareholder.[15] Although at first blush this might seem like a generous rule, it is not. Note that if the proceeds of the policy are payable to the corporation, or to one of its creditors, there will be a resulting increase in the value of the stock held by the shareholder, which is included in the shareholder's gross estate under § 2033. To also include the proceeds of the policy under § 2042 would amount to including the proceeds twice. Nevertheless, if the proceeds are paid to a third party and not for the corporation's benefit (to the shareholder's children, for example), that transfer has no effect on the value of the corporation, and will result in inclusion of the proceeds under § 2042. In that case, the incidents of ownership are attributed to the shareholder, and the proceeds will be included in the shareholder's gross estate.[16]

To illustrate, consider the following example:

Example #5: D owns 75% of the single class of stock issued by D Corp. D Corp. purchases a $1,000,000 life insurance policy on D's life. D Dies. In the alternative, the proceeds are payable to (i) D Corp. or (ii) D's daughter.

In (i) where the proceeds are payable to D Corp., the incidents of ownership are not attributable to D. The corporation's value will increase by $1,000,000, and because he owns 75% of the stock, D's estate will increase in value by roughly $750,000. In (ii), no portion of the life insurance proceeds will increase the value of the corporation or D's stock. In this case, since D owns more than 50% of the combined voting power in D, D is attributed the incidents of ownership of the policy and the full $1,000,000 will be includible in D's gross estate.

Moving Forward

We have almost finished the discussion of items included in the gross estate. We have seen that both probate and non-probate transfers are included, as well as items the decedent may have transferred away during life, if she retained certain powers or interest. The final section to address involves rights that the decedent may hold in property transferred by others, known as "powers of appointment". Those powers are the subject of our last inclusion chapter, **Chapter Six**.

---

[15]   § 20.2042–1(c)(6).

[16]   Id.

CHAPTER SIX

POWERS OF APPOINTMENT (§ 2041)

■ ■ ■

Part A. What Is a "Power of Appointment"?

Powers of appointment, like property interests, are creatures of state law. New York law, for example, defines a power of appointment as:

> An authority created or reserved by a person having property subject to his disposition, enabling the donee to designate, within such limits as may be prescribed by the donor, the appointees of the property or the shares or the manner in which property shall be received.[1]

The holder of a power of appointment over property does not have an actual "interest" in the property. What she does have is the ability to direct the holder of the property to transfer beneficial ownership of it to another. Certain terminology is used in connection with powers of appointment. The property subject to the power is the "appointive property." The "donor" of the power is the person that created it, and the "donee" is the holder of the power. A power is "exercised" when the holder of the power makes use of it, and is "released" when the holder expressly waives or limits his right to exercise.[2] The "appointee" is the person that benefits from the exercise. Typically instruments creating powers name "takers in default," who are the parties that receive the property if a power is not exercised. Powers can be exercisable during life ("intervivos") or at death ("testamentary"). The power often designates how it must be exercised, e.g., testamentary powers are usually exercisable by will.

Depending upon the breadth of a power, it may give the holder something very close to an actual ownership interest in the property. Powers are categorized under state law as general or non-general (the latter are sometimes referred to as "special powers"). How a power is categorized depends upon the identity of the permissible appointees: typically state law defines a general power as one that is exercisable in

---

[1] New York Estates, Powers and Trust Law (EPTL) § 10–3.1.

[2] See, e.g., EPTL § 10–9.2: "(a) Any power of appointment, whether exercisable only by deed, only by will, or by either deed or will, and whether general or special, exclusive or nonexclusive other than a power which is imperative, is releasable, either with or without consideration, by written instrument signed by the donee of such power and delivered as hereinafter provided."

favor of the donee, her estate, her creditors, or the creditors of her estate.[3] Any power that is not a general power is a non-general, or "special" power. These distinctions become important for state law purposes, and state law governs how and if powers are exercised, and who is entitled to the property in the absence of exercise.

Part B. Powers of Appointment and the Transfer Taxes in General

Powers of appointment are very frequently used in estate planning; they allow planners to build enormous flexibility into estate plans. A firm understanding of their tax treatment is therefore essential. Because they are not property interests, an exercise of a power by the holder may not be a "transfer of property" by the holder under the gift tax, and powers held by a decedent are not "property" included in the estate under § 2033. Nevertheless, the Code treats certain types of powers over property as essentially equivalent to ownership of the underlying property; § 2514 treats the exercise or release of a "general power of appointment" as a transfer of property for gift tax purposes, and § 2041 includes property subject to a "general power of appointment" in the holder's gross estate. The fundamental question is what types of powers are "general" within the meaning of §§ 2514 and 2041.[4]

In contrast with §§ 2036–2038 and 2042, which ensure that wealth that originated with the decedent will be included in the decedent's estate, § 2041 acts to include in a decedent's estate wealth that had its source in another person. If the decedent holds a "general power" over such wealth, at the time of her death, it will be included in her gross estate.[5] Consider X, who transfers stock outright to D. When D dies owning that stock, it is clearly an asset of her estate. When it is distributed to her beneficiaries, she is clearly making a transfer of wealth to them. What if instead X transferred that stock into trust for D's benefit, giving her an income interest for life, and a remainder interest to her issue, or their estates? As we have seen in the preceding chapters, because D's interest in the trust terminates at her death, nothing will be included in her gross estate. This makes sense, because she is not transferring wealth; the transfer of wealth to her issue was made by X. These examples create the two ends of a spectrum of rights that D can have in the stock. At one end is fee ownership, which will clearly result in inclusion in her gross estate under § 2033. At the other end of the spectrum is the bare right to the income from the stock,

---

[3]   See, e.g., EPTL § 10–3.2(b).

[4]   The estate tax and gift tax definitions of general powers are the same, and in the following discussion we refer mostly to § 2041 for that definition.

[5]   While one can transfer property and retain a power for state law purposes, for tax purposes those would be picked up by §§ 2036 or 2038. Section 2041 steps in if the decedent didn't make a transfer with the retained power.

which will not result in inclusion. The issue addressed by § 2041 is what additional rights or powers over the stock can we give D along that spectrum, and avoid inclusion in her estate.[6]

To illustrate, in addition to the income interest, we could give D the right to demand distributions of principal during her life. We could limit that right to principal to a specific dollar amount, or limit it to amounts needed for medical emergencies. We could allow her to designate the shares that her issue will take in the remainder. We could allow her to leave the remainder to someone other than her issue. The question is when these rights and powers will rise to the level of a "general power of appointment."

Section 2041 answers the question by drawing a bright line along the spectrum. One crosses that line when one holds a "general power of appointment" as defined by the statute.[7] If D's powers over the property rise to the level of a general power of appointment, then the property is included in her gross estate; if they don't, then it will not be included. There are two ways that a general power can result in inclusion in the holder's estate. First, § 2041(a)(2) includes in the gross estate any property with respect to which the decedent has a general power of appointment at the time of death. **Examples #1 and #2** below deal with this issue. Second, even if the decedent no longer holds a general power at death, if she exercised or released one during life in such a manner that it would have resulted in inclusion under §§ 2035–2038 had she transferred the underlying property, the resulting property is included in her estate. Both the gift and estate tax consequences of that exercise or release are illustrated in **Examples #3 and #4** below.

For all intents and purposes, the Code treats the holder of a general power of appointment as if she owned the property outright, and at death § 2041 taxes her estate on the transfer of wealth associated with that power. Consistent with this view of the holder of a general power, § 2514 treats the intervivos *exercise or release* of a general power of appointment as a transfer of the property subject to the power for purposes of the gift tax.

Both §§ 2041 and 2514 distinguish between pre- and post-October 21, 1942 powers. Prior to that date, powers were taxed only if they were exercised, the release of power was not taxed as a gift, and jointly held powers were exempted from the rules. Our discussion will be limited to post-October 21, 1942 powers.

---

[6] While powers can be created outside of trusts, this is rarely done. So we will confine our examples to powers of appointment in trusts.

[7] As you will see, the Code's definition differs from that under state law. From this point on, when we refer to a general power, we will be referring to the Code definition in §§ 2041 and 2514.

General Power of Appointment Defined

While the term "general power of appointment" may be defined by state law, §§ 2041(b) and 2514(c) supply the definition that governs for federal transfer tax purposes. That definition creates a bright line rule for distinguishing between general and non-general powers for tax purposes. Initially, the definition is consistent with the state law definition, i.e., a power is general if it is "exercisable in favor of the decedent, his estate, his creditors, or the creditors of his estate." Sections 2041(b) and 2514(c) refine the definition, however, to provide:

> (1)   Powers limited by an ascertainable standard relating to the health, education maintenance and support of the decedent are deemed non-general.[8]

> (2)   Certain jointly held powers are deemed non-general, including those exercisable only in conjunction with the creator of the power, and those exercisable in conjunction persons who have a substantial interest that is adverse to the exercise of the power.[9]

Any power that is not a general power falls outside of the statute.[10]

In evaluating a power-holder's rights with respect to property, we must take into account powers she holds in her individual capacity (e.g., a beneficiary's right to demand principal distributions) and powers she may hold in a fiduciary capacity (e.g., if a trustee who is also a beneficiary has the power to determine if she is entitled to a principal distribution.) Both individual and fiduciary powers can give rise to a general power, which means that in drafting trusts, planners must consider carefully both the question of who should be trustee, and what the relevant distribution provisions can permit. Fortunately, the statute provides a blueprint: If one wants to avoid § 2041, then a power must be drafted to fall on the non-general side of the bright line rule. It cannot be exercisable in favor of the holder, her estate, her creditors, or the creditors of her estate, unless it is limited by an ascertainable standard, or jointly exercisable with the creator of the power or another person having a substantial adverse interest. If the grantor wants the beneficiary to have access to the principal beyond that permitted by the ascertainable standard (e.g., for her "comfort and happiness"), then the beneficiary should not be the trustee of the trust. There may be circumstances in which a planner may specifically want to

---

[8]   §§ 2041(b)(1)(A) and 2514(c)(1).

[9]   §§ 2041(b)(1)(C) and 2514(c)(3).

[10]   There is one limited exception, which we will not address in detail here. Under § 2041(a)(3) if a decedent exercises a non-general power by creating another power which, under the law of the state in question, would postpone the vesting of the property for "a period ascertainable without regard to the date of creation of the first power," then exercise of the non-general power is taxed. This is a problem in states that do not have a rule against perpetuities, and is generally referred to as the "Delaware Tax Trap".

create a general power of appointment, in which case the job of the drafter is to craft a power that falls on the general power side of the bright line.

General Powers Held at Death

To illustrate the definition of a general power of appointment, consider the following examples. Ignore any possible application of the GST tax.

Example #1: **Decedent's will created a testamentary trust that provides for income to her nephew, N, for his life, remainder to N's children, A, B and C, in such shares as N appoints by will. In default of appointment, the remainder passes equally among A, B and C, or their estates. N is Trustee, and dies while acting in that capacity.**

The testamentary power is held by N in his individual capacity, he holds no fiduciary powers for his own benefit. N has a power to designate the beneficiaries of the trust after his death. In this case, the permissible appointees are limited to A, B and C, and do not include himself, his estate, his creditors, or the creditors of his estate. It is a non-general power, and hence will not be included in N's estate under § 2041.

Variation 1(a): **Same as *Example #1* except that the trust also provides that during N's lifetime, in addition to income distributions, the Trustee is authorized to distribute as much principal to N as the Trustee deems necessary for his health, education, maintenance and support.**

As before, the testamentary power held by N in his individual capacity is non-general. But in this case N holds a fiduciary power to distribute trust principal to himself. Nevertheless, because this power is limited by an ascertainable standard, it is not a general power within the meaning of the statute.[11] No portion of the trust will be includible in N's estate.

Variation 1(b): **Same as *Example #1* except that the Trustee may distribute principal to N in such amounts as the Trustee deems appropriate for any reason.**

While N's testamentary power is still non-general, now the fiduciary power held by N, as Trustee, is a general power of appointment because it is unconstrained. If N chose to do so, he could terminate the trust and distribute the entire principal to himself, so the general power essentially gives him ownership of the property. Therefore, if N dies while acting as Trustee, the entire value of the trust will be included in his gross estate. Note that if the trust appointed someone other than N as Trustee, so that

---

[11] § 2041(b)(1)(A).

N did not have the power to distribute the property to himself, then no portion of the value of the trust would be includible in N's estate.

> *Variation 1(c):* **Same as *Variation 1(b)* except that N and Local Bank are named Co-Trustees. The trust agreement requires that both Trustees agree before any discretionary distribution to N can be made.**

Although the Co-Trustees must agree to distributions to N, jointly held general powers come within § 2041, *unless* they can be exercised only in conjunction with either (i) the creator of the power or (ii) a person who has a substantial interest adverse to its exercise, under § 2041(b)(1)(C). Local Bank did not create the power nor does it have any beneficial interest in the trust,[12] let alone a substantial adverse one.[13] N therefore holds a general power of appointment, and the entire value of the trust will be included in his estate.

> *Variation 1(d):* **Same as *Example #1*, except that on N's death the remainder passes to A, B, and C, or their estates, in equal shares (i.e., N does not hold the testamentary power to divide the remainder among A, B and C.) As Trustee, N has the power to make intervivos principal distributions to N, but only if C consents.**

In this case, C has a vested remainder in one third of the trust, which would be reduced if principal was distributed to N. Therefore, C holds a substantial interest in the trust which is adverse to the exercise of the power, As a result, N's fiduciary power is not a general power of appointment, and the trust will not be included in his estate.

> *Example #2:* **Testator's will creates a testamentary trust that provides for income to his sister A for life, remainder to Testator's children, or their estates, in equal shares. A and her two adult children B and C, are named co-Trustees. During A's lifetime, the Trustees (if they all agree) may make principal distributions to A, B or C in such amounts they deem appropriate. A dies.**

While B and C might well object to principal distributions to A and not to them, the regulations make it clear that their status as permissible appointees is not a substantial adverse interest (note D's children would clearly have a substantial adverse interest if one of them were co-Trustee.)[14] Therefore, A dies holding a general power of appointment over

---

[12] Although Local Bank has an economic interest in the fees it will earn, this does is not an interest in the trust property and therefore is not an adverse interest. § 20.2041–3(c)(2).

[13] Reg. § 20.2041–3(c)(2) elaborates on the meaning of "substantial adverse interest." The interest must not be "insignificant" relative to the value of the property subject to the power, and an interest is adverse if it would be reduced by exercise of the power. Takers in default of a power have a substantial adverse interest, because if the power is exercised their interests will be reduced.

[14] § 20.2041–3(c)(2).

the trust. The remaining question is to what extent? The statute assumes that if A wanted a principal distribution, B and C would permit it only if equal distributions were made to them.[15] As a result, one third of the trust would be included in A's estate.

What if B died before A? Would her power as co-Trustee be a general power? The answer is no, so long as A is acting as co-Trustee. A's income interest gives her a substantial interest that is adverse to distributions to B.[16]

General Powers Exercised or Released During Life

The exercise or release of an intervivos power can result in a taxable gift under § 2514, and possibly inclusion in the estate under § 2041. These rules are explored in the following examples.

Gift Tax Consequences

Example #3: **Testator's will creates a $500,000 testamentary trust for the benefit of her daughter D and D's nephews. The trust provides for income to D for life, with a remainder to D's nephews A and B in equal shares, or their estates. In addition, during D's life she has the right to direct the Trustee to make principal distributions to whomever she directs, for whatever reason. Assume that during all relevant times the trust principal is $500,000, and that a bank is Trustee. In the current year, D directs the Trustee to distribute $100,000 to her friend X.**

D holds a general power over the trust, because she can direct the Trustee to pay principal to anyone, including herself. If she dies holding the power, we know that the trust assets will be included in her estate under § 2041. When she *exercises* that power during life, by directing that the Trustee pay out $100,000 of principal to X, she has made a taxable gift to X, to the same extent she would have had she written him a check.[17] This is entirely consistent with the notion that the holder of a general power is treated as the owner of the underlying property for transfer tax purposes.

> *Variation 3(a):* **Instead of exercising her power in favor of X, in the current year D executes a release of the power and delivers it to the Trustee. Assume this is a valid release of the power under local law, so that she no longer has the right to direct principal distributions.**

---

[15] See § 2041(b)(1)(C)(iii).

[16] § 2041(b)(1)(C)(ii).

[17] § 2514(b). Ignore possible application of the annual exclusion.

If D waives, or "releases" her power, we now know that A and B (or their estates) will ultimately receive the entire principal upon her death. Section 2514(b) treats the *exercise or release* of a power as a transfer of the property subject to the power. Thus, D has made a taxable gift to A and B. Of what? She has not gifted the entire $500,000 of principal, because A and B won't receive it until D dies. And in the meantime D will continue to receive the income from the property. So D has made a gift of the remainder to A and B, which will be valued under § 7520, as we learned in *Chapter Two*.[18]

> *Variation 3(b):* **Instead of having an unlimited power to direct principal distributions, D has the right to withdraw principal of up to $100,000 each year. The right is non-cumulative, so that any amounts not withdrawn by year's end remain part of the principal of the trust. In the year of D's death she does not exercise her right to withdraw.**

Rights to withdraw principal can be "cumulative" or "non-cumulative." If a right is cumulative, amounts not withdrawn will be available in subsequent years, along with amounts subject to withdrawal in those years.[19] If it is non-cumulative then the right to draw down each year's amount will disappear at the end of the year (we say the power has "lapsed"). Section 2514(e) treats a lapse of a power the same as it does a release of the power, and thus the lapse is taxed as a gift. There is an important limitation on this rule, referred to as the "five and five" rule. Section 2514(e) provides that a lapse is treated as a release *only* to the extent that the amount that could have been withdrawn exceeds the greater of (i) $5000, or (ii) 5% of the assets subject to the right. This can act a de minimis rule, so that lapses of small amounts can be disregarded, but a lapse of any amount will be reduced by amount defined by the rule.

In this case, D has allowed her right to withdraw $100,000 to lapse. That will be treated as a release to the extent that it exceeds the greater of $5000 or 5% of the value of the trust (let's assume the trust value remained constant at $500,000). We will therefore subtract the five and five amount ($25,000)[20] from the amount subject to the lapsed power ($100,000) and D has made a transfer of $75,000 as a result of the lapse. Again the question is of what? And again the answer is that D has not made a gift of the entire $75,000 but only a remainder interest in the $75,000 subject to the power, which will be valued actuarially.

---

[18] Note that if A and B were D's children, rather than nephews, D's "retained" income interest would be valued at zero, and she would make a taxable gift of the full $1,000,000 under the rules of § 2702.

[19] So, for example, if D's right of withdrawal was cumulative, if she did not withdraw the $100,000 available in year one, she could withdraw up to $200,000 in year two.

[20] 5% of $500,000 is $25,000, which is greater than $5,000.

Estate Tax Consequences

As we noted at the beginning of our discussion of general powers and the estate tax, there are two ways that a general power can result in inclusion in the holder's estate. We've seen that § 2041(a)(2) includes in the gross estate any property with respect to which the decedent has a general power of appointment at the time of death. *In addition*, even if the decedent no longer holds a general power at death, if she *exercised or released* one during life in such a manner that it would have resulted in inclusion under §§ 2035–2038 had she transferred the underlying property, the resulting property is included in her estate. We'll now explore that second prong of the statute.

In *Variation 3(a)* above, we noted that by releasing her power over the entire principal, D made a gift of the remainder interest in the entire trust to her nephews. D is essentially treated as transferring the trust assets to a new $500,000 trust, which gives income to her for life, and a remainder to A and B. Had D made this transfer directly, using funds in her bank account, you should have no doubt that at death those trust assets would be included in D's estate under § 2036, as she would have made a transfer with a retained income interest. Consistent with the notion that the holder of a general power is essentially the owner of the underlying property, when D releases her power, and the assets remain in the trust that provides her with income for life, § 2036 won't apply because she hasn't technically made a "transfer," but § 2041(a)(2) will include that property in D's estate. The words of the statute are as follow:

> The value of the gross estate shall include the value of all property . . . to the extent of any property with respect to which the decedent has at the time of his death a general power of appointment . . . , *or* with respect to which the decedent has at any time *exercised or released* such a power of appointment by a disposition which is of such nature that if it were a transfer of property owned by the decedent, such property would be includible in the decedents estate under sections **2035 to 2038**, inclusive. [Emphasis added]

As a result, in *Variation 3(a)*, where D released a general power over the $500,000 trust, not only will D be taxed on the resulting gift of the remainder at the time she executes the release, the entire date of death value of the trust assets will be included in her estate at death, under § 2041(a)(2).

Variation 3(b) creates a slightly more complicated problem, because D's power was limited to a portion of the trust ($100,000 per year), and she has not actually exercised or released it, but allowed it to lapse. While we've seen how the gift tax applies to that lapse, computing the amount to include in D's estate at death is more difficult. We refer to this as "the lapse problem," and discuss it in detail below.

The Lapse Problem

Recall the facts of **Variation 3(b)** above. Testator has created a testamentary trust of $500,000 that provides income to D for life, remainder to D's nephews A and B. D has a non-cumulative right to withdraw $100,000 per year. In the first year of the trust she does not withdraw any principal, and the power for that year lapses. Let's assume she dies in the second year of the trust, without exercising her withdrawal power for that year.

First, D clearly has a general power of appointment over $100,000 of the trust assets that she is entitled to withdraw during the second year of the trust's existence, and because she dies holding that power § 2041 would include that $100,000 in her estate. Is there anything else to include in her estate under § 2041? Above we saw that in year one D was deemed to have released $75,000 in year one, making a gift of the remainder value of that amount. The reality is that D had the right to withdraw the $100,000, but she chose not to do so, and we taxed her on the resulting gift of a remainder interest in $75,000. So in a very real way D has essentially become the creator of the trust to the extent of the $75,000 released power. Consistent with result we found in **Variation 3(a)**, where we included all of the trust on her death, here it appears that a similar result should occur when D allowed the partial withdrawal power to lapse.

The first piece of the puzzle is § 2041(b)(2), which, like § 2514(e), tells us that the lapse of a power of appointment is treated as a release of the power to the extent is exceeds $5,000 or 5% of the trust value.[21] So the released amount is again $75,000. Second, we know that § 2041(a)(2) includes in the estate NOT ONLY powers held at death, but any property with respect to which a decedent has released a power in such a way that would result in inclusion under §§ 2035–38 had it been transferred by the decedent. So consider what has happened in our example. If D had transferred $75,000 (the amount treated as released) into a trust in which she has retained the income for life, that transfer would clearly be included in her estate under § 2036. By allowing her power to lapse she has essentially done just that, and that portion of the trust will be included in her gross estate. To calculate the portion of the trust included under § 2041 we would compare the amount of the deemed release ($75,000) to the trust principal at the time of the release ($500,000). Therefore not only will § 2041 include in D's estate the amount ($100,000) she had the right to withdraw on her date of death, it will also include 15% of the remaining value of the trust in her estate.

---

[21] This "five and five" rule is identical to the gift tax version in § 2514.

What if the trust principal was $5,000,000, rather than $500,000 like the trust used in our example? In the earlier case D's right of withdrawal represented a significant portion of the trust's assets, and it makes sense to treat her as a partial grantor of the trust. But consider the larger trust: it is not at all unusual for a grantor to want to provide access to principal to an income beneficiary, and let's assume that the trust allows D to withdraw $100,000 (i.e., 2%) of the principal every year. The right of withdrawal is non-cumulative. Now consider the complexity involved in determining what percentage of the principal of the trust is attributable to the lapsed power if G allows the power to lapse year after year. It could be very difficult to trace. This is where the five and five rule provides relief: so long as the lapsed power is within the rule, no release is deemed to take place, and no inclusion in the estate will result.

Example #4:   **Testator dies in year one, and his will creates a trust that provides income to his daughter A for life, remainder to A's nephew B or B's estate. A is also given an annual non-cumulative power to withdraw up to $400,000 of principal. Assume that the initial value of the trust is $8,000,000, at the end of year one the trust's assets are worth $10,000,000, at the end of year two they are worth $15,000,000 and at the end of year three, $20,900,000. On December 31, year three, A dies having never exercised her powers.**

A's power to withdraw up to $400,000 of principal each year is clearly a general power of appointment. Because she died in year three at a time that she held that power, her estate will include $400,000 attributable to the year three power under § 2041. We then must consider the powers that lapsed in years one and two. The lapse of the power at the end of each of those years will be treated as a release of the power to the extent that the amount she had the right to withdraw ($400,000) exceeded 5% of the trust's assets at the time of the lapse. On these facts, at the end of year one, 5% of the trust's assets was $500,000 (5% of $10,000,000) and at the end of year two, 5% of the trust's assets was $750,000 (5% of $15,000,000). Because A's withdrawal power did not exceed those amounts, neither lapse will be treated as a release of the power for purposes of § 2514 or § 2041. So there will be no taxable gifts in years one and two, and when A dies in year three her estate will only include the $400,000 she had the right to withdraw at the time of her death.

Variation 4(a): **Same as *Example #4,* except that A's annual non-cumulative power to withdraw $400,000 can only be exercised during the month of November each year. If it is not exercised by December 1 of any particular year, it lapses. Assume that A dies on October 15, year three.**

The withdrawal power is still a general power of appointment. Nevertheless, A did not hold it at the time of her death, because it was not exercisable on October 15, her date of death. As a result, there will be no inclusion of the year three power under § 2041. Had she died during the month of November then it would have been includible, as in the above example, and had she died in December it would have lapsed, and would be analyzed with the lapsed powers. It is for this reason that withdrawal powers are frequently drafted so that they can be exercised during a narrow period of time, and frequently at the end of the year. The analysis of the lapsed power in years one and two is the same as in *Example #4*. Because the lapsed powers did not exceed 5% of the trust principal, the lapse is not a release, and there are no further gift or estate tax consequences. So A has made no gifts, and nothing will be included in her gross estate under § 2041.

Variation 4(b): **Same as *Example #4* except that A has the annual non-cumulative power to withdraw $900,000 of the principal.**

As in *Example #4*, A dies holding the power to withdraw in year three, and as a result the gross estate will include $900,000 under § 2041(b)(2). The major difference here is that A's power now exceeds 5% of the trust principal, and the lapse problem looms.

Gift Tax

At the end of year one, 5% of the $10,000,000 assets in the trust was $500,000. A's lapsed power exceeds that amount by $400,000, and she will therefore be treated as releasing a $400,000 power of appointment, under § 2514. This represents 4% of the value of the trust at that time. Because this amount is held in the trust, she has made a completed gift of the remainder to B, with a retained income interest in herself.[22]

The analysis is essentially the same for year two except that 5% of the $15,000,000 assets in the trust is $750,000. This means that A will be deemed to have made a transfer to the trust of $150,000 (the excess of the $900,000 withdrawal right over $750,000). This represents 1% of the value of the trust at that time. Once again the remainder will be considered a completed gift, and she has retained an income interest.[23]

Estate Tax

A dies in year three, when the trust is worth $20,900,000 The $900,000 year three power that she held at death must be included in her gross estate under § 2041(b)(2). The question that remains is how much of the

---

[22] Note that if A and B are related within the meaning of § 2702 A's retained interest will be valued at zero, and the full $400,000 will be the amount of the gift.

[23] Once again § 2702 may apply to tax the entire amount.

balance of the trust, $20,000,000, must be included because of the lapsed powers.

As we noted above, A's lapsed powers resulted in deemed transfers to the trust of a total of 5% of its value (4% in year one, and 1% in year two). As a result, at death she is treated as though she is the grantor of a total of 5% of a $20,000,000 trust (which would have a value of $1,000,000) that provides her with income for life. Had she actually made such a transfer, that portion of the trust would have been included in her estate under § 2036. She didn't actually make the transfer, so § 2036 won't operate, but § 2041(b)(2) will. This means that § 2041(b)(2) would require the inclusion of $900,000 for the year three power, plus $1,000,000 for the 5% of the trust she is deemed to have created.[24]

Drafting to Allow Principal Distributions While Avoiding the Lapse Problem

When a trust provides for income to one beneficiary for life, remainder to another, it is common (and good practice in many cases) to allow the Trustee to invade the principal for the benefit of the income beneficiary; she is often the prime object of the grantor's bounty and the income may be insufficient to meet her needs. Because of the obvious complexities that arise when one encounters the lapse problem, planners typically draft trusts in a manner to avoid the problem, and to avoid inclusion of the trust in the beneficiary's gross estate. Sophisticated planners have many tools in their toolbox, but a few standard items to consider are:

First, if the beneficiary is NOT the Trustee of the trust, then the Trustee can have discretionary powers to distribute principal to the income beneficiary, drafted as narrowly or broadly as is consistent with the Grantor's goals. Because the Trustee, not the beneficiary, holds the power, the standard for distribution does not need to meet the "health, education, support or maintenance" language used to avoid a general power of appointment.

Second, if the beneficiary is to be the Trustee, then she can have the power to distribute principal to herself, so long as that power falls short of a general power, meaning it must be limited by the necessary ascertainable standard of "health, education, support or maintenance."

Third, whether or not the beneficiary is acting as Trustee, if the Grantor of the trust wants the beneficiary to have the ability to access some portion of the principal each year without asking the Trustee to exercise discretion (if the beneficiary is not Trustee) or without needing to justify it under the ascertainable standard

---

[24] We subtract the $900,000 of the current years power prior to applying the 5%, to avoid double counting.

("I want a giraffe"), then the trust can give him that right. But such rights are typically expressed in terms of the five and five rule: the beneficiary can demand principal each year up to the greater of $5000, or 5% of the value of the trust at that time (as opposed to a provision entitling him to a fixed sum, as in our examples). Such powers are referred to a "five and five powers." When used, the lapse problem is entirely avoided. The only potential inclusion will be the power that exists on the date that beneficiary dies, so, as discussed in *Variation 4(a)*, such powers are often limited to exercise during a particular month, or on the 15th day of any month, etc., in order to reduce the risk that the power will exist on the date of death.

Moving Forward

This concludes our discussion of amounts *included* in the gross estate under the various provisions of the Code. In the following chapter we will address items *deductible* from the gross estate in arriving at the tax base, the taxable estate, after which we will have concluded the estate tax portion of the text!

CHAPTER SEVEN

DEDUCTIONS
(§§ 2053, 2055 & 2056)

■ ■ ■

Having arrived at the gross estate, applying all of the inclusion sections studied in the previous chapters, we have still not reached the tax base for the estate tax, the "taxable estate," which is defined in § 2051. Under the estate tax, there are a number of permitted "deductions," found in §§ 2053 through 2058, which reduce the amount subject to tax. Similarly, there are a number of deductions allowed against the gross amount of transfers by gift in arriving at the tax base of "taxable gifts" under § 2503. The deductions allowed under the gift tax parallel the corresponding provisions of the estate tax, and in the following discussion we will focus primarily on the estate tax rules.

In this chapter we will discuss the three most commonly applicable deductions, those found in §§ 2053, 2055, and 2056. The rationale for each of these deductions, and the role that they play in the transfer taxes, are very different, and in the detailed discussion that follows we will identify the most common issues that arise in each. Briefly, the deductions we will consider are as follows:

Section 2053 allows a deduction for funeral expenses, the costs of administering the estate, and debts of the decedent (mortgages and "claims against the estate"), so that the taxable estate reflects the actual wealth transferred by the decedent. Logically, if the decedent owned assets of $10 million but had debts of $11 million, no wealth is transferred to the beneficiaries. There is no analog to § 2053 in the gift tax.

Section 2055 allows a deduction for amounts transferred to charity.[1] While arguably amounts transferred to charitable beneficiaries represent wealth transfers that should be taxed like any other, Congress long ago decided that amounts passing to charity should not be subject to the estate or the gift tax. To the extent that the justification for the transfer taxes is to prevent the

---

[1] The gift tax charitable deduction is found in § 2522.

buildup of dynastic wealth, the deduction certainly makes sense, and it acts to encourage charitable giving.[2]

Section 2056 allows a deduction for amounts passing to the decedent's surviving spouse, and is commonly referred to as the "marital deduction."[3] In its current form, the deduction has the effect of exempting from tax all amounts passing from a decedent to her surviving spouse, and the gift tax analog makes gifts to a spouse tax-free. Essentially, this deduction has the effect of treating each married couple as a single tax paying unit. Under current law, the marital deduction is the most important deduction in estate planning.

Part A. Expenses, Indebtedness, etc.: § 2053

The deduction allowed by § 2053 provides a useful context to discuss the legal process that follows a decedent's death. The laws vary substantially from state to state, but can be generally described as follows:

Introduction to Probate

If a decedent dies with assets in his or her name, those assets must be subjected to a legal process that will ultimately vest title in the beneficiaries of the decedent's will, or her heirs. That process is called "probate." All these assets go into a "probate estate" and an individual will be appointed to manage the estate.[4] That person is sometimes referred to as the "personal representative." If the decedent died with a will, that will is submitted to the local probate court (or "Surrogate's Court") and the court will appoint the personal representative (usually referred to as "Executor"). The Executor may be nominated in the will, or may be chosen by the court. If a decedent dies without a will, the personal representative is the "Administrator" of the estate, and the laws of intestacy, rather than the will, dictate distribution of the estate. The court then authorizes the personal representative by issuing "Letters Testamentary" (to an Executor) or "Letters of Administration" (to an Administrator) to act on behalf of the estate.

The personal representative's task is generally described as (1) marshalling the decedent's assets, (2) paying off creditors, and (3) distributing the remaining property to the beneficiaries entitled to it. That process involves a multitude of tasks and court filings, and in some cases court hearings. An inventory of the estate's assets must be filed with the

---

[2] See Miranda Perry-Fleischer, *Charitable Contributions in an Ideal Estate Tax*, 60 Tax L. Rev. 263 (2007).

[3] The gift tax provision is § 2523.

[4] The assets in the probate estate are essentially those assets included in the gross estate by § 2033.

court. The personal representative may invest liquid assets of the estate, and may need to manage estate property. The estate is a separate entity for income tax purposes, and must file returns for the period that it is under administration. The personal representative will file the decedent's final income tax return, for the period ending on his date of death. The personal representative must file the estate tax return within 9 months following the decedent's death, subject to possible extensions. Estate tax returns are frequently audited, and the personal representative will participate in that audit. The personal representative must account to the court for all of its activities during the administration process. Assets may be liquidated for distribution, or to generate funds to pay estate taxes. Even in relatively simple estates, the process can be expensive and time-consuming, requiring payment of legal fees, appraisal fees, accounting fees, broker fees, etc. Given the $5,000,000 plus exemption amount, it is unlikely that many estates that are concerned with estate tax will be simple.

Virtually all decedents die with some amount of outstanding debt, including loans made to the decedent, credit card bills, rent and utility bills, etc. Some states require that notice of the decedent's death be published in a local newspaper, and the creditors often have a limited period of time to submit their claims to the personal representative for payment (seven months in New York). If a claim is not submitted within that time the personal representative may not be required to pay it. The creditor can try to collect from other property outside of the probate estate, but that is much more difficult. Because outstanding debts are usually paid during probate, the probate estate is sometimes referred to as the "property subject to claims."

Revocable Living Trusts, Non-Probate Property

Because of the perception (true or untrue) that the probate process is unnecessarily time consuming and expensive, there has been a "probate revolution" over the last 30 years or so. Estate planners have in many cases structured estate plans to avoid probating assets. We have already discussed some non-probate property that is subject to the estate tax, including retirement plans, joint tenancy property, and life insurance. Yet those do not cover many assets that might otherwise need to be probated. The device used to transmit those assets to the decedent's beneficiaries is commonly referred to as a Revocable Living Trust. A properly planned Revocable Living Trust plan involves the creation of a trust by a Grantor during her lifetime (we will focus on a single Grantor for simplicity purposes), which she funds by transferring to it the bulk of the assets held in her name, including homes, investments, and even personal property, like jewelry and home furnishings. The Grantor is the sole beneficiary of the trust so long as she lives, and she has the right to amend or revoke the trust.[5] She can be the trustee for herself, but if she becomes unable to care for herself the trust names someone to step in as successor trustee to take care of the her finances. To this extent, the trust acts as a substitute for a conservatorship for an elderly individual. In addition, the trust directs to whom the property will pass upon the Grantor's death, in this way it acts as a substitute for a will. If all of the Grantor's assets are effectively transferred to the trust while she is alive, then when she dies there will be no assets in her name; they will all be held in the name of the trust.[6] The then-acting Trustee can then distribute the assets to the trust beneficiaries, without intervention of the probate court, by simply transferring title.

Just because the assets in a revocable living trust avoid probate does not mean that there are not still substantial expenses incurred in administering the trust after the Grantor's death. Those assets also must be managed, divided, distributed, etc. The trust instrument may require the Trustee to account to the beneficiaries. The Trustee, if she holds all of the assets, may be the one to file the estate tax return. The trust must file income tax returns. But what is missing are the many probate court procedures that can prolong the process and add to the expense.

Funeral Expense: § 2053(a)(1)

Section 2053(a)(1) allows a deduction for the decedent's funeral expenses. The regulations expand the term to include a "reasonable expenditure for a tombstone, monument, or mausoleum, or for a burial lot, either for the decedent or his family."[7]

Administration Expenses: § 2053(a)(2) & (b)

A major category of expenses deductible under § 2053 is administration expenses under § 2053(a)(2). Into that category fall all of the expenses incurred by the estate in the probate process described above, such as legal fees, accounting fees, brokerage fees, property management fees, the personal representative's fees and other expenses that are allowable by the probate court administering the estate. While § 2053(a)(2) applies to amounts payable from property subject to claims,[8] if the decedent had a revocable living trust, then § 2053(b) allows a deduction for similar expenses incurred by the trustee in managing the assets prior to distribution.

---

[5]   Obviously, the assets of the trust are includible in her estate for estate tax purposes under § 2038.

[6]   The trust is usually executed along with a "pour over will" that directs that any property remaining in the Grantor's name at death will be added to the trust. Those assets will need to be probated. They are added to the trust so that all of the assets can be administered as a group.

[7]   § 20.2053–2.

[8]   § 20.2053–1(a).

One issue that comes up in this context is whether the expenses are for the benefit of the estate, or whether they are for the benefit of the beneficiaries. The period of administration can be protracted and the personal representative may also be named as a trustee of a testamentary trust created by the will (or the revocable living trust may continue to be held in trust). In some cases the line between expenses necessary to administer the estate and those necessary to administer the trust can blur. The regulations provide that "expenditures not essential to the proper settlement of the estate, but incurred for the individual benefit of the heirs, legatees, or devisees, may not be taken as deductions."[9]

Claims Against the Estate: § 2053(a)(3)

To the extent that estate assets are being used to satisfy debts owed by the decedent at death, they should and do reduce the gross estate under § 2053(a)(3). The regulations define claims against the estate as personal obligations of the decedent existing at the time of death.[10] This will include amounts owed by the decedent on personal loans, credit cards, and rent or mortgage payments due as of the date of death, and a host of other obligations, including tort and contract obligations.

An important limitation on deductibility is that the claim must be bona fide in nature. Bequests that are cloaked as claims are not allowable as deductions.[11] Imagine a decedent who had three children, and the eldest lived with and cared for the decedent during her last years. The will divides the estate equally among the three children. Shortly before death, the decedent signed a document recognizing an obligation to the eldest for $50,000, in recognition of the loving care he has received. Is this a claim against the estate, or a disguised bequest to the child? If it is a claim against the estate for services rendered, then it will be deductible for estate tax purposes, but should be taxable income to the child. If it is a disguised bequest, then there will be no estate tax deduction, and will be excluded from the child's income under § 102.

Mortgages: § 2053(a)(4)

Many homes and other real property owned by decedents are subject to some sort of mortgage. A mortgage loan is secured by the property, and the mortgage agreement entitles the lender to take the property ("foreclose") in the event of default.[12] A mortgage can be "recourse" or "nonrecourse." The difference between the two is important in the income

---

[9] § 20.2053–3(a)(1). So, although an estate is entitled to expenses in preserving and distributing its assets, if the administration of the estate is extended for a prolonged period of time, the expenses related to preserving the estate's assets may not be deductible under § 2053.

[10] § 20.2053–4(a)(1).

[11] § 20.2053–1(b)(2).

[12] Non-real property can also be subject to a secured loan, a good example is a margin brokerage account.

tax, less so under the transfer taxes. A mortgage is recourse if the borrower has personal liability to pay any shortfall if the value of the property at foreclosure is insufficient to satisfy the loan. In the case of a nonrecourse loan, if the value of the property at foreclosure is less than the outstanding loan then the bank's rights are limited to retaking the property; the borrower has no personal liability to make up the shortfall. In that case the lender suffers the loss.

Unlike most creditors' claims (credit card debt, rent, utilities) mortgages are not current debts typically paid off in probate.[13] Rules on "exoneration of liens" vary from state to state, and can be varied by the will, but frequently the property is distributed to the beneficiary subject to the debt, and the beneficiary takes over payments.[14] Whether they are to be paid off or not, mortgages certainly reduce the value of the property passing to the beneficiaries, and if the full value of the property is included in the estate, we need to reduce the value to reflect the outstanding debt.

Section § 2053(a)(4) specifically authorizes a deduction for outstanding mortgages, and would seem by its terms to apply to both recourse and nonrecourse obligations. Nevertheless, the regulations distinguish between recourse and non-recourse mortgages. Property subject to a recourse mortgage is included in the gross estate at its full value, and the mortgage is deducted under § 2053(a)(4). Property subject to a non-recourse mortgage is included in the gross estate at its value *net of* the mortgage, meaning no deduction is taken.[15] Although the amount of the taxable estate will not differ, the amount of the gross estate will, and that may be relevant for issues such as the filing threshold.

Part B. The Charitable Deduction: §§ 2522, 2055

As in the income tax, the transfer taxes allow amounts passing to charity to pass free of tax. Unlike the income tax, the deduction is unlimited, so that if decedent leaves his entire estate to charity there will be no tax. The list of qualifying charities is similar, though not identical, to those qualifying for the income tax deduction. Differences do exist among the income tax, gift and estate tax rules, so no charitable gift or bequests should be made before establishing that the recipient is qualified.

The § 2055 deduction is available for all "bequests, legacies, devises or transfers" to a qualified organization. Property transfers through the exercise of a general power of appointment are considered a bequest of the

---

[13] Interest accrued up to the date of death will be a claim against the estate.

[14] This can, of course, be varied by will, if the testator instructs the personal representative to satisfy to distribute the property free and clear of the mortgage. State rules vary.

[15] § 20.2053–7. The regulations seem to indicate the net treatment for non-recourse debt is optional, although the instructions to the Form 706 Estate Tax Return direct the disparate treatment.

property.[16] If the will or local law requires that the assets going to charity bear a share of the estate's transfer tax liability (whether federal or local) the deduction is reduced by the amount of those taxes.[17]

Bequests to qualified organizations are deductible to the extent of the value of the property given. The deduction is limited to the value of the transferred property that is included in the gross estate.[18] Outright bequests, made directly to a charity, are easy to value; the estate simply deducts the amount that was included in the gross estate. So if a will leaves property included in the gross estate at a value of $2,000,000, it deducts $2,000,000 in arriving at the taxable estate. The deduction is neither more nor less than the value of what the charity is getting.

The major limitation to the estate and gift tax deduction arises when the decedent/donor wishes to divide the property over time between charitable and non-charitable beneficiaries. Some charitable donors do not choose to make gifts outright, and instead leave the property in trust. They may want family members to enjoy the property either before it goes to charity, or after the charity has had the use of it for some time. For example, the decedent may want to support his brother during his lifetime, and thereafter have the property go to charity (referred to as a "charitable remainder trust"). Alternatively, the charity's interest may precede the non-charitable beneficiary's, for example, the decedent may want the charity to have the use of the property for ten years, and then have it pass to the decedent's children (a "charitable lead trust").

If our goal is to make sure we give a deduction for the value of what the charity is actually receiving, then valuing transfers made in trust is problematic. Recall the rules we discussed in **Chapter Two** regarding valuing transfers in trust. In the case of a trust creating an income interest for life and a remainder, we saw that § 7520 divides the value of the property between the interests created, using an interest rate equal to 120% of the AFR and mortality tables that predict the life expectancy of the income beneficiary. This gives us, at best, an estimate of the value of each interest, which will be inaccurate to the extent that the trust earns more or less than the predicted interest rate, and the mortality assumptions prove to be untrue. Should we allow the estate to deduct this estimate, when we don't really know the value of what the charity will get? Consider the following example.

Example #1: **Assume that D wants to leave his $10,000,000 estate to Harvard University, but wants to provide support to his brother B for the balance of his lifetime. His will could create a trust that would pay the income to B for life, with a remainder to**

---

[16] § 2055(b).

[17] § 2055(c).

[18] § 2055(d).

Harvard. **The will divides D's estate temporally between B and Harvard, creating two interests. Clearly B's income interest won't qualify for the charitable deduction, but should the remainder to Harvard?**

If we were to allow a deduction for the remainder, we would need to determine its actuarial value under § 7520, with reference to the Table S in the regulations that we have seen before. Assume that the trust will contain assets of $10,000,000, that the § 7520 interest rate is 2.8%, and that B is 68 years old. The tables assume that the income payments to B will be 2.8% each year, and will value Harvard's remainder at $6,659,000. That would be the amount of the deduction. A serious problem with valuing charitable deductions this way is that it does not take into account the ability of a Trustee to control the trust's investments, and to favor one beneficiary over another. Suppose, for example, that the Trustee wants to maximize the income payments to B, and to that end, buys junk bonds that currently pay interest at a rate of 8%. The reason that the current yield on these bonds is so high is that the bonds are very risky and it is possible that the borrower will not be able to pay the bonds at maturity. For this reason, value of Harvard's remainder interest these bonds determined under Table S would be significantly overstated. Similarly, if Harvard had been given an income interest for a term of years and B held the remainder, the Trustee could favor B by investing in stock in companies that do not currently pay dividends, but rather reinvest their profits for future growth. In this case, the value of Harvard's income interest the tables would be significantly overstated.

These concerns prompted changes in the law in 1969, and under current law split-interest transfers (a transfer of an interest in the same property to both a charitable and non-charitable beneficiary) must comply with a specific set of rules, designed to avoid manipulation, to qualify for the deduction. By limiting the deduction to situations in which the payout rate to the current beneficiary is defined as a dollar amount or fixed percentage of principal, the Code minimizes the ability of the Trustee to overvalue the interest going to charity. Because the amount is defined, the Trustee cannot manipulate the payments going to the current beneficiary, meaning that the risk of over or under valuing that interest is reduced. One variable still remains in the tables if the income beneficiary's life is the measuring stick for an annuity or unitrust interest, and that is the life expectancy of the beneficiary. But presumably the Trustee has no control over that.

Section 2055(e) provides that if a decedent splits property temporally between a qualified charitable beneficiary and a non-charitable beneficiary, then

A remainder interest will qualify for the deduction *only* if the trust is a charitable remainder annuity trust or a charitable remainder unitrust (both defined in § 664(d) of the Code), or a pooled income fund (defined in § 642(c)(5)).

Any other interests in trusts (i.e., lead interests) are deductible *only* if the charity receives a guaranteed annuity or a fixed percentage of the annual value of the trust.

Charitable remainder annuity trusts are defined in § 664(d)(1). The trust must provide a fixed amount to be paid at least annually to the non-charitable beneficiary, and that amount must be at least 5% and no more than 50% of the initial trust principal.[19] The amount can be paid for a set term of years (maximum 20), or for the life of the beneficiary. The remainder must pass to a qualified charity. Charitable remainder unitrusts, described in § 664(d)(2), are similar, but the annual amount going to the non-charitable beneficiary (also ranging from 5 to 50%) is determined based on the value of the trust each year. Pooled income funds are assets managed by the charity itself, which will pay out the amount to the non-charitable beneficiary.[20]

Consider the following variations on *Example #1:*

Variation 1(a): **Assume instead that the trust provides for payment to B of $100,000 per year for life, remainder to Harvard. Recall that the trust was funded with $10,000,000.**

This appears to be a charitable remainder annuity trust, because the amount going to B is a fixed amount per year.[21] It will not, however, qualify as such because B is receiving less than 5% of the initial value of the trust per year. If the annuity amount is $500,000 or more, then the deduction will be allowed for the value of the remainder.

Variation 1(b): **Assume instead that the trust provides for payment to B of 10% of the value of the trust's principal, determined annually, for life, remainder to Harvard.**

This is a charitable remainder unitrust, and the value of the remainder will be deductible under § 2055. The main distinction between an annuity trust and a unitrust is the method of calculating the payment.

---

[19] The 5% restriction is imposed for an unrelated income tax reason, having to do with charitable foundations. The 50% rule was imposed in 1997 to stem an abusive transaction called "accelerated charitable remainder trusts."

[20] Fewer restrictions apply to pooled income funds, because the charity is in charge of investments, and the manipulation possibilities described below do not exist. We will not deal with them in detail here.

[21] Annuities can be expressed as a dollar amount, or as a percentage of the trust's initial fair market value. In either event the amount does not vary during the term of the trust. This annuity is the same as one that was expressed as 1% of the initial fair market value of the trust.

An annuity trust pays a fixed amount based on the trust's *initial value*, a unitrust pays a fixed percentage of the trust's assets as *valued each year*.

Variation 1(c): **Assume instead that the trust provides for payment to Harvard of $100,000 per year for ten years, remainder to decedent's issue, by representation.**

The estate will be allowed a deduction for the value of the ten year stream of payments to Harvard. This is an example of a charitable lead trust. Section 2055(e)(2)(B) allows a deduction for interests other than remainder interests (such as this stream of payments) only if the interest is in the form of an annuity or a unitrust payment. There are no restrictions on the amount or term of the payments going to the charity, so the $100,000 amount is sufficient. The estate will receive a deduction for the present value of the ten year stream of payments, using the § 7520 rate.

Variation 1(d): **Assume instead that the decedent left B a life estate in decedent's personal residence, with a remainder to Harvard.**

There is an exception to the rule for split interests in property when the property being divided is either a farm or the decedent's personal residence.[22] In the case of a personal residence this exception can be justified in that it is not possible to manipulate the income interest in the property; it is simply the use of the property for a period of time. On these facts, the estate would be permitted a deduction for the charity's remainder interest.

Variation 1(e): **Assume instead that the decedent transferred $10,000,000 to a pooled income fund[23] maintained by and for the benefit of Harvard University, directing that the income should be distributed to B for life.**

This type of transfer is specifically blessed by the statute and the estate will be allowed a deduction for the value of the remainder. Pooled income funds are frequently established by charities so that donors can easily donate irrevocable remainders without the expense of setting up their own charitable trusts. All property given to the fund is commingled, and all income beneficiaries receive an amount of income based upon the fund's actual income each year. Since the charity has a vested remainder in all of the property in the fund, it is in the charity's interest to invest conservatively and preserve the value of the remainder, and still pay a reasonable return to the income recipients in order to attract future donations.

---

[22]　§ 2055(e)(2) excepts "an interest described in section 170(f)(3)(B)."

[23]　Pooled income funds are defined in § 642(c)(5).

Part C. The Marital Deduction: §§ 2523, 2056

Introduction

The role of the marital deduction changed dramatically with the Economic Recovery Tax of 1981 (known as "ERTA"). Prior to ERTA the role of the deduction was limited; it was intended to equalize the treatment of decedents in common law states with those in community property states. Since ERTA, however, the deduction has played and continues to play a major structural role in the estate and gift taxes. As applied to married persons, it essentially transformed the estate and gift tax from taxes on individuals to taxes on couples.

Pre-ERTA

To illustrate the role that the deduction played prior to ERTA, consider a married couple (H and W) with $5,000,000 in assets, all the result of the earnings of H. H died in 1980, leaving his entire estate to W by will. W dies the following year.[24]

If the couple lived in a community property state, H's estate would consist of his half of the community property, or $2,500,000. On W's later death, her estate would be $5,000,000, consisting of her half of the community plus the amounts received from H. The estate tax would apply to an aggregate of $7,500,000 in transfers.

If the couple lived in a common law state, however, H's estate would include all $5,000,000 of his assets, which would be taxed again when W died leaving an estate of the same amount. Absent a special rule, the estate tax would apply to an aggregate of $10,000,000. To alleviate this inconsistency, prior to ERTA H's estate would be entitled to a deduction for amounts passing to W of up to one-half of his estate.[25] As a result, H's estate would receive a marital deduction for $2,500,000, and the total amount subject to tax after both deaths would be $7,500,000, consistent with the community property couple.

The basic statutory architecture for the marital deduction was created during these years and is found in § 2056. Only amounts "passing" to the surviving spouse were eligible for the deduction, and the deduction was only allowed if the amounts going to the spouse would be included in her estate on her later death. Section 2056(b) therefore denied the deduction for "terminable interests," i.e., those interests that would terminate on the survivors death, and hence escape taxation. This meant that, as a general

---

[24] For these examples we make several simplifying assumptions. First, that in the common law state the assets are held in H's name alone. Second, that H predeceases W, and that the value of assets passing to her in all situations are not consumed, and have a constant value.

[25] There was a minimum deduction of $250,000, which could also benefit couples in community property states. We will not address that here.

proposition, marital bequests in trust did not qualify for the deduction. There was an important statutory exception, however. Under § 2056(b)(5) a gift in trust would qualify for the marital deduction if the surviving spouse was entitled to all of the net income from the trust, and held a general power of appointment over the trust assets (generally referred to as a "GPA trust"). In addition, an exception would exist if the trust provided that the trust assets passed to the estate of the surviving spouse ("estate trust"). The latter is not a statutory exception per se; it qualifies because it does not come within the definition of a "terminable interest," which we explore more closely below.

ERTA

With the enactment of ERTA in 1981, Congress began its gradual dismantling of the estate and gift taxes, as we discussed in **Chapter One**. As a part of that process, Congress changed the marital deduction from a maximum of 50% of the estate to an unlimited amount, so that beginning in 1982, all amounts passing to a surviving spouse are eligible for the marital deduction. The deduction is available equally in community and non-community property states, and its role as equalizer became moot. Its current role is to essentially treat the spouses as a single economic unit, and so long as assets stay within that unit there is no tax. Only when the surviving spouse leaves the assets to her beneficiaries will the transfer taxes apply. Thus, the tax is not forgiven, but deferred until the surviving spouse's death.

The change was a dramatic one, and increased the appeal of leaving assets to a surviving spouse in order to defer estate tax liability, even for individuals whose first priority might not be the support of the surviving spouse. For example, individuals in a second marriage, who each have children from a prior marriage, might wish to leave only a portion of their assets to their surviving spouse, in order to preserve the rest for their children. Prior to ERTA, if they wanted to take advantage the marital deduction, they could leave assets in trust for the survivor's life, with a remainder to their children, but to qualify for the deduction the trust would have to leave the remainder to the survivor's estate, or give the surviving spouse a general power of appointment over the trust assets. One could hope the survivor would not exercise the power to cut out the children, but there was no guarantee that the wishes of the predeceased spouse would be fulfilled.

In a bow to these concerns, ERTA also amended § 2056(b) to add an additional exception to the terminable interest rule. Under § 2056(b)(7), a decedent may leave assets in trust for the benefit of his surviving spouse, with a remainder to his children (or any other beneficiary he chooses) so long as certain requirements discussed below are met. Assets qualifying for the deduction are referred to as "qualified terminable interest property," and the trusts that hold them are referred to as "QTIP trusts." An election to qualify the trust for the marital deduction must be made on the estate tax return of the predeceased spouse, and one result of the election is that assets remaining in the trust at the surviving spouse's death will be included in her estate.

Marital Deduction Requirements

In the following discussion we will detail the requirements of the marital deduction. As we noted above, the basic statutory structure pre-dated ERTA, with the most major "recent" amendment being the addition of § 2056(b)(7) for QTIP trusts.

The "Passing" Requirement

As a threshold matter, under § 2056(a) only property that "passes" to a "surviving spouse" qualifies for the deduction. There is an overarching limitation that property will only qualify for the deduction to the extent it is included in the decedent's estate.

Section 2056(c) fleshes out the "passing" requirement. Not only do bequests to the survivor under the deceased spouse's will qualify, so do amounts received by inheritance if the deceased spouse died without a will. Also qualifying are amounts passing under an elective share statute or similar state rule that protects surviving spouses from disinheritance. In addition, amounts that are not part of the probate estate are treated as passing from the decedent, such as insurance, joint tenancy property, and property passing pursuant to a power of appointment. Under § 2056(c) all of these amounts will be treated as "passing" from the decedent to the surviving spouse.

Amounts that the survivor receives from the decedent's estate by virtue of a disclaimer raise the "passing" problem. Assume, for example, that the decedent's will leaves $1,000,000 to her aunt, and the residue to her husband. If the aunt disclaims the bequest it will go to the husband as residuary beneficiary. Did the amount pass from the decedent to the husband, or did it come from the aunt? The regulations make clear that so long as the aunt's disclaimer was "qualified" under § 2518, amounts going to the husband will be deemed to have passed from decedent to her husband.[26] The flip side is that if the husband disclaims property left to him in the will, it will not be treated as passing to him.

The recipient must be the decedent's "surviving spouse," and legal status as such is determined under state law as of the date of the decedent's

---

[26] § 20.2056(d)–2(b).

death. The 2013 Supreme Court case of *U.S. v. Windsor*[27] made it clear that the term includes legally married same sex couples.

Terminable Interest Rule

The trickiest aspect of the marital deduction is the so-called "terminable interest" rule of § 2056(b)(1). As a basic principle, it is designed to ensure that the tax on amounts qualifying for the deduction is delayed, not forgiven; if a deduction is allowed for an interest then that interest should (unless consumed by the survivor) be taxed on the survivor's death. The rule applies when the decedent splits property into two or more interests, giving one to the surviving spouse and the other to a non-spouse. If the interest going to the surviving spouse will terminate upon some event, and at that point the property will go to the non-spouse, then that is a "terminable interest" that will not qualify for the deduction.

To illustrate, consider the following examples:

Example #2: **D's will leaves his estate for the benefit of his wife W under the following variations:**

Variation 2(a): **D's will leaves his estate to a trust that provides income to W for life, remainder to W's estate.**

This is NOT a terminable interest. Although the income interest going to W will terminate upon her death, D has not split his property; for this purpose the wife and her estate are one person.[28] This type of trust, sometimes called an "estate trust," qualifies for the marital deduction.

Variation 2(b): **D's will leaves real property to W and D's child C as co-tenants**.

Here D has split his property, but the half interest going to W will not fail or terminate upon some event (at her death it will be part of her estate). The interest left to W will therefore will qualify for deduction. We don't need the terminable interest rule here, because W's share of the property will be a part of her estate at death. Thus, the one-half of the property passing to W will qualify for the marital deduction.

Variation 2(c): **D owns a copyright, and his will leaves it to W. The copyright will expire in eight years.**

Notice that D did not split up the rights he held in the copyright. He gave all the rights he had to W. Although these rights will terminate in

---

[27]   133 S. Ct. 2675 (2013).

[28]   § 2056(b)(1)(A) provides that an interest in terminable if it the property is divided between the spouse and any person other than the surviving spouse, or her estate. Here the entire property went to the spouse and her estate.

eight years, they will not pass to another. For this reason, they do NOT constitute a terminable interest.[29]

Variation 2(d): **D's will instructs his executor to purchase an annuity for the exclusive benefit of W for her life.**

Under § 2056(b)(1)(C), this is treated as a terminable interest, but it is unclear exactly why. If D had merely suggested to the Executor that she should consider purchasing an annuity for W, or if W on her own had purchased the annuity with funds that passed from D, no terminable interest would have been created. This amounts to no more than a trap for the unwary.

Variation 2(e): **D's will leaves his estate outright to W if she survives him by one year.**

This type of survivorship requirement, designed to avoid unnecessary double probate of assets if the spouses die within a relatively short time period, is common, and may create a terminable interest problem. D has split his property between W and the other beneficiaries of his will, each receives a contingent right to take the property. W's interest will terminate if she dies within the one year period. Therefore, this is a terminable interest that will fail to qualify for the deduction. Nevertheless, there is a statutory exception to the terminable interest rule found in § 2056(b)(3), which permits survivorship requirements of up to six months. Requirements for longer periods, as in this Variation, will render the bequest ineligible for the deductions.

Statutory Exceptions to the Terminable Interest Rule for Transfers in Trust

Absent a special rule, and except for "estate trusts," the terminable interest rule prevents marital bequests made in trust from qualifying for the deduction. Prior to ERTA there was only one major statutory exception that allowed some trusts to qualify, the power of appointment trust. Since ERTA, however, the QTIP trust has been the principal vehicle for marital deduction trusts. Both are discussed below.

General Power of Appointment Trusts. Prior to ERTA, the major exception to the terminable interest rule that permitted marital deduction gifts to be made in trust was § 2056(b)(5), which allows a deduction for a transfer in trust so long as the survivor is entitled to all of the income from the property for her life, payable at least annually, and she is given a general power of appointment over the property.[30] No other person can have a power to appoint the property to anyone other than the survivor

---

[29]   § 2056(b)(1)(A).

[30]   Section 2056(b)(6) contains a similar rule for life insurance and annuity payments held by an insurer and paid out in installments.

during her life. If the statute is complied with, the property escapes the terminable interest rule because the statute deems the entire property has passed to the spouse, and none has passed to another person. As a result, the *full amount* passing into the trust is deductible. While these "GPA" trusts were quite common prior to ERTA, they are less frequently used since 1981, when Congress authorized the "QTIP" trust, for reasons that we discuss below.

Qtip Trusts. Section 2056(b)(7) carves out an exception to the terminable interest rule for "qualified terminable interest property." If the statutory requirements are complied with, then the entire amount of property passing into the trust is treated as passing from the decedent to the surviving spouse, and hence is not a terminable interest.

The basic requirements are that the surviving spouse must have a "qualifying income interest" in the property for life, and the executor of the first spouse to die must make an election to have § 2056(b)(7) apply. For this purpose, a specific portion of property will qualify, i.e., the election can be made with respect to a fractional interest in a trust.

A qualifying income interest for life is defined in § 2056(b)(7)(B)(ii). The surviving spouse must be entitled to all of the income from the property, payable at least annually, and during the spouse's lifetime no one can hold a power to distribute the property to any person other than the surviving spouse. So long as the surviving spouse has this income interest, the remainder of the trust can go to anyone that the predeceased would like. Frequently it is his children or grandchildren, but it could be anybody. In stark contrast with the GPA trust, the survivor is not given a general power of appointment over the trust, so that she cannot vary the wishes of the predeceased spouse.[31]

If a QTIP election is made with respect to a trust, then the assets of the trust will be included in the surviving spouse's estate under § 2044. This is how the statute accomplishes deferral of the tax until the survivor's death.

Example #3: **Consider the following variations, in which a decedent H leaves his estate in trust for the benefit of his wife W under the following alternative scenarios:**

Variation 3(a): **The trust provides for income to W, payable quarterly, and remainder to H's children. The trust will continue for W's life, but will terminate in the**

---

[31] A QTIP trust may well give the surviving spouse interests in the trust beyond her qualifying income interest. She might be given a right to principal distributions that falls short of a general power of appointment, and she might be given a testamentary special power over the remainder, perhaps to vary the shares of the children. But the only interest she is required to receive is the qualifying income interest for life.

event of her remarriage, and be distributed to the children.

This trust does not create a qualifying income interest for life, because the surviving spouse's interest does not exist for her lifetime. W's interest is terminable, and the estate will not be entitled to a marital deduction.

Variation 3(b): **The trust provides for income to W for life, payable quarterly, remainder to H's children. The Trustee has discretion to invade trust principal as it deems necessary for the support of W or the children.**

Again W does not have a qualifying income interest because of the Trustee's power to distribute principal to the children during W's lifetime. Therefore, W's interest is terminable and the estate will not be entitled to a marital deduction. The same would be true if W had the power to direct distributions to the children.

Variation 3(c): **The trust provides for income to W for life, payable quarterly, remainder to H's children. The Trustee has discretion to invade trust principal as the trustee deems appropriate for the support of W in her accustomed standard of living.**

In this case W does have a qualifying income interest for life, and if the executor makes the QTIP election it will qualify for the marital deduction. The power to invade principal for W's benefit does not violate the statutory requirement. Indeed, it is not uncommon for the Trustee to have the flexibility to distribute principal to the surviving spouse. Nevertheless, the statute does not require such a provision; it is sufficient if the surviving spouse gets all of the income, and no one else has access to principal.

If H's executor makes a QTIP election with respect to the trust, then assets remaining in the trust will be included in W's estate upon her subsequent death under § 2044. What would happen, however, if W gave away all or a portion of her rights in the QTIP trust? In such a case, the trust would not be includible in her estate. Congress recognized this possibility and enacted § 2519. Under this provision, if a surviving spouse disposes of all or any portion of a qualified income interest, then she shall be treated as transferring *all* interests in the property, *except* the qualified income interest. To illustrate:

Variation 3(d): **Assume H's will created the trust created in *Variation 3(c),* and H's executor made a QTIP election under § 2057(b)(7). Some years later, when W's income interest was worth $10 Million and the remainder is worth $15 Million, W makes a gift of one-half of her income interest to her daughter.**

It is clear that, under general principles, the transfer of ½ of W's income interest, worth $5,000,000, will be taxed as a gift. Under § 2519 W will *also* be treated as making a gift of the entire remainder interest ($15,000,000), resulting in total gifts of $20,000,000. This achieves the goal of eventually taxing amounts that qualified for the marital deduction on D's death. Had W not made the transfer, then the entire trust would have been taxed on her death under § 2044. When W does make the transfer of all or a part of the income interest, that transfer accelerates the taxation of the remainder. When W later dies, no portion of the trust will be included in her gross estate.[32]

Charitable Remainder Trusts. Section 2056(b)(8) allows a deduction for the surviving spouse's interest in a charitable remainder trust in which the surviving spouse is the only non-charitable beneficiary. To qualify, the trust must otherwise meet all of the requirements for a charitable remainder trust that we discussed in Part B, above. If it does qualify, then the unitrust or annuity trust interest going to the surviving spouse is eligible for the marital deduction, and the remainder qualifies for the charitable deduction.

Consider a couple who wish to provide for the surviving spouse during his or her lifetime, and want their property to go to a charity following the survivor's death. One possibility is to create a charitable remainder trust that would specify the annuity or unitrust interest going to the survivor, and would designate the specific charity to receive to the remainder. Prior to ERTA, that would have been the only possibility. But since ERTA, the availability of the QTIP makes it possible for the couple to accomplish their goal in a simpler way. The trust would need to provide the survivor with income for life, and in addition there could be an invasion power to provide additional support to the survivor as necessary. The trust would designate a charity to receive the remainder, although it could give the survivor a special power to vary the charity if she or he chose. Such a trust would never qualify as a charitable remainder trust, but so long as the executor makes the election it would qualify as a QTIP. On the survivor's death it would be included in his or her estate, but because it passes to charity at that point it would be eligible for the charitable deduction in the survivor's estate.

The Marital Deduction and Estate Planning

We've learned that all amounts passing outright to a surviving spouse will qualify for the marital deduction. As a result, spouses who have "simple wills," i.e., mirror wills that say "I leave all of my estate to my spouse if he/she survives me, and if not to my children who survive me," can be assured that there will be zero estate tax to pay on the death of the

---

[32]   § 2044(b)(2).

first spouse, regardless of the size of the estate. Under this simple will, the surviving spouse will own all of the assets outright, and to the extent she does not consume them, they will be included in her estate when she dies (unless, of course, she remarries and leaves them to her new spouse).[33]

Prior to 2010, this was not a good estate plan for many spouses. By zeroing out the estate of the first spouse to die, no use was made of his exclusion amount. The assets were all included in the survivor's estate, and only her exclusion amount was available to offset the tax. To illustrate, consider the following example and variations. In all cases, assume a fixed $5,000,000 exclusion amount.

Example #4:   **H and W, each 65 years old, have simple wills as described above. The issue is whether that estate plan is advisable if they own property of the following amounts:**

Variation 4(a): **H and W have jointly held assets of $1,000,000.**

In this case it would seem that simple wills are adequate. If W predeceases H, all of her share of the assets will pass to H, and her estate will owe no tax. On H's later death all of the remaining assets will be included in his estate, but that estate is highly unlikely to exceed the $5,000,000 exemption amount. In arriving at this conclusion, we would take into account the ages of H and W. If they are nearing retirement age, it is unlikely that they will experience a marked increase in their assets prior to death. One might come to a different conclusion, for the reasons described below, if H and W were younger and still actively engaged in their businesses.

Variation 4(b): **H and W have jointly held assets of $7,000,000.**

In this situation, W's estate would once again be zeroed out by the marital deduction, and her estate will owe no tax. But in this case, the assets remaining at H's death may well exceed H's exclusion amount of $5,000,000. The problem here (if there is one) is that W's exclusion amount was essentially "wasted," because it went unutilized at her death. Prior to 2010 this would indeed have been a problem, and something fancier than simple wills were needed to prevent this result. But with the addition of the concept of "portability" to the Code in 2010,[34] H's estate may not only make use of his exclusion amount, but also any of W's that was not utilized at her death. We discussed the concept of portability more thoroughly in ***Chapter One.*** The one thing to remember about portability is that the estate of the predeceased spouse *must* file an estate tax return, even if one

---

[33] For ease of explanation we are assuming outright transfers to the surviving spouse. The same analysis would apply if the wills left all of the property to marital deduction trusts, either GPA or QTIP trusts.

[34] § 2010(c)(4).

would otherwise not be required, in order for her exclusion amount to be preserved. Under our facts, if W's estate filed the requisite return and made the appropriate election, then H's estate would have $10,000,000 of available exclusion amount, which would likely result in no tax due. Now that portability is available, the simple wills may be adequate.

Variation 4(c): **H and W have jointly held assets of $15,000,000.**

In this variation, simple wills may not be optimal. If W predeceases, and her entire estate passes to H, then there will be no estate tax due at W's death because of the marital deduction. Portability will make W's exclusion amount available to H's estate when he dies, but there will be some estate tax payable because (absent a catastrophe) H's estate will exceed the combined exclusion amounts. Let's assume that H outlives W by ten years. Is W's exclusion amount worth the same when she dies as it is ten years later? It is not. The exclusion amount is fixed at $5,000,000,[35] but the value of the assets that it offsets isn't fixed. For example, under the simple wills all would go to H. If he were to invest the funds at 4%, when H dies the $5,000,000 in assets that would have been offset by W's exclusion will have grown to $7,400,000, but W's unused exclusion amount will only offset $5,000,000 of that value. If instead W's will had left $5,000,000 of her estate in manner that did not qualify for the marital deduction, then W would have had a taxable estate of $5,000,000, and there would be no tax.[36] Neither that $5,000,000, nor the $2,400,000 of appreciation in those assets, would be a part of H's estate on his later death. The bottom line is that it may be better to use the predeceased spouse's exclusion amount sooner rather than later.

Making use of W's exclusion amount does not mean that H cannot benefit from the property not left outright to him. It can be left to the children, which would be fine if H and W were sufficiently wealthy. But if the couple is concerned that H may need access to those funds, that $5,000,000 can be left to a trust for H's benefit. Such trusts are usually referred to as "bypass" or "credit shelter" trusts. So long as the trust does not qualify for the marital deduction (and no QTIP election is made with respect to it) and there is nothing in the trust that gives H a general power of appointment, it will not be included in his estate. Thus, a typical bypass trust would provide for income to H for life, potential invasions of principal (circumscribed by an ascertainable standard if he is Trustee), a five and five power, and a special testamentary power over the remainder that gives him the ability to adjust shares going to his children. This type of trust can give H as "close to complete ownership as is consistent with excludability

---

[35] Even though we are ignoring inflation adjustments to the exclusion amount for these examples, it is worth noting that W's unused exclusion amount will remain fixed at its amount in the year of her death, it won't be further adjusted for inflation.

[36] The remaining $2,500,000 would pass to W.

of those assets from his estate."[37] And the result will be that the $7,400,000 in assets that were sheltered by W's exclusion amount will not be taxed in H's estate.

It is worth noting also that the exemption amount for the GST tax is not portable. That amount is tied to the exclusion amount under § 2010. As a result, if later generations were to benefit from W's will, her GST exemption would expire with her. In such a situation it would be necessary to craft the will to take advantage of her GST exemption at her death.

Moving Forward

Now that we have arrived at the tax base, the "taxable estate," we have largely completed our exploration of the estate tax. We will now turn our attention back to the gift tax, and discuss some of the more important and complex issues under that tax.

---

[37] We give credit to this phrase to the late Melvin H. Morgan, Esq.

CHAPTER EIGHT

ADVANCED GIFT TAX ISSUES (§§ 2503, 2702 & 2518)

■ ■ ■

In *Chapter Two* we learned the basics of the gift tax. In that chapter we briefly introduced the annual exclusion, the rules for valuing retained interests in trusts, and disclaimers. In this chapter we will return to those topics for a more detailed discussion.

Part A. Annual Exclusion Gifts in Trust

Introduction

As discussed in *Chapter Two*, § 2503 excludes certain amounts from the computation of taxable gifts. We saw that under § 2503(b), each year the first $10,000 of gifts from each donor to each donee is excluded from the tax base. We also saw that the inflation-adjusted amount of the "annual exclusion" is currently $14,000, and demonstrated how that amount can be effectively doubled for married donors through the "gift splitting" mechanism of § 2513. We also discussed in that chapter the exclusion of § 2503(e) of transfers for education and medical care.

We return now to the limitations on the availability of the annual exclusion for gifts made in trust. The principal limitation on the availability of the annual exclusion is the so-called "present interest rule" contained in the parenthetical of § 2503(b). That section allows the exclusion for gifts *other than* future interests, i.e., only present interests in property qualify for the exclusion. A present interest is "an unrestricted right to the immediate use, possession or enjoyment of property or the income from property."[1] Future interests include remainder and reversionary interests, and any other interest that will commence in use, possession or enjoyment at a future time.

That present interest rule is consistent with the original reasoning behind the annual exclusion, which was to exempt from tax traditional holiday and wedding gifts. It is also consistent with the "per donee" aspect of the exclusion, because identifying the person who will ultimately enjoy a future interest can often be difficult. Outright gifts of property certainly qualify for the exclusion. But in many cases the donor may not want to

---

[1]   § 25.2503–3(b).

implement a giving plan using outright gifts. The donor may have concerns about the donee's age, and may be concerned that the donee is too unsophisticated to manage the money; the donor may prefer to make the gift in trust. If a donor makes a gift in trust, only the present interests created will qualify for the annual exclusion. So, for example, if G transfers $14,000 in a trust that provides of income to the beneficiary until age 30, remainder to the beneficiary, or his estate, only the actuarial value of the income interest will qualify for the exclusion. The remainder, as a future interest, will not qualify for the exclusion. Hence, the search for ways to circumvent the present interest rule.

Gifts to Minors

One reason a donor might not be willing to make an outright gift eligible for the annual exclusion to a donee is that the donee is a minor. While many parents and grandparents want to take advantage of the annual exclusion by transferring funds to their minor children and grandchildren, many are not willing to make those transfers outright, and in fact it may not be possible to so without the appointment of a legal guardian for the benefit of the child. Donors in such situations have a number of options available.

Custodianships

One of the simplest and least expensive ways of making a gift to a minor is under the Uniform Gifts to Minors Act, or the Uniform Transfers to Minors Act, versions of which have been adopted in most if not all of the states. Under those acts, funds or property can be transferred to a custodian for the benefit of a minor, who is vested with powers to manage the property and use it for the minor's benefit, and who must distribute the funds to the minor when he reaches majority (or age 21, in some states). Because a custodian holding property for the benefit of a minor has substantially the same powers as a legal guardian, the IRS has long held that those gifts will qualify as present interests.[2] In some states the beneficiary of such a transfer is entitled to the property at age 18, and the Service has ruled that the annual exclusion is still applicable.[3] Custodianship gifts have income and estate tax pitfalls, however, that may make them unattractive. The minor's parent is taxable on the income from the property to the extent it is used to defray her obligation of support; the balance of the income will be taxed to the minor, but the "kiddie tax" rules may tax that income at the parent's rate.[4] If the donor acts a custodian, the broad powers over the custodianship will cause the property to be included

---

[2]   Rev. Rul. 59–357, 1959–2 C.B. 212.

[3]   Rev. Rul. 73–287, 1973–2 C.B. 321.

[4]   Rev. Rul. 56–484, 1956–2 C.B. 23, § 1(g).

in his estate under § 2038 if he is acting as custodian at death.[5] Finally, custodianships automatically terminate at either age 18 or 21 under the Uniform Acts, a result that concerns many donors who may want the gifts to be available at a later date.

"Minor's Trusts": § 2503(c)

Section 2503(c) provides that a gift to an individual under age 21 will not be considered to be a future interest if it meets certain requirements.[6] Specifically, the exclusion is available only if the property and the income from it (1) may be expended by, or for the benefit of, the donee before he attains age 21, and (2) any remaining property must pass to the donee when he reaches age 21, and if he dies before then it must be either paid to his estate or as he appoints under a general power of appointment. These requirements are intended to ensure that the donee has essentially the same access to the funds that he would have had a legal guardian been appointed, and the regulations impose the additional requirement that there cannot be substantial restrictions imposed on the Trustee's discretion to make distributions to the donee.

In many cases donors may prefer to place assets for the minor in a trust that extends beyond the beneficiary's 21st birthday. This is possible, within the limits imposed by the regulations. During the beneficiary's minority (note that the age of majority in many states is age 18, but for this purpose we'll use the term to describe someone under 21) the Trustee can have discretion to distribute the principal and the income to the beneficiary, but that discretion cannot be subject to "substantial restrictions."[7] The Trustee's power must be analogous to the power of a guardian under local law, so reference must be made to the law of the relevant state. Powers limited to "accident, illness or other emergency" have been held not to qualify;[8] broader powers relating to "support, care, education, comfort and welfare" have been held to qualify.[9] This is an area where careful drafting is important, and resorting to language typically used to create an ascertainable standard for other purposes may be dangerous.

Although the statute requires that the trust terminate at age 21, the regulations authorize the exclusion if the beneficiary has the right to choose at age 21 to continue the trust rather than terminate it. The Tax Court has allowed the exclusion for a trust that continued until age 25, subject to the beneficiary's right to terminate it at any time after he

---

[5]   Rev. Rul. 59–357, 1959–2 CB 212.

[6]   Note that the age of majority in many states is 18, nevertheless § 2503(c) in all events treats the age of majority as 21.

[7]   § 25.2503–4(b)(1).

[8]   See e.g., *Faber v. U.S.*, 439 F.2d 1189 (6th Cir. 1971).

[9]   Rev. Rul. 67–270, 1967–2 CB 349.

reached age 21.[10] The Commissioner has acquiesced in that decision, and further allowed the exclusion for a trust that provided the beneficiary with a limited time after reaching age 21 to terminate. In Revenue Ruling 74–43, the Service ruled:

> Accordingly, a gift to a minor in trust, with the provision that the beneficiary has, upon reaching age 21, either (1) a continuing right to compel immediate distribution of the trust corpus by giving written notice to the trustee, or to permit the trust to continue by its own terms, or (2) a right during a limited period to compel immediate distribution of the trust corpus by given written notice to the trustee which if not exercised will permit the trust to continue by its own terms, will not be considered to be the gift of a future interest as the gift satisfies the requirements of *section 2503 (c) of the Code*, and the exclusion provided for in *section 2503 (b)* is allowable.

In *Commissioner v. Herr*, the Third Circuit held that in determining whether a trust meets the requirements of § 2503(c), each interest created in the trust should be separately tested. In that case, during the beneficiary's minority the trustee had the discretion to distribute the income and principal to the beneficiary, and at age 21 the beneficiary was entitled to any accumulated income, but not the principal. The trust continued thereafter until the beneficiary reached age 30.

Under those terms, the income interest met the requirements of § 2503(c), because even though the income could be accumulated, those amounts were distributed at age 21. The remainder interest did not satisfy the statute. The court held that the income interest separately qualified for the annual exclusion, even though the remainder interest did not.[11]

"Crummey Trusts"

Apart from the rules of § 2503(c) for minor's trusts, the present interest requirement would seem to preclude the ability to make gifts in trust that qualify for the annual exclusion, beyond the actuarial value of the income interest. This may be particularly problematic in the case of life insurance trusts, where the donor/insured will usually need to fund continued premium payments, and will want those payments to qualify for the annual exclusion. Nevertheless, the courts have carved out an exception that makes it quite easy to qualify any gift in trust for the exclusion. So easy, in fact, that § 2503(c) trusts are rarely used, because of the restriction that they impose on distributions, and the fact that they

---

[10] *Heidrich v. Commissioner*, 55 TC 746 (1971).

[11] *Commissioner v. Herr*, 303 F.2d 780 (3rd Cir. 1962). To illustrate the distinction being drawn, suppose a donor today were to contribute $14,000 to a trust with the same terms as in *Herr*. Assuming that under § 7520 the income interest was worth $8,000, and the principal $6,000, then under *Herr* the $8,000 would be eligible for the annual exclusion.

generally must end at age 21. Instead, trusts with withdrawal rights, known as "*Crummey* Trusts" have become far more common.

The case credited with blessing these trusts is *Crummey v. Commissioner*,[12] decided by the Ninth Circuit in 1968. In *Crummey*, the donors created trusts for the benefit of their four children, some of whom were minors. The trusts were not drafted to qualify under § 2503(c). Each donor claimed four annual exclusions ($3000 per child)[13] for amounts contributed to the trust. This claim was based on a withdrawal right given to the beneficiaries under the trust: following any contribution by the donors to the trust, each child had the right to demand the lesser of (i) the amount contributed, or (ii) $4000. That right lapsed at the end of the calendar year of the contribution.[14] The Tax Court found that the transfers to the trusts for the adult children qualified for the annual exclusion, because of the child's ability to withdraw the contributed funds (which constituted a present interest). As to the minor children, however, it held that because there was no guardian appointed for the children who could exercise the withdrawal right, the contributions to their trusts were future interests. The Ninth Circuit reversed, holding that the right in the minor children to demand withdrawal was sufficient, however unlikely it was that the right could or would be exercised: "All this is admittedly speculative since it is highly unlikely that a demand will ever be made or that if one is made, it would be made in this fashion. However, as a technical matter, we think a minor could make the demand." Thus, the existence of the withdrawal right meant that the donors were each allowed a total of $12,000 in annual exclusions for their contributions to the trust. Thus was spawned the "*Crummey* Trust."

The rule of the *Crummey* case has been extended well beyond the facts of the original case. Whereas in *Crummey* the withdrawal right was limited to the children, who were the primary beneficiaries of the trust, the Tax Court has since extended the rule to allow annual exclusions based on withdrawal rights granted to contingent beneficiaries as well.[15] The government argued that *Crummey* should be limited to vested beneficiaries, but the Tax Court disagreed:

> The likelihood that the beneficiary will actually receive present enjoyment of the property is not the test for determining whether a present interest was received. Rather, we must examine the ability of the beneficiaries, in a legal sense, to exercise their right

---

[12]   397 F.2d 82 (9th Cir. 1968).

[13]   The amount of the annual exclusion at the time was $3,000.

[14]   Powers like these are known "*Crummey* powers."

[15]   *Cristofani's Estate v. Comm'r*, 97 T.C. 74 (1991). See also *Kohlsaat v. Comm'r*, 73 T.C.M. 2732 (1997).

to withdraw trust corpus, and the trustee's right to legally resist a beneficiary's demand for payment.[16]

In order to bolster the fiction that the withdrawal right is real, and might actually be exercised by a beneficiary, the trustee must give notice to the beneficiary when a trust contribution subject to withdrawal is made, and allow a reasonable time for the right to be exercised.

One issue that comes up in the context of *Crummey* Trusts is the lapse problem that we discussed in **Chapter Six**. A withdrawal right under such a trust is essentially a general power of appointment over the amount subject to withdrawal, and if that right lapses unexercised, and the amount involved exceeds the five and five rule,[17] then (as we saw in **Chapter Six**) a number of additional gift and estate tax problems may arise.

If the courts are willing to extend *Crummey* to contingent beneficiaries, how about individuals who otherwise have no interest in the trust? Suppose, for example, the owner of a corporation sets up a trust for her children and annually grants to each member of her Board of Directors a *Crummey* power. Should the owner be entitled to an annual exclusion for each of these powers, even though they are not exercised? Surely not, but it is not exactly clear why. At any rate, the rule of *Crummey* has pretty much eviscerated the present interest rule, and has generated periodic calls to amend the statute to limit the annual exclusion to outright gifts. Congress has yet to act on any of those proposals.

Part B. Gift Tax Valuation of Retained Interests: § 2702

Introduction

Section 2702 of the Code was added by Congress in 1990 to address a particular type of transaction considered abusive. Presumably the cure isn't worse than the disease, but the cure has spawned yet another set of abusive transactions.

Section 2702 was aimed at a "GRIT," or Grantor Retained Income Trust. A GRIT is an intervivos trust created by a Grantor who reserves an income interest in the trust (and possibly another interest) and makes a gift of the remainder. An example is as follows:

Example #1: **D (age 70) transfers $100,000 to a trust that provides for income to D for 15 years, remainder to C or C's estate. If we apply a discount rate of 10%,[18] the actuarial value of D's**

---

[16] *Id.,* at 83.

[17] This was not a problem when, as in *Crummey*, the annual exclusion was $3,000, because the lapsed power was always less than the five and five rule. But with the increase in the annual exclusion it has become a problem.

[18] While that rate may seem unrealistically high, it is actually entirely consistent with rates during the 1980s, when this type of planning was extensively used.

retained interest is $76,000, hence the taxable gift of the remainder is $24,000.[19]

If D dies within 15 years, clearly the full fair market value of the assets in the trust will be included in his estate under § 2036. So at no further estate tax cost or risk, D can reduce the amount of the taxable gift further by also retaining a reversion to his estate if he dies within 15 years.[20] If the actuarial value of the reversion is $14,000, then the amount of the taxable gift by D is reduced to $10,000.

But what if D survives the 15 year term? When he later dies, nothing will be included in his estate, because the trust will have passed to C by that time, and all of the strings retained by D have expired. So $100,000 has passed to C, while the amount subject to the transfer tax was only $10,000.

This result is not necessarily abusive. If we assume that the value of the principal of the trust remains fixed at $100,000, and that the income of the trust was at least 10% a year, the values we used in taxing the gift are appropriate, and the income payments will have replaced the property in D's estate. But in reality will they? The Trustee is required to pay income to D, and the Trustee has substantial discretion in choosing how to invest the trust's assets. Suppose the Trustee invests in growth stocks that generate little current income, but are expected to increase in value over time. In this case the income interest that D retains is overvalued and the remainder undervalued, and the tax benefits to D can be substantial. Assume, for example, that the Trustee invested the $100,000 in a growth stock that quadrupled in value during the 15 year trust term, but paid little or no dividends. The result in that case would be to shift $400,000 to C, while only $10,000 was subject to the gift tax.

Congress enacted § 2702 in 1990 to deal specifically with the GRIT problem. Section 2702 is a valuation rule that applies only for gift tax purposes. It applies to determine *if* a gift has been made, and the *value* of the gift. It applies when a transferor (i) transfers an interest in trust to a family member (as defined in the statute), and (ii) simultaneously retains an interest in the trust. When § 2702 applies, it usually values the interest retained by the transferor as zero. Hence, in the above example, if C were a member of D's family, under § 2702 both D's retained income interest and reversion would be assigned a value of zero, and the value of the gift made upon creation of the trust would be $100,000, the entire value of the amount transferred. The statute doesn't prevent the shift of appreciation

---

[19]   We are taking the liberty of rounding numbers.

[20]   There is no estate tax risk, because even though § 2037 will be triggered by the reversion, the entire trust will be included anyway under § 2036.

to C, but at least it requires D to pay gift tax on the full amount transferred.[21]

> *Variation:* Same as *Example #1*, except the terms of the trust provide for income to C for 15 years, remainder to C or his estate. D is named Trustee, and in that capacity has the power to distribute all or a portion of the income to his spouse S in his sole discretion.

In this case D has not retained an interest in the trust in the normal sense; he will not benefit from the income. But he has retained a power over the property, the power to divert income away from C and give it to S. This power is sufficient to render the gift of the income interest incomplete, although the gift of the remainder is complete. It appears that the value of the gift will be limited to the actuarial value of the remainder. But that is not the case. The regulations state that:

> An interest in trust includes a power with respect to a trust if the existence of the power would cause any portion of a transfer to be treated as an incomplete gift under Chapter 12.[22]

Thus, even though D did not expressly reserve an interest in the trust for his own benefit, because of the power retained by D over the income interest, D is treated as having retained that interest. Therefore, the trust will be subject to § 2702 and the value of that retained "interest" will be treated as zero. The same result as in *Example #1* will occur, and the full $100,000 transferred will be taxed as a gift.

Qualified Retained Interests

The statute permits certain reserved interests to be valued actuarially, these "qualified interests" are described in § 2702(b), and are basically the types of interests that are not susceptible to manipulation by the Trustee's choice of investment. Thus, if instead of retaining a right to income, D retains the right to receive a fixed amount each year (an annuity interest), or a fixed percentage of the trust's fair market value each year (a unitrust interest), then the actuarial value of those interests can be subtracted in valuing D's gift. Presumably, Congress believed that such interests are accurately valued by the valuation tables, limiting opportunities for abuse. This is not necessarily true.

The "Zeroed Out GRAT"

The § 7520 rules assume that the principal of the trust will remain constant, and the entire investment return is in the form of current income, at the § 7520 rate. What if a donor owns an asset with an extremely volatile

---

[21] If D had simply transferred the $100,000 outright to C, C would be entitled to all of the appreciation without further gift tax. § 2702 essentially treats D as if he had done that.

[22] § 25.2702–2(a)(4).

value, for example stock that has dropped precipitously in value following a market downturn? The donor may believe that the stock will appreciate rapidly in value, and would like to take the opportunity created by the downturn to shift future appreciation out of his estate. The donor could contribute it to a "GRAT," or grantor retained annuity trust, and retain an annuity sufficiently large that the value of the remainder is essentially zero. In order to avoid the possibility that the value of the stock will average out over time, and to limit the risk that the donor will die during the trust term (which would result in inclusion in his estate under § 2036) the term for the trust should be very short. If the stock does not go up in value, it ends up back in the hands of the donor, at no gift tax cost, and the donor can try the transaction again. But if the stock does increase dramatically in value, the donor will have successfully transferred all of that appreciation to the remainderman at no gift tax cost.

A good example is found in the case of *Walton v. Commissioner*.[23] In that case, the grantor created two trusts, in which she retained an annuity interest, and the remainders went to her daughters. To each trust she transferred Walmart stock worth approximately $100,000,000 (yes, that's one hundred million dollars). The grantor retained an annuity in the trust for two years, which was payable to her estate in the event of her death, and the sum of the value of those annuities zeroed out the value of the remainders. The reported gift tax on the transfer was zero.

In fact, in *Walton* the Walmart stock did not appreciate as hoped, and the trust actually had insufficient assets to pay the annuity to Mrs. Walton. But what if Walmart had increased in value above the § 7520 rate? The potential wealth transfer is staggering.

Before examining how § 2702 operates, it will be useful to take a closer look at terms used in the statute: Section 2702 is triggered any time an individual makes a "transfer of an interest in trust" to a "member of the transferor's family" if that individual (or an "applicable family member") retains an interest in that trust. Unless the retained interest is "qualified," the value of that interest shall be treated as zero.

Transfer of Interest in Trust

The term, "a transfer of an interest in trust" is broadly defined and encompasses transfers of any interest in property in which there are 1 or more "term interests." A term interest includes both a life interest as well as a term of years. The creation of a trust with one or more term interests is the most common example. However, the term would also encompass a transfer by the owner of Blackacre of a term of years in Blackacre, or a transfer of a remainder in Blackacre, retaining a term of years.

---

[23]   115 TC 589 (2000).

In addition, the term also includes certain joint purchases. If two family members purchase property in which there is a term interest, the transaction will be treated as though the person who acquires the term interest acquired the entire property and then transferred the other interests in the property (i.e., the remainder interest) to the other family members in exchange for whatever they paid for their interests. To illustrate, suppose Mother and Daughter jointly purchase Blackacre for $2,000,000. Instead of taking title as tenants in common, Mother takes a legal life estate in the property, and Daughter receives the remainder. Each contributes an amount to the purchase price equal to the actuarial value of their interests; Mother contributes $1,300,000 and Daughter contributes $700,000. Under § 2702(c)(2) the transaction is treated as if Mother purchased the entire property for $2,000,000, and then transferred the remainder in the property to Daughter in exchange for $700,000. Mother's retained life interest will be valued at zero, and the amount of Mother's taxable gift will be $1,300,000, which is the total amount transferred, $2,000,000 less the consideration received, $700,000.[24]

Members of Family & Applicable Family Members

For purposes of § 2702(a), a "member of the transferor's family" is broadly defined. Section 2702(d) sends us to § 2704(c)(2), which defines members of the family to include the transferor's spouse, brothers and sisters (and their spouses) and all ancestors and lineal descendants of the transferor (and their spouses). Note that it does not include the transferor's nieces and nephews, i.e., descendants of brothers and sisters.

Section 2702 can be triggered if the transferor or an *"applicable family member"* retains an interest in the property. Applicable family members are defined in § 2701(e)(2) differently from members of the transferor's family. They include the transferor's spouse, ancestors of the transferor and her spouse, and spouses of those ancestors. It does not include siblings or descendants of the transferor.

The following examples involve several members of the same family: Father (F), Daughter (D), Son (S), and Father's Mother (M). For purposes of these examples, please disregard the annual exclusion.

Example #2: **Father (F) transfers $10,000,000 in assets to an irrevocable trust. The terms of the trust provide that F (or his estate) is entitled to the income from the trust for 10 years. At the expiration of 10 years the remainder passes to F's Son (S), or his estate. If the § 7520 rate is 4%, the value of S's remainder interest is $6,700,000.**

---

[24] Note that the property will not be included in Mother's estate under § 2036, because of the exception in that statute for transfers for adequate and full consideration.

This transaction is an example of a GRIT and clearly falls within § 2702: F has made a completed gift of the remainder of this trust to S, a family member,[25] while retaining an interest in the trust, the 10-year income interest. Under § 2702(a)(2)(A), F's retained 10-year income interest is valued at zero. Therefore, F is treated as making a taxable gift to S of $10,000,000.

If F subsequently makes a gift of his income interest, then that gift would be taxed at its then actuarial value. This seems somewhat unfair, given that he was taxed on the full transfer at the time he created the trust. The regulations recognize that it would be unfair not to take into account the prior transfer and allow for a reduction of the amount of the subsequent taxable gift so that F would not be double taxed.[26]

Variation 2(a): **Same as *Example #2* except that F retained the right to payment of $500,000 each year for 10 years, with the remainder going to S or his estate.**

F's right to the annual payment, which is an annuity interest, is a qualified interest under § 2702(b)(1). Therefore, its value is determined under § 7520, and that value will be subtracted in determining the amount of the gift.[27]

Variation 2(b): **Same as *Example #2* except that F retains the right to change the remainderman to his Daughter (D).**

F's power to change the remainderman renders the gift of the remainder incomplete.[28] Because F has retained the income interest, no completed gift has taken place, and § 2702 will not apply. This is one of the express exceptions that is contained in the statute.[29]

Variation 2(c): **Same as *Example #2* except that S paid F $6,700,000 for the remainder interest, which is equal to its fair market value.**

In addition to valuing interests in property, § 2702 also is used to determine whether there has in fact been a gift.[30] Since F has transferred an interest in trust to S and retained an interest that is not qualified, F's retained interest is valued at zero. Therefore, F has transferred a remainder interest with a value of $10,000,000 to S in exchange for $6,700,000, resulting in a gift of $3,300,000.

---

[25] §§ 2702(e) & 2704(c)(2).

[26] § 25.2702–6(a), (b)(1).

[27] § 2702(a)(2)(B).

[28] § 25.2511–2(c).

[29] § 2702(a)(3)(A)(i).

[30] § 2702(a)(1).

Variation 2(d): Same as *Example #2*, except the trust instrument designated F's Mother (M), not F, as the income beneficiary for the 10-year term, remainder to S.

This transaction is not described in § 2702 because F did not retain an interest in the property, but did an "applicable family member" do so? Although M is an "applicable family member" under § 2701(e)(4), she did not "retain" an interest in the trust. Under the regulations, retained means held by the same person both before and after the transfer to the trust.[31] This transaction would simply be treated under the normal rules. We don't need § 2702, because in any event F has made a gift of the full amount transferred, $10,000,000.

If, however, F transfers an interest in a trust in which M holds an interest, then § 2702 could apply. Assume that, apart from the trust that he created, F is the remainder beneficiary under a trust created by his father's will, and M is the income beneficiary of that trust. If F makes a gift of his remainder interest, M will have held an interest in the trust (the income interest) both before and after the transfer. Therefore, the value of M's retained interest will treated as zero, and F's gift will equal the full value of the trust principal.

The concern with this transaction is that, just like the garden variety application of the statute in *Example #2*, the remainder interest's value under § 7520 may be understated if the Trustee manipulates the trust investments to favor the remainder over the income interest.

Exception for Personal Residences

We have already seen that there is an exception in § 2702 for transactions in which there is no completed gift.[32] Another significant exception has to do with personal residence property.[33] The zero valuation rule will not apply if the transferor transfers his personal residence into a trust, reserving an interest in the trust, and leaving the remainder to a family member. To illustrate, consider the following example:

Example #3: In addition to his $20,000,000 condo in Manhattan, G owns a summer home in the Hamptons worth $10,000,000. When he is 65, he transfers the Hamptons home into a trust that provides that G will continue to have the right to occupy the home for 10 years, at which time it will pass outright to G's children, or their estates, in equal shares.

Absent an exception, the trust would clearly be subject to § 2702. Because G's retained term interest is not a qualified interest, it would be

---

[31]   § 25.2702–2(a)(3).

[32]   See *Variation 2(b)*, above.

[33]   § 2702(a)(3)(A)(ii).

valued at zero, and G would have made a taxable gift of $10,000,000. However, there is an exception that can apply, and that is the one found in § 2702(a)(3)(A)(ii). Under that rule, § 2702(a) does not apply:

> If such transfer involves the transfer of an interest in trust all of the property in which consists of a residence to be used as a personal residence by persons holding term interests in such trust. . .

The regulations describe two types of trusts that will qualify for this exception. The first, a "personal residence trust," is quite restrictive. The trust is not permitted to own any property other than the residence and generally the property must be used by the holder of the term interest as a residence.[34] The second, a "qualified personal residence trust," is far more flexible.[35] Among other things, it permits the trust to hold cash or other property as long as the purpose for holding the additional property is related to expenses related to holding the residence.[36]

This creates quite an opportunity for tax planning under certain conditions. If the G outlives the set term of his interest, his children will own the property at that time. If in fact the property has increased in value, then all of that appreciation goes straight to the children, without transfer tax cost. In an era of rising real estate values and relatively high interest rates, this can result in a substantial benefit. Let's assume that when G creates the trust, the § 7520 rate is 6%. The value of the remainder is roughly $5,500,000, and that would be the amount of G's gift. If the property continues to go up in value at an annual rate of 5%, then when the children get the property, it will be worth close to $18,000,000. Which means, if all works out as hoped, Grantor will have removed $12,500,000 in value from his transfer tax base at no gift tax cost. Grantors can hold interests in two such trusts, so if our Grantor was so inclined, he could transfer his Manhattan condo into a trust as well. What's not to like?

Well, first of all, if G does not live out the ten year term then the property will be included in his estate at its full date of death value under § 2036. This is not the end of the world, however, because he will be no worse off than if he had done nothing, except for paying a bunch of ultimately unnecessary legal fees.

Second, as we have learned in recent years, the real estate market does not dependably increase each year. There is a chance that the property will not grow in value as much as expected, which will reduce the amount of the tax savings. Interest rates fluctuate as well, so in a time of uncertainty

---

[34] § 25.2702–5(b). There is an exception for "qualified proceeds." These would be amounts that the trust receives as a result of the destruction or involuntary conversion of the property.

[35] § 25.2702–5(c).

[36] This latter exception goes beyond the precise language of the statute, but was presumably issued under the authority given Treasuring in § 2702(a)(3)(A)(iii) to add additional exceptions deemed consistent with the statute's intent.

in the market the rates may drop, and there will be less to gain from creating the trust. To illustrate, at this writing the § 7520 rate is 2.4%. Using that rate, the value of the trust remainder that would be subject to gift tax would be roughly $7,900,000. And if the property increases at an annual rate of 3% over the ten year term, its value would grow to roughly $12,700,000. The savings is not as significant. And what if the trust ends during a severe drop in the market? There may be no savings at all, and a potential cost.

What all of this means is that Congress has left open a planning opportunity, the rationale for which is hard to fathom, that may or may not result in significant tax savings.[37] Offset against the potential savings are the fact that, if he survives the ten year term, his children will own the house, and if he wants to continue to live there he will have to pay them rent at a market rate to avoid inclusion under § 2036. There are also transaction costs, and the rules applicable to qualified trusts are quite detailed and somewhat restrictive. The bottom line is that planning for such trusts must be done carefully, with an eye on any available crystal ball.

Part C. Disclaimers: § 2518

In *Chapter Two* we briefly discussed the disclaimer rules of § 2518. In short, if an individual makes a "qualified disclaimer" of a transfer of property interest, then for purposes of the transfer taxes (i.e., the estate, gift and GST tax), the interest will be treated as if it were never transferred to that person. We have seen several examples of how disclaimers can be important, and here we turn to a more detailed examination of the rules for qualified disclaimers.

Prior to 1976 the transfer tax treatment of disclaimers was in disarray, largely because of the substantial variations in local law requirements for effective disclaimers. With § 2518 Congress created a uniform set of rules to govern the tax treatment of disclaimers, regardless of their effectiveness under local law. Under that section, the formal requirements for a qualified disclaimer are fairly mechanical and straight-forward. First, the disclaimer must be in a writing that describes the property interest disclaimed, and is signed either by the person disclaiming ("the disclaimant") or her legal representative. Second, it must be delivered to the transferor of the interest, her legal representative, the holder of legal title of the property, or the person in possession of the property, within 9 months following the date of the transfer creating the interest. The clock is tolled if the disclaimant is under age 21, in which case the 9 month period does not begin to run until her 21st birthday. Third, the disclaimant must not have

---

[37] It is worth noting that there is a similar provision in § 2055(e)(2) for charitable contributions of remainder interests in personal residences.

accepted the interest or any of its benefits. And finally, the disclaimed interest passes without any direction of the disclaimant to a person other than the disclaimant or the spouse of the decedent.

Notice that the last requirement allows the spouse of the decedent to disclaim property even though the disclaimer will result in an interest in the property passing to her. This rule is utilized often in post-mortem estate planning. To illustrate, suppose the Decedent leaves his entire estate outright to his Spouse with instructions that any disclaimed amount will pass to a trust in which Spouse has an income interest, with a remainder to the children. This will allow for the decision whether or not to create a "bypass trust," as discussed in *Chapter Seven*, to be deferred until after the death of the predeceased spouse.

Timing of Disclaimers

Identifying the deadline for disclaiming can be tricky in some cases, as the date on which the clock starts running depends on the nature of the underlying transfer. The governing rules are contained in § 25.2518–2(c)(3) & (4). The key is to determine when the interest was created.

> *Intervivos gifts.* If the interest being disclaimed is an intervivos gift, then the 9 month period begins on the date that the transfer is a completed gift for gift tax purposes. This is true even if the interest in property is subsequently brought back into the donor's estate.

> *Testamentary transfers.* If the interest is received by reason of the death of the transferor (e.g., gifts by will, through intestacy or by transfers that become irrevocable on the transferor's death), then the 9 month period commences with the date of death.

> *Powers of appointment.* If the interest passes to the transferee by reason of the exercise or release of a *general* power of appointment, then the clock starts ticking on the date the power is exercised or released. A different rule, however applies to *non-general* powers. In that case, any person who might benefit from the power, including the holder of the power, and any permissible appointee and any taker in default, must disclaim within 9 months after the special power is created. This somewhat confusing rule is consistent with the notion that the holder of a general power is essentially treated as the owner of the property, whereas the holder of a special power is not. Indeed, the holder of a special power can be viewed as an agent of the creator of the power. This means that the relevant transfer in the case of a general power takes place when the power is exercised or released, whereas the relevant transfer in the case of a special power takes place upon creation of the power.

Remainder interests. The recipient of a remainder interest, whether vested or contingent, must disclaim within 9 months of the transfer that originally created the interest.

Residuary beneficiaries. Disclaimed property typically passes under state law as though the disclaimant had predeceased the transferor. In the case of testamentary transfers, that means that the disclaimed property will usually pass to the residuary beneficiary of the will. If that beneficiary (or any other person to whom disclaimed property would pass) wants to disclaim the property, she must do so with 9 months of the decedent's death.

Joint tenancy property. If the recipient of a joint tenancy interest in property transferred intervivos wants to disclaim her interest, she must do so within 9 months of the transfer. If she does not, however, then she has 9 months from the date of her co-tenant's death to disclaim the one-half portion of the property to which she succeeds as a result of the death. This is true regardless of how much of the property is included in the decedent co-tenant's estate, how much consideration either co-tenant supplied, and whether or not the tenancy was severable.

Notice that in many cases the clock to disclaim may be running even though the potential disclaimant may be entirely unaware that she has received an interest that could be disclaimed. While the clock is tolled until the beneficiary is 21, no other provision is made for other legal disabilities, or for lack of notice to the beneficiary.

To illustrate these timing rules, consider the following examples. The principal issue in each example is when the clock starts to run for purposes of § 2518. Assume that all parties are 21 years of age or older.

Example #1:   On February 1, 2016 D creates an irrevocable trust with the following terms: D is to receive all the income from the trust for life, with the remainder to be distributed to B or her estate. On March 1, 2017, D dies and the entire value of the trust is included in D's estate under § 2036(a)(1).

On February 1, 2016 D makes a completed gift of the remainder interest; this is the date the vested remainder interest is created. Therefore, the clock begins to run on that date and B must disclaim that interest within 9 months, i.e., before November 1, 2016. The fact that the value of the trust was later included in D's estate is irrelevant for this purpose.

Example #2:   On March 1, 2016 D creates an irrevocable trust with the following terms: the trust's income is to be distributed between A and B for 15 years in whatever amounts the Trustee deems appropriate; the remainder is to be distributed to C or C's

estate. D is named as Trustee and acts in that capacity until his death on April 1, 2018. The entire value of the trust is included in D's estate under § 2036(a)(2).

The gift of the remainder interest to C was complete on March 1, 2016. Therefore, C has 9 months from that date to disclaim her gift. The fact that the value of the remainder is included in D's estate is irrelevant. The gift of the income interest to A and B, however, is not complete because D has retained the discretion to distribute the trust's income between them as she deems appropriate.[38] The transfer of the income interest becomes complete on April 1, 2018, the date of D's death. Therefore, the clock begins to run for A and B on that date and they each have 9 months thereafter to disclaim their interests.

Example #3:   On February 1, 2017, D transfers to H and W Greenacre (real estate) as joint tenants with right of survivorship. On December 1, 2017, H dies.

D's gift of Greenacre was complete on February 1, 2017. Therefore, H and W each have 9 months from that date to disclaim their one-half interests in the property. Assuming that neither disclaims their interest, following H's death on December 1, 2017, W has 9 months to disclaim the one-half portion of Greenacre to which she succeeds as a result of H's death.

Example #4:   On May 1, 2017, D dies. D's will grants A a special power to appoint the residue of D's estate among X, Y and Z in such shares as A chooses. On December 1, 2017, A exercises the power in favor of X.

On these facts, the transfer that created X's interest in the property is the creation of the special power in A on the date of D's death Because X was one of the set of possible appointees, X's clock for purposes of § 2518 begins on that date and she must disclaim within 9 months. This is true, even if X was totally unaware of the possibility that she might receive the property. This would also be true even if the special power was broadly drafted, so that A could appoint to anyone other than herself, her estate, creditors or the creditors of her estate.

Example #5:   D dies on June 1, 2017, survived by A. D's will grants A a general power of appointment over the residue of the estate. The will also provides that if A does not survive D, then the residue passes to Z, or Z's estate.

A's general power of appointment was created on June 1, 2017 by D's death, and therefore A has 9 months from that date to disclaim the power. If she does disclaim the power, then Z will be entitled to the residue. What

---

[38] Note, however, that to the extent D made distributions to A and B before her death, these would be treated as completed gifts of the amounts distributed on the dates they were made.

is curious is that if Z wants to disclaim all or part of the residue, she *also* must do so within 9 months of D's death, not from the date that A disclaims.

Suppose, however, that A does not disclaim the power but instead exercises the power in favor of Z. In this case, Z's interest in the property will be created by the exercise of the power. Therefore Z's clock begins to run on the date of the exercise of power.

Disclaimers of Partial Interests

A disclaimant must not have accepted the property or any of its benefits prior to making the disclaimer. Thus, if the disclaimant uses the property, or accepts any income from it, prior to disclaiming, the disclaimer will not be qualified. This rule ties into the rule of § 2518(c)(1), which permits a disclaimer of an undivided portion of an interest in property. Thus, accepting one interest in a piece of property does not *necessarily* preclude the disclaimer of another interest in the same property. The rules governing the disclaimer of less than an entire interest in property are found in § 25.2518–3.

An undivided interest in property means just that: the disclaimed interest must consist of a fraction or percentage of the disclaimant's interest in the property, and must extend over the term of a property interest. To illustrate, if D leaves Blackacre to T by will, T can disclaim 50% of Blackacre. T cannot disclaim a remainder interest in Blackacre and reserve a life estate. If, however, D leaves T a life estate in Blackacre, with a remainder to X, T can disclaim an undivided 50% interest in his life estate.

To illustrate disclaimers of less than an entire interest in property, consider the following example in which various beneficiaries attempt to disclaim a portion of their bequest. Assume throughout that all the disclaimers are timely.

Example #6: **D dies on June 1, 2017. D's will included the following specific bequests:**

(1) **100 shares of IBM stock to A;**

(2) **Blackacre (50 acres of real estate) to B;**

(3) **$1 million in trust, income to C for life, remainder to Y.**

In addition, D grants to X a general power of appointment over the residue of the estate.

In the alternative,

(a) **A disclaims 75 shares of IBM stock.**

This constitutes a qualified disclaimer. A is disclaiming an undivided interest in the stock.

(b) B disclaims 10 acres of Blackacre.

This is a qualified disclaimer. B is disclaiming an undivided portion of Blackacre.

(c) B disclaims a 30 year leasehold in Blackacre, retaining the remainder.

This is not a qualified disclaimer. The leasehold is not an undivided interest in Blackacre.

(d) C disclaims 40% of her income interest in the trust.

This is a qualified disclaimer. She is disclaiming an undivided portion of the interest.

(e) X disclaims the power to appoint any portion of the residue to herself, her creditors, her estate or the creditors of her estate, thereby converting the general power of appointment into a special power.

This is not a qualified disclaimer. The power to appoint property to oneself, is not an undivided interest. X could disclaim the right to appoint some percentage of the property and that would be a qualified disclaimer of an undivided interest.[39]

Moving Forward

We have now completed our study of the estate tax and the gift tax. In **Chapter Nine** we take on the GST tax, a difficult but worthy endeavor. Finally, in **Chapter Ten** we will offer an overview of the valuation rules that can arise in all three of the transfer taxes, and introduce some estate planning techniques.

---

[39] See § 25.2518–3(a)(iii) & (b).

CHAPTER NINE

THE TAX ON GENERATION SKIPPING TRANSFERS

■ ■ ■

Part A. Introduction

At this point we have learned about the primary transfer tax, the estate tax. We also seen how it is "backed up" by the gift tax, and that those two transfer taxes are "unified," so that neither is incurred until lifetime and death transfers exceed the exclusion amount. What remains is the tax on generation skipping transfers (the "GST tax").

The impetus behind the GST tax was the notion a transfer tax should be imposed on family wealth as it moves from one generation to the next, and that if the estate or gift tax didn't apply at each generation, an additional tax should step in and fill the gap. Congress made its first attempt to enact such a tax in 1976, but because of its complexity and several serious shortcomings, it was retroactively repealed. In 1986 Congress enacted the current version of the GST tax, which remains in effect today. Although the 1986 version was a vast improvement on the earlier legislation, the GST tax remains exceedingly complex.

Before the GST tax, it was possible for wealthy families to limit their transfer tax liability by having wealth "skip" a generation, and avoid estate or gift tax at that generation. There were several ways to do this. To illustrate, suppose a Grandparent (GP) has one child (C) and one grandchild (GC). A "normal" movement of wealth through this family would impose an estate tax when GP leaves her estate to C, and then another estate tax would be imposed when C dies and leaves the assets to GC.[1] If the family was very wealthy, one obvious way to eliminate one of these two levels of tax would be for GP to leave her assets directly to GC, entirely skipping C. If, however, that wasn't consistent with C's wishes, the same result could be accomplished by having GP's estate remain in trust for C's benefit for his life, with a remainder going to GC. As we've learned, C could receive the entire net income of the trust, together with access to principal as needed; C could be trustee of the trust, and so long as he was not given a general power of appointment over the trust, those assets would not be included in his estate. Except as limited by the rule against

---

[1]   If gifts were made those would be taxed as well.

perpetuities, the trust could continue indefinitely, through multiple generations. What the current GST tax does is to impose a transfer tax at the level of C's generation, as a substitute for the gift or estate tax.

The GST tax plays an increasingly important role in the transfer tax system, as a growing number of states have largely repealed the rule against perpetuities, allowing for the creation of "dynasty trusts" that can span multiple generations.

As we begin to explore the statute, it is important to keep in mind the basic type of transaction at which the tax is aimed: a transfer from a grandparent to a grandchild or more remote descendant. The statute goes well beyond that basic transaction, however, and achieves new heights of complexity in order to capture less common but possible transactions that could avoid the transfer tax. So as we explore the trees, try to keep the forest in mind.

Part B. Who Is a Skip Person? §§ 2613 & 2651

Central to an understanding of the GST tax is an understanding of the terms "skip person" and "non-skip person," which are defined in § 2613. The statute uses these terms to identify those transactions targeted by the tax: those that allow wealth to pass free of gift or estate tax at one generation level. Both natural persons and trusts are treated as "persons" for purpose of the statute, and how they are categorized will depend upon the generation assignment of a natural person. A natural person is a skip person if she is assigned to a generation two or more generations below the transferor's generation assignment. Trusts are skip persons depending upon the identity of the trust's beneficiaries under rules discussed in detail below. Any individual or trust that is not a skip person is a "non-skip person".

Generation Assignments of Natural Persons: § 2651

Section 2651 provides different rules for assigning natural persons to a generation depending on whether the person is a lineal descendant of the grandparent of the transferor (or of her spouse) or not. Section 2651(b) governs the assignment of these lineal descendants, and § 2651(d) governs the assignment of those that are not in that category.

Lineal Descendants of Grandparents

Section 2651(b) governs the generation assignment of any lineal descendant of the transferor's (T's)[2] grandparents, and of T's spouse's

---

[2]   Transferor is defined in § 2652(a) as the donor of a transfer taxable under gift tax or the decedent of a transfer subject to the estate tax. If under § 2513 a gift is treated as being made ½ by the husband and ½ by the wife, then each is treated as a transferor of her share. Note that if the trust is a QTIP trust, the assets in the trust will be included in the surviving spouse's estate under § 2044. Thus, ordinarily the surviving spouse is the transferor with respect to those assets.

grandparents. The spouse of any lineal descendant is assigned to the same generation as the descendant.[3] Starting with the simplest case, if the individual in question (let's call him X) is a lineal descendant of the transferor's grandparent, we assign X to a generation by comparing the number of generations between the transferor and the transferor's grandparent (which will always be two), to the number of generations between X and the transferor's grandparent. Thus we start with the transferor, and create a family tree for him, going up to his grandparent. We have created such a family tree in the Table below.

The Transferor's Family Tree

Generation

+2			Grandparents
+1		Parent	Uncles & Aunts
0	Tranferor & Spouse	Brothers & Sisters	1st Cousins
-1	Children	Nieces & Nephews	1st Cousins Once Removed
-2	Grandchildren	Grand Nieces & Nephews	1st Cousins Twice Removed
-3	Great Grandchildren	Great Grand Nieces & Nephews	1st Cousins Thrice Removed

With the help of this Table, it is a fairly simple matter to determine which lineal descendants of T (and/or of her spouse) are skip persons. Note

---

However, § 2652(a)(3) allows for a "reverse QTIP election" which permits the estate of the first spouse to die to elect to remain the transferor of that trust for GST purposes.

    [3]   § 2651(c)(2).

first that the Table only includes the issue of T's grandparents.[4] Also note that the way the Table is constructed, each row of the Table represents a single generation, each of which is numbered, and T's generation assignment is zero. We can see that the number of generations between T and his grandparent is two, and we number the grandparent's generation plus two (+2). Under the general rule, skip persons are those who are two or more generations below T's, or in generation "-2" and lower.

From this Table it is clear that nieces and nephews are not skip persons because they are assigned to generation "-1," only one generation below T. It is equally clear that T's grandchildren, grand nieces and nephews, and first cousins twice removed are skip persons, because they are assigned to generation "-2."

If T makes a transfer to a lineal descendant of his spouse's grandparent, then we would create a mirror image of this table for the spouse, and would compare the transferee's generation assignment to that of the spouse, who is a member of generation "0."[5] Thus, if T makes a transfer to a descendant of his spouse (e.g., the spouse's nephew or grandnephew), we would simply compare the transferee's generation assignment to that of the spouse. Again, only when we reach the generation two levels below the spouse would we encounter skip persons. Thus the spouse's nephew, who is assigned to generation "-1" would not be a skip person, but the spouse's grandnephew, who is assigned to generation "-2" would be.

Deceased Parent Exception

Under § 2651(e) there is a special rule (sometimes referred to as the "orphan's rule") for assigning generations to certain persons whose parent is dead at the time of a transfer subject to the estate or gift tax. When this rule applies, the individual is assigned to the generation which is one generation below the lower of (i) the transferor's, or (ii) that of the youngest living ancestor of the individual who is also a descendant of a parent of the transferor. The generation assignments of all of the orphan's descendants are adjusted as well.

To illustrate the underlying purpose for this rule and to see how it works, suppose that a deceased transferor (T) had only one child (C), who predeceased her, and only one grandchild, (GC). Who would be the natural object of T's bounty? Because C is deceased, it would clearly be GC. If she left her estate to GC, should her estate be subject to the GST tax? On facts such as these, Congress' answer was no. The GST tax was intended to tax transfers that were designed to reduce or avoid the transfer taxes by

---

[4]   More remote relatives, such as T's second cousins (who are descendants of T's great-grandparents, but not T's grandparents), are not governed by this rule and will be assigned a generation under § 2651(d), discussed below.

[5]   T's spouse (or former spouse) is always assigned to T's generation. § 2651(c)(1).

skipping a generation; that purpose would not be served here. In this situation, the transferor *could not* have left her estate to her deceased child. For this reason, Congress enacted § 2651(e), which changes the generation assignment of GC; it essentially moves GC up one generation, to his parent's generation, so that he is not a skip person with respect to T.

The orphan's rule is subject to substantial limitations and applying it can be tricky. The rule primarily applies to lineal descendants of the transferor, but can also apply to certain other relatives on our chart. If the transferor has no living descendants, it can also apply to other lineal descendants of the transferor's parent (or her spouse's parent), i.e., those relative described in the middle column in our chart.[6] Thus, the transferor's grandnieces and grandnephews may be moved up a generation under the rule, but only if the transferor did not leave descendants.[7] The rule does not apply to more remote relatives, those in the third column. To review, the orphan's rule can apply when the transferee is described in the first column, sometimes applies when the transferee is described in the second column, and never applies when the transferee is described in the third column.

The following examples illustrate how the rule applies.

Example #1: **T makes a $1,000,000 gift to her grandchild, GC. At the time of the transfer, T's child, the father of GC, is dead.**

GC is assigned to one generation below T's (i.e., C's generation) and so is not a skip person. Note that if T's child (GC's father) is living at the time of the transfer, but GC's mother were deceased, the orphan's rule does not apply: the deceased parent must be a lineal descendant of the transferor's parent.[8]

Example #2: **T makes a $1,000,000 gift to her grandniece (GN) at a time when GN's father, T's nephew, is dead.**

Application of the orphans rule will depend on whether T had living lineal descendants at the time of the gift. If T had none, then GN would be moved up one generation, and she would not be a skip person.[9] If T did have living descendants at the time of the gift, then GN's generation assignment would not change.

---

[6] § 2651(e)(2).

[7] One's eyes start to cross at some point in this inquiry. But stepping back, if T in our example above, left her estate to C then C would be moved up a generation because her parent was dead. But if T had children and grandchildren, then amounts passing to her grandnieces and nephews would be subject to the tax, even if their parents predeceased T.

[8] This is where the term "orphan's rule" proves to be a bit of a misnomer. We are only concerned with the death of a parent who was related to the transferor (or spouse) by blood. Thus if T had one child C who was married to S, and they had one child GC, the orphans rule would apply if C died, but not if S died.

[9] § 2651(e)(2).

Example #3:   T makes an intervivos transfer of $1,000,000 to an irrevocable trust for the benefit of T's child C for life, remainder to C's child GC. Several years after the transfer, C dies, and the trust assets are distributed to GC.

As we'll learn later in this chapter, if GC is a skip person when C dies, then C's death will be a taxable event under the GST tax.[10] If GC is not a skip person at that time, then the tax will not apply. This raises the question of when do we decide whether GC is an "orphan?" Under the statute, the parent of the transferee must be dead at the time the transfer was first subject to the gift or estate tax.[11] The gift of GC's remainder was complete at the time of the initial transfer. As a result, the orphan's rule does change GC's generation assignment, because C was alive at the time that T made the initial transfer to the trust.

Example #4:   T makes a $1,000,000 intervivos gift to her great grandchild, GGC. At the time of the transfer, T's child is alive, but T's GC (GGC's parent) is dead.

On these facts, the orphan's rule applies, but does not eliminate the GST tax. The generation assignment of GGC will indeed be changed; GGC is assigned to the generation that is one below the lower of T's, or that of the GGC's youngest living ancestor, C. In this case, since C is in a lower generation than T, GGC will be assigned to her parent's generation and will still be a skip person.

Non-Lineal Descendants

The GST tax applies to transfers to more remote relatives, and to non-family members as well. If the individual being assigned a generation is not governed by the rules of § 2651(a), then under § 2651(d) she will be assigned to a generation based upon the difference in age between her and the transferor. For this purpose, each generation is deemed to be 25 years. Under this rule, if the individual is not more than 12 ½ years younger than the transferor, she is assigned the transferor's generation; if the individual is more than 12 ½ years, but less than 37 ½ years younger, she will be assigned to the generation just below the transferor. Each additional 25 years of age difference is considered another generation. For example, suppose a 70 year old transferor makes a gift to an unrelated 30 year old individual. Since the difference in age between the transferor and the individual is 40 years, the 30 year old individual would be assigned to a generation two below the transferor and would be considered a skip person.[12]

---

[10]   It will be a taxable termination.

[11]   § 2651(e)(1)(B).

[12]   The transferor and her spouse (or former spouse) are always assigned to the same generation, regardless of the difference in their ages. § 2651(c)(1).

When Is a Trust a Skip Person?

Under § 2613(a)(2) a trust will be considered a skip person under two circumstances:

(i)   if all interests in the trust are held by skip persons, or

(ii) if no one holds an interest in the trust, and at no time can a transfer be made to a non-skip person.

Essential to understanding this provision is the special definition in the statute of an "interest in trust," which is found in § 2652(c). The phrase is misleading because it appears that it encompasses both present and future interests. It does not. For this purpose, a natural person has an interest in a trust if and ONLY if:

(i)   she has a current (not future) right to receive trust income or corpus, or

(ii) she is a permissible current recipient of trust income or corpus.[13]

We will refer to interests defined by the statute as "§ 2652 interests."

To illustrate when a trust will be characterized as a skip person, consider the following three irrevocable trusts, each of which has an independent Trustee. Grandparent (GP) created all three. GP, has one Child (C), one Grandchild (GC), and one Great Grandchild (GGC). At the time each of the trusts is created, everyone is living.

Trust #1:   The terms of the trust require all income to be paid to GC for life, and, at her death, the remainder will be distributed to GGC. This trust is a skip person: only one individual, GC, has a § 2652 interest in the trust, and she is a skip person.

Trust #2:   Same as *Trust #1*, except that the Trustee, in her sole discretion, may distribute income and/or corpus to C for her maintenance and support. This trust is not a skip person: C, who is a non-skip person, has a § 2652 interest in the trust because she is a permissible current recipient of income and/or corpus.

Trust #3:   The terms of the trust require the Trustee to accumulate all trust income for 20 years, and add it to corpus. After 20 years, the Trustee is to distribute the corpus equally between GC and GGC, or their estates. This trust is a skip person. Note that no one holds a § 2652 interest in this trust (i.e., no beneficiary has a current interest in the income or the corpus of the trust), and that all future distributions must be made to skip persons (i.e., GC or GGC).

---

[13]   There are special rules for charitable organizations described in § 2055(a). § 2652(c)(1)(C).

Part C. Taxable Events

Section 2601 imposes a tax on every "generation-skipping transfer," and § 2611 defines that term as including three events: taxable distributions, taxable terminations, and direct skips. The definitions of these three terms are found in § 2612.

Direct Skips

Direct skips are defined in § 2612(c) and may be the easiest to understand. A direct skip occurs any time a transferor makes a transfer subject to either the gift or the estate tax to a skip person. The simplest example of a direct skip is an outright transfer by gift or bequest by a grandparent to a grandchild or a great grandchild. Assuming the orphan's rule does not apply, such transfers would be subject to the gift or estate tax, and would be direct skips. In the case of a direct skip, liability for the tax falls on the transferor.[14]

To illustrate, consider the following examples. In each example assume that no transferee's parent has died, and ignore the potential application of the annual exclusion, the unified credit, and the transferor's GST exemption.

Example #5: **Grandparent (GP) gives her great granddaughter (GGC) $100,000 outright as a wedding gift.**

This is a direct skip because both requirements are met: GP has made a transfer that is subject to the gift tax, and the transfer is to a skip person. This transfer is subject to ***both*** the gift tax and the GST tax. Even though the gift to the great-grandchild skips two generations, it is subject to only one level of tax.[15]

Example #6: **GP dies and in her will leaves $500,000 outright to GGC.**

This is a direct skip because (i) GP has made a transfer that is subject to the estate tax and (ii) GGC is a skip person. The taxable transfer is $500,000 and it will be subject to both the estate and GST tax.

Example #7: **GP's will creates a testamentary trust with $500,000 for the benefit of GC and GGC. Under the terms of the trust, GC is given an income interest for life, and at GC's death the remainder passes to GGC or her estate.**

This is also direct skip. The only difference between this example and ***Example #6*** is that the testamentary trust is the skip person.[16]

---

[14] § 2603(a)(3).

[15] See § 26.2612–1(f) Ex. 2.

[16] GC, who is a skip person, holds the only § 2652 interest in the trust.

Example #8:   **GP pays GC's $50,000 bill for college tuition.**

This transfer is not a direct skip. Section 2503(e) provides that "qualified transfers" under that section, which include tuition and medical care payments made directly to the school or provider, are not treated as transfers of property by gift. Therefore, the transfer cannot be a direct skip, because it is not subject to the gift or estate tax.[17]

As we shall see later in this chapter, in the case of intervivos transfers there is a (qualified) exception to the GST tax generally for gifts that are covered by the annual exclusion in § 2503(b). If an annual exclusion gift is made outright, then it will be excluded from the GST tax as well as the gift tax. If, however, the gift is made in trust, then the rules are more complicated.[18]

Taxable Terminations

The second group of events that give rise to the GST tax are taxable terminations; they are defined in § 2612(a) and are somewhat more complicated. A taxable termination occurs whenever a § 2652 interest in a trust terminates (e.g., by death or lapse of time), *unless*

(i)   immediately after the termination a non-skip person has a § 2652 interest in the trust, or

(ii)   at no time after the termination may a distribution be made to a skip person.

To illustrate, suppose GP's will creates a testamentary trust with income for life to her spouse, then income for life to her child C, then the remainder to her grandchild GC. Creation of the trust is not a direct skip because the trust is not a skip person: the only § 2652 interest in the trust is the income interest held by GP's spouse, who is not a skip person. If the spouse dies survived by C, his income interest terminates, but this is not a GST event.[19] It is not a taxable termination because immediately after the termination of the spouse's income interest, C, a non-skip person has a § 2652 interest in the trust. Note, however, that when C dies and her income interest terminates, there will be a taxable termination: immediately after C's death the only § 2652 interest in the trust is held by GC, a skip person. When a taxable termination occurs, the liability for paying the tax falls on the trustee of the trust.[20]

---

[17]   Section 2611(b) excludes from the definition of a generation skipping transfer any transfer that, if made by an individual, would not be treated as a taxable gift by reason of § 2503(e). This could apply if a trust under a decedent's will made payments for education or health care.

[18]   Only certain types of trusts will qualify, and a typical *Crummey* trust will not. These rules are discussed in more detail later in this chapter.

[19]   It is certainly not a direct skip (i.e., the spouse's death does not trigger either the gift or the estate tax with respect to the trust) or a taxable distribution (there was no distribution).

[20]   § 2603(a)(2).

Taxable Distributions

The last of the three taxable events is a taxable distribution. This is any distribution from a trust to a skip person that is *not* either a taxable termination or a direct skip.[21] To illustrate, suppose GP's will creates a testamentary trust with the following terms: The Trustee shall distribute all income to GP's spouse for life, and at her death, the Trustee shall distribute the remainder to GP's grandchild, GC, or her estate. In addition, the Trustee, in its sole discretion may distribute income and/or corpus during the life of GP's spouse for the support and maintenance of GC.

This trust is not a skip person because GP's spouse has a § 2652 interest in the trust. Therefore, although creation of the trust is subject to the estate tax, it is not a GST. Suppose, however, that the Trustee decides to make a distribution to GC for her support and maintenance. This distribution does not terminate anyone's interest in the trust, so it is not a taxable termination. The distribution is also not subject to either the gift or estate tax, so it is not a direct skip. This places us squarely within the definition of a taxable distribution: ". . . any distribution by a trust to a skip person (other than a taxable termination or a direct skip)."

In the case of a taxable distribution, liability for the GST tax falls on the distributee.[22]

Identifying the Taxable Event

To illustrate how the three taxable events interrelate, consider the following example and its variations:

Example #9:   **GP's will creates a testamentary trust granting to her only child, C, an income interest for life. Following C's death, the income is to be distributed to GP's two grandchildren, A and B, or the survivor, until the death of the survivor. When the survivor of the two grandchildren dies, the remainder is to be distributed to GP's then-living great grandchildren, in equal shares. During the term of the trust, the independent Trustee has the discretionary power to make distributions of principal to C, A or B, or to any great grandchild (GGC), as needed for health, education, maintenance and support.**

On these facts, GP is the transferor, and § 2652 interests in the trust are held by C, A and B, and the GGC's; C is a current income beneficiary[23] and A, B, and the GGC's are permissible distributees of principal.[24]

---

[21]   § 2612(b).

[22]   § 2603(a)(1).

[23]   § 2652(c)(1)(A).

[24]   § 2652(c)(1)(B).

Because C is not a skip person, the trust is not a skip person, and creation of the trust at GP's death is not a direct skip.

Variation 9(a): **During the first year of the trust, the Trustee distributes $100,000 to A for her support and maintenance.**

The distribution to A, a skip person, is a taxable distribution. It is not a taxable termination, because no interest in the trust has terminated. It is not a direct skip, because the transfer is not subject to either the gift or estate tax. A, as beneficiary, is liable for the tax due, if any.

Variation 9(b): **C dies ten years after GP's death.**

C's death is a taxable termination: C's interest in the trust terminated at her death, and thereafter all § 2652 interests in the trust are held by A and B and GGC's, all of whom are skip persons. Although this fact by itself would be sufficient to characterize C's death as a taxable termination, since C was the only beneficiary who is not a skip person, it would not be possible for the trust to make a distribution to a non-skip person.

Consider the result if we vary the facts for a moment: what if C had a general power of appointment over the trust? The existence of that power would mean that the trust assets would be included in C's estate under § 2041, so it would appear that imposition of the GST is unnecessary: the assets have been taxed at C's generation. Yet it still seems that C's death falls within the definition of a taxable termination.

The statute avoids this inappropriate result in the definition of the "transferor" under § 2652(a). Where property is subject to the estate tax, the "transferor" within the meaning of the statute is the decedent, and if the property was subject to the gift tax, the "transferor" is the donor. The effect of this rule is that once the assets of the trust are taxed in C's estate, C becomes the transferor of this trust for GST purposes. Because A and B are not skip persons with respect to C, following C's death a non-skip person holds a § 2652 interest in the trust, and the GST will loom again only after their death, or if distributions are made to great grandchildren.

For purposes of the remaining two variations, assume C did ***not*** hold a general power over the trust, and that C's death was a taxable termination.

Variation 9(c): **One year after C's death, the Trustee makes income and principal distributions to A and B, and makes a principal distribution to one of the GGC's.**

The first issue is whether the distributions to A and B are (or should be) considered taxable distributions: isn't the trust making distributions to skip persons? Stepping back for a moment, it is clear that these distributions should not be considered GST events. When C dies, the GST tax is imposed because there was no transfer tax imposed on C's generation—now one has been imposed. It seems, from a policy point of view, that A and B should be able to receive distributions tax-free, and only future distributions to GGC's should be subject to the GST tax. With the help of § 2653, this is precisely what happens.

Under § 2653, whenever there is a generation skipping transfer of any property, and immediately after the transfer the property is held in trust, then for subsequent transfers from the trust, the beneficiaries get new generation assignments; basically everyone moves up. This is accomplished by reassigning the original transferor (GP) to the 1st generation above the highest generation of any person who has a § 2652 interest in the trust. This rule clearly applies to these facts: C's death is a generation skipping transfer, and the property is thereafter held in trust. Therefore, for purposes of subsequent distributions from the trust, GP is assigned to the generation just above that of A and B: C's generation! For this reason, from the point of view of the trust, A and B are no longer considered skip persons. The only beneficiaries who are skip persons now are the GGC's.

Thus, the distribution to the great grandchild is a taxable distribution: it is a distribution from the trust to a skip person; it is not a taxable termination or a direct skip. Because of § 2653, however, distributions to A and B are not taxable events.

> *Variation 9(d):* **A dies two years after C, and B dies two years later. At B's death, the trust terminates and the principal is distributed to the GGC's.**

A's interest in the trust terminates with his death. However, since B, a non-skip person, holds a § 2652 interest in the trust, this is not a taxable termination. When B dies and her interest in the trust terminates, there is a taxable termination because after B's death all interests in the trust are held by skip persons.[25]

Part D. The Taxable Amount

The amount taxed and the liability for the tax will vary depending upon the event that gives rise to the tax. Because of these variations, in some cases the GST tax is tax exclusive, like the gift tax, and in some cases it is tax inclusive, like the estate tax.

  1.   In the case of a taxable distribution the amount taxed is the value of the property received by the trust beneficiary, and the distributee is liable for the tax.[26] If the trustee pays the GST tax out of trust funds, then that payment is treated as

---

[25] See § 26.2612–1(f) Ex. 4.
[26] §§ 2621 & 2603.

an additional taxable distribution to the beneficiary.[27] Thus, when applied to taxable distributions, the GST tax base is tax inclusive, like the estate tax.

2. In the case of a taxable termination, the entire value of the property subject to the termination is taxed, i.e., the entire corpus of the trust.[28] The trustee is liable for the tax, so that amounts used to pay the tax are included in the amount taxed.[29] Thus, when applied to taxable terminations the GST tax base is tax inclusive.

3. In the case of a direct skip, the taxable amount is the amount received by the transferee, and the transferor is liable for the tax.[30] Thus, like the gift tax, amounts used by the transferor to pay the tax are not themselves subject to tax, so the tax base is tax exclusive.[31]

These characteristics are summarized in the Table below. The tax rate on these transfers is the highest rate under § 2001, currently 40%.[32] As with the gift and estate taxes, there are certain exceptions (discussed below) and each individual is entitled to an exemption from the tax in an amount equal to the basic exclusion amount under § 2010 of $5,000,000 (adjusted for inflation). § 2631.

---

[27] § 2621.

[28] § 2622.

[29] § 2603.

[30] §§ 2623 & 2603.

[31] To mitigate this disparate treatment of direct skips, Congress enacted § 2515, which requires the donor of a gift that is characterized as a direct skip to increase the amount of the gift by any GST tax paid. To illustrate, suppose grandparent, GP, gives grandchild (whose parents are both alive) $1 million. Assuming that GP has used her GST exemption, and ignoring the annual exclusion, GP would owe $400,000 in GST taxes. In addition, she would owe a gift tax on $1.4 million ($1 million gift plus the $400,000 gift tax) or $560,000 for a total transfer tax of $960,000 on a gift of $1 million.

[32] § 2641.

Type—§ 2612	Taxable Amount	Liability—§ 2603	Tax Base
Taxable Distribution—(a)	Distribution— § 2621	Distributee	Inclusive
Taxable Termination—(b)	Corpus— § 2622	Trustee	Inclusive
Direct Skip—(c)	Amount Rec'd— § 2623	Transferor	Exclusive

Part E. Computation of the GST Tax: Exemption and Exclusions

As illustrated in note 31, when the GST tax hits, it hits hard: it is imposed in addition to any federal estate or gift tax that may result from the same transfer. Nevertheless, there is a generous exemption from the tax, and many transfers are entirely excluded. The amount of the GST exemption is tied to the estate tax exclusion amount under § 2010(c). Thus, at this writing the GST exemption is $5,490,000. In addition, many intervivos direct skips will escape the tax, because amounts treated as nontaxable gifts under § 2503(b) (the annual exclusion) and § 2503(e) (medical care and education) are similarly excluded from the GST tax. While it's tempting to say that anything qualifying for the annual exclusion is free of GST tax as well, that's not actually true. As noted below, when an annual exclusion gift is made in trust it may still be subject to the GST tax.

Implementing the GST Exemption: The Applicable Rate

The following discussion describes how the GST tax is calculated. It is important to keep in mind that the complexities are all designed to implement the exemption from the tax. Basically, the rate of tax applied to a taxable event will depend upon whether it is covered by the exemption or not.

The amount of tax due on a GST is equal to the "taxable amount," as described above, multiplied by the "applicable rate." The statute implements the GST exemption by manipulating the rate applied to the taxable amount. In sum, if there is no available exemption to apply to a GST, then the transfer will be taxed at the maximum estate tax rate. If, however, some or all of the exemption is allocated to the transfer, then the applicable rate of tax will be less than the maximum rate, and perhaps zero.

The "applicable rate" is defined in § 2641 as the product of the maximum Federal estate tax rate (currently 40%) and the "inclusion ratio." The latter term is defined in § 2642, and the role of the inclusion ratio is to take into account the transferor's GST exemption. As noted above, under current law each transferor is entitled to an exemption of $5,490,000, and the statute allows substantial flexibility in how the transferor can allocate it.[33] The inclusion ratio is defined in § 2642 as 1 over the applicable fraction.[34] The numerator of the applicable fraction is amount of the GST exemption allocated to the trust (or in the case of a direct skip, to the transfer) and the denominator is generally the value of the property transferred to the trust.[35]

We know, it sounds impossible! But it's not so bad. To illustrate, consider the following three transfers to trusts. The sole beneficiaries of each of the trusts include GP's grandchildren and great grandchildren, so each trust is a skip person.[36] Assume that before these transfers, GP had not used any of her GST exemption. For each trust determine its inclusion ratio and its applicable tax rate. For ease of calculation, assume the GST exemption is $5.5 million.

Transfer #1:   In the first year, GP transfers $3,000,000 of securities to Trust #1. GP allocates $3 million dollars of her GST exemption to this trust.

The applicable fraction in this case is 1 because the numerator (i.e., the GST exemption allocated to the trust) and the denominator (i.e., the value of the property transferred) are both $3 million. Therefore, Trust #1's inclusion ratio is equal to 1 minus 1, or zero. This means that the applicable rate of tax for Trust #1 is zero, and, in the absence of any additional contributions, Trust #1 will never be subject to the GST tax.

Transfer #2:   The following year GP transfers $4 million in securities to Trust #2, and allocates the balance of her GST exemption of $2.5 million to this trust.

The applicable fraction for Trust #2 is 5/8 (i.e., 62.5%): the numerator is the amount of the GST exemption allocated to the Trust, $2.5 million, and the denominator is the value of the property transferred, $4 million. Therefore the inclusion ratio for Trust #2 is equal to 1-5/8, or 3/8 (i.e., 37.5%). This means that Trust #2's applicable tax rate on future generation skipping transfers will be 3/8, or 37.5% of the maximum Federal estate rate

---

[33] In the absence of an election to the contrary, if a person makes an inter vivos direct skip, any unused portion of the exemption is allocated to it. § 2632(b) & § 26.2632–1(b)(1). Similarly, if the person makes an inter vivos transfer into a trust that may eventually trigger a taxable distribution or termination, in the absence of an election, the exemption is also allocated to it. § 2632(c). Any remaining exemption on the death of the person is to be allocated by the executor. In the absence of a timely allocation by the executor, § 2632(e)(1) provides default rules for its allocation.

[34] Note different rules for direct skips under § 2642(a)(1)(B).

[35] The value of the property would have to be reduced by any Federal estate taxes or State death taxes paid out of the trust as well as any allowed charitable deductions. § 2642(a)(2)(B)(ii).

[36] Assume that their parents are alive at all relevant times.

at that time of the taxable event. At the current maximum rate of 40%, the applicable GST rate of tax for Trust #2 would be 3/8 of 40% or 15%.

> **Transfer #3:   In the third year GP dies and leaves her $10,000,000 estate to Trust #3. No portion of her exemption is available to offset the transfer, and the transfer is a direct skip.**

The applicable fraction for the transfer to Trust #3 is zero. This is because the numerator of the fraction, the amount of the GST exemption allocated to Trust #3 is zero. For this reason the inclusion ratio for the transfer to Trust #3 is 1 and its applicable tax rate will be the highest Federal estate tax rate at the time of the transfer, currently 40%. Thus, in addition to any estate tax owing by reason of GP's death, her estate will owe an additional $4 million in GST taxes.

It should be noted that, except for certain non-taxable gifts, discussed immediately below, once an individual allocates her entire exemption, the inclusion ratio will always be 1, and GST's will be taxed at the maximum federal estate tax rate.

Transfers Excluded from the Tax

As we've learned, § 2503(b) and § 2503(e) exclude certain transfers from the gift tax. Section 2503(b) excludes $14,000 (currently) of gifts per donor, per donee. Section 2503(e) excludes transfers made directly to educational institutions and medical care providers. As we've seen in earlier chapters, these provisions can allow substantial amounts of wealth to escape the gift tax, and the estate tax. We have also seen how *Crummey* trusts enable grantors to essentially multiply their annual exclusions by making the gifts in trust.

In general, transfers eligible for exclusion under § 2503(b) and (e) also escape the GST tax. As we have already seen, amounts excluded by § 2503(e) are not subject to the GST tax. The treatment of amounts eligible for the annual exclusion is somewhat more complicated. In general, if the transferor makes a "nontaxable gift," the statute assigns that transfer an inclusion ratio of zero, which has the effect of reducing the tax rate to zero.[37] However, the statute does not extend the protection to ALL transfers that qualify for the annual exclusion. Under § 2642(c)(2), if the gift is made in trust for the benefit of an individual, then it is treated as a "nontaxable gift" for this purpose ONLY IF: (i) during the individual's life, no person other than that individual may receive income or corpus from the trust, and (ii) if the trust does not terminate before the individual dies, the assets of the trust must be included in the individual's estate.

---

[37] See §§ 2641(a) & 2642(c)(1). The statute extends the same rule to transfers under § 2503(e), though that would seem to be excess statutory baggage, given the existence of § 2611(b).

Recall the discussion in ***Chapter 8*** about *Crummey* trusts, and how cases such as *Kohlsaat* and *Cristofani* have enabled taxpayers to multiply their annual exclusions by giving withdrawal powers to multiple beneficiaries of a trust. Even though the courts authorize this use of the annual exclusion from gift taxes, § 2642(c)(2) prevents extending that principle to the GST tax. If one wants to utilize a *Crummey* trust and exclude transfers to the trust from the GST tax, a separate trust for each annual exclusion gift needs to be created. It is worth noting that trusts drafted to comply with § 2503(c) (minor's trusts) will comply.

Moving Forward

We have now completed our exploration of workings of the transfer taxes. What remains is ***Chapter Ten,*** where we discuss valuation methods that are used for all of the taxes, and explore some tax planning techniques used to minimize transfer tax burdens.

CHAPTER TEN

VALUATION

■ ■ ■

Part A. Introduction

Valuation is the Achilles' heel of the transfer tax system.[1] Although valuation issues arise in the income tax, the determination of value in a non-market transaction is central to the transfer taxes. Thus far we have focused on whether a gift has taken place, whether an asset is included in the gross estate, or whether a generation-skipping transfer has occurred. But the transfer tax story does not end there. An essential part of determining transfer tax liability is the *value* of the property subject to the tax, and much litigation in the area involves disputes over valuation.

At first glance, the definition of "fair market value" is easy enough. It is:

> "the price at which the property would change hands between a willing buyer and a willing seller, neither being under compulsion to buy or sell and both having reasonable knowledge of relevant facts."[2]

The problem is that in the case of a gratuitous transfer, we have neither a willing buyer nor a willing seller, and in many cases it is not at all clear how to apply this definition.[3] In earlier chapters we explored how to value interests in trusts and insurance policies. In this chapter we will survey several of the basic valuation methods that are used to value property, and then turn to some of the complications and planning opportunities that arise when interests in small closely-held businesses are transferred.

---

[1] Professor Bill Andrews once observed that the "realization rule" was the Achilles' heel of the income tax *in A Consumption-Type or Cash Flow Personal Income Tax*, 87 Harv. L. Rev. 1113 (1974).

[2] § 20.2031–1(b) and § 25.2512–1.

[3] Many find this definition, which is also used for income tax purposes, is deficient. For example, Bittker & Lokken quote an early critic of the definition (James Bonbright) asserting in 1937 that "the willing-buyer, willing-seller incantation is a great bar to clear thinking in the law, and . . . has no more place in legal opinions than it has in the literature of economic theory." Bittker & Lokken, FEDERAL TAXATION OF INCOME, ESTATES AND GIFTS @ ¶135.1.2 (2nd/3rd Ed. Warren, Gorham & Lamont). Nevertheless it has survived.

Part B. Date of Valuation: § 2032

As a threshold matter, we need to determine the date for determining value.

The date that property is valued for transfer tax purposes can be important. For gifts, valuation takes place when the gift is complete. For purposes of the GST tax, valuation occurs as of the date of the generation skipping transfer. For estate tax purposes, unless the estate elects the "alternative valuation date" under § 2032, valuation must be made as of the date of the decedent's death.

Section 2032 generally allows an estate to elect to value its assets six months *after* the death of the decedent. If the estate disposes of an asset within that six month period, it is valued on the date of disposition. The provision was first enacted in 1935, in response to the stock market crash of 1929. Congress thought it unfair to tax an estate using date of death values when the assets held by the decedent precipitously dropped in value shortly after his death. Indeed it was possible that an estate's tax bill could exceed the value of its assets when it came time to pay the tax. Section 2032 was generally available to all estates until 1984, and it provided some unintended consequences. Even when the assets of an estate went up in value, executors might elect the alternative valuation date to get a larger step up in basis under § 1014. This was advantageous in cases where the increased value did not significantly increase the estate tax bill.[4] This allowed an income tax benefit (higher basis) at no significant estate tax cost. Congress amended the statute in 1984, and under current law an estate can elect the alternative valuation *only* if the election decreases the value of the gross estate and reduces the transfer taxes due.[5]

There is a special rule under § 2032 for "any interest or estate [whose value] is affected by the mere lapse of time."[6] In such a case, the change in value due to the lapse of time is not taken into account. So, for example, suppose that the decedent owned a patent, which on the date of her death had an unexpired term of 5 years. On the alternative valuation date, there would be only 4 ½ years left on the patent. Therefore, as a result of the mere lapse of time the patent would be less valuable.[7]

To illustrate how § 2032 works, consider the following example:

---

[4]   This would be the case if the estate tax rate of tax was lower than the income tax rate of the beneficiary, something which is not going to be the case under current law, when the estate tax rate is essentially 40%.

[5]   These taxes would include both the estate tax as well as the GST.

[6]   § 2032(a)(3).

[7]   The type of property that Congress had in mind property includes patents, income interests for a period of years, annuities, remainders and reversions. The latter two would actually increase in value. See § 20.2032–1(f).

Example #1:   D died on May 1, 2008. On the date of her death, she held marketable securities worth $100 million, a personal residence worth $20 million, and an antique Studs Bearcat worth $5 million. On July 1, 2008, the executor sold the personal residence for $17 million, and the Studs Bearcat for $6 million. In late September, the stock market crashed and on November 1, the estate's marketable securities had fallen in value to $60 million. On that date, the personal residence was worth $12 million and the Studs bearcat $3 million.

In the absence of an election under § 2032, D's total gross estate, valued as of her date of death, would be $125 million. If the executor elects under § 2032 to use the alternative valuation date, the gross estate would only be $83 million. This is the sum of the value of the securities on November 1 ($60 million) plus the values of the personal residence and the Studs Bearcat as of July 1, the date they were sold ($17 million and $6 million respectively).

Part C. Survey of the Basic Methods of Valuation

There are a number of methods traditionally used to value different types of property. We explore those here.

Historical Cost

If the property to be valued was acquired close in time to the valuation date in an arm's length transaction, the price paid will be the starting point for determining its value. So, for example, if a decedent purchases a new residence one month before she dies, the best evidence of its value at her date of death is going to be her purchase price. In this case, there would be no need to use the "comparable sales" method, discussed below.[8]

In an early case, the Supreme Court had to determine the value of a gift where the taxpayer purchased a single premium life insurance policy for $850,000 and immediately gave it to her children. The policy had an initial cash surrender value of $717,000, which the taxpayer argued was the value of the gift. The Court rejected that argument on the basis that the policy was obviously worth more than its cash surrender value as evidenced by the fact that the taxpayer paid more than that to acquire it.[9]

Although a recent purchase price is very helpful, it is not necessarily determinative. People sometimes make good purchases and bad purchases. Suppose, for example, the decedent shortly before she dies purchases a

---

[8]   The Tax Court held that if property was recently acquired in an arm's length transaction, the purchase price was "much more reliable evidence of the fair market value . . ." than the comparable sales method. *Ambassador Apartments, Inc. v. Comm'r*, 50 T.C. 236, 243 (1968).

[9]   *Guggenheim v. Rasquin*, 312 U.S. 254 (1941).

desk for $100 at an auction that turns out to be a valuable antique worth $10,000. In this case, the fair market value of the desk is $10,000.

Sales of Comparable Property

When the property to be valued has not been recently purchased, the estate must find other ways to value it. One of the most common methods is the "comparable sales" method. Under this method, the courts look for the actual sales of similar property within a short period of time before and/or after the valuation date. For certain types of property, this method can be relatively straight-forward and reliable. For example, to determine the value of stock or securities in a publicly traded company, all one has to do is open up the Wall Street Journal to see what they were trading for on the valuation day. For unique properties, however, the method is more complicated and less precise. For example, this method is used quite often to value real property. Since all real property is unique, the sales prices are merely the starting point and must be adjusted for the actual features of the property being valued. Not surprisingly, there is a great deal of room for disagreement, the estate and the government will offer dueling appraisals, and often a court has to sort it out.

Capitalization of Income

One common method of valuing income producing property, particularly commercial real estate and some types of businesses, is based on the amount of income the property or business is likely to produce. The appraiser values the property by "capitalizing" its earnings. The underlying assumption is that theoretically the fair market value of any business or investment asset is the present value of its expected income stream.

This method is frequently used when valuing an asset that has a predictable cash flow, such as a commercial office building. To illustrate, suppose we wanted to value a building that generates $100,000 in net income each year, under long term leases. From a prospective buyer's standpoint, the most important measure of the value is apt to be the expected income from the property. In order to translate those annual earnings into the value of the building, one needs to apply a discount rate, often called a "capitalization rate," or "cap rate." The appraiser will look at the selling prices of comparable property, to determine the relationship of their values to the annual net income of the property. For example, if a building in the area recently sold for $3,000,000, and it generated rents of $240,000 per year, that building was valued using a cap rate of 8%.[10] Capitalization rates will vary across types of property, and locations. So this can be viewed as a variation of the "comparable sales" approach. Once

---

[10] The formula is income/sales price = capitalization rate. So 240,000/3,000,000 = .08, or 8%.

the cap rate is chosen, one simply divides the annual income by the cap rate, to determine value. As applied to our example, if we apply an 8% cap rate to our building that generates net income of $100,000 per year, we get a value of $1,250,000.[11]

When this method is used to value a business, in addition to choosing a capitalization rate by looking at sales of comparable businesses, one needs to estimate the future income stream from the business. The starting point for estimating the future earning of a business is undoubtedly its past earning record. Have these earnings been stable, or have they been volatile? Needless to say, a lot of judgment calls must be made and not all experts will agree.

Special Rule for Valuing Certain Real Property Including Family Farms: § 2032A

In determining the fair market value of property, normally one assumes that it will be used in as profitable a manner as possible, its "highest and best use." Section 2032A creates an exception to this general rule for valuing "qualified real property." Qualified real property is certain real property that has been used as a family farm or in another family trade or business. If qualified, the real property can be valued with reference to how the property is actually being used, rather than how it could be used. This provision was enacted in 1976 in an effort to help preserve family farms and businesses. The thought behind the provision is that if the family plans to continue using the property as a family farm or business, they might be forced to sell if it were valued based on its development potential. Under this provision, an estate can reduce the amount otherwise includable in a decedent's gross estate by a maximum of $750,000, adjusted for inflation. The limitation in effect for decedents dying in 2017 is $1,120,000.[12]

Section 2032A is extremely complex, and the details are beyond the scope of this book. Nevertheless, a simple illustration will help you better understand the purpose behind, and the operation of, this provision. Suppose in 2017, D dies owning a farm in Eastern Long Island, D leaves the farm to his children, who plan to continue operating the farm. If the property were valued as a farm it would be worth $2 million dollars. The demand for residential real estate on Eastern Long Island, however, has increased dramatically and the value of the farm to developers would be $3 million. If the property is qualified, the estate would be entitled to value the farm at $2 million.

---

[11] $100,000/.08 = $1,250,000.

[12]   Rev. Proc. 2016–55.

Part D. Valuing Business Interests

Even after one determines the value of a business as a whole, when an interest in that business is gifted, or held at death, that interest's value may differ from its proportional value of the business as a whole. For example, if a business is valued at $1,000,000, a 10% interest in the business is not necessarily worth $100,000. It may be necessary to take into account certain factors that could affect the value of the interest. In this section we will explore some of these factors, including blockage, lack of marketability, control premiums and minority discounts.[13]

Blockage

One of the easiest types of assets to value for transfer tax purposes is publicly traded securities. The regulations provide that the value is the mean between the highest and lowest quoted selling prices on the valuation date.[14] Suppose, however, that the decedent held a substantial portion (i.e., a "block") of the outstanding shares, say 20%. In such a case, if the estate had sold such a large block of shares on the valuation date, that would flood the market and depress the market price significantly. In that case, the estate would claim a "blockage discount."[15]

The blockage discount issue could arise when a founder of a successful business takes her company public, retaining most of the stock.[16] When the founder dies, she might very well own a block of stock too large to be valued accurately on an exchange, and the estate may be entitled to a discount.

The blockage discount has been applied to the estates of artists where the estate includes a large number of work by the artist herself. It has also been applied to the estate of the owner of a very successful art gallery that included a very large collection of art by multiple artists.[17]

Lack of Marketability

If ownership interests in a business are not publicly traded, they are much more difficult to value. Once the value of the business as a whole has been determined under one of the methods described above, the estate may be entitled to a discount to account for the fact that the decedent's interest in the business would be very difficult to sell. Although the regulations do not explicitly authorize a discount for the lack of a market for interests in a closely held business (whether a corporation, LLC or partnership) both

---

[13] While we speak in terms of corporate stock, the same rules are applied in valuing partnerships and LLCs.

[14] §§ 20.2031–2(e)(1) & 25.2512–2(b).

[15] §§ 20.2031–2(e) & 25.2512–2(e). In the gift context, the determination of the blockage discount is made on the basis of each gift.

[16] See, for example, *Maytag v. U.S.*, 125 F 2d. 55 (8th Cir. 1942)(Maytag family retained 85% ownership).

[17] *Janis v. U.S.*, 461 F.3d 1080 (9th Cir. 2006).

the IRS and the courts acknowledge that in certain cases one would be appropriate. For example, in the *Estate of O'Connell v. Comm'r*[18] the government allowed the estate a 20% discount for its closely-held stock, but the discount was raised to 30% by the Tax Court. This discount is available whenever there is no ready market for the stock. Most of the cases that have permitted a discount base their decisions on the comparison of sales prices for comparable companies that are registered and those that are not.[19] The absence of a ready market makes the interest more difficult to sell, and thus worth less when compared to publicly traded companies.

Control Premiums and Minority Discounts

The regulations recognize that a block of stock that "represents a controlling interest" in a non-publicly traded corporation is worth more per share than a block that does not.[20] The value of the block should reflect a "control premium." From the willing buyer's perspective, she would attach extra value to the fact that a controlling shareholder has a great deal of power over the operation and future of the enterprise, much more so than minority shareholders. The shareholder would have the power to appoint the board of directors, which in turn determines the management of the company, its dividend policy, as well as the salary of its employees, including, in many cases, the shareholder herself.

The flip side of the control premium is the "minority discount." It accounts for the fact that the willing buyer would pay less for a minority interest in a corporation because of the *lack* of control held by minority owners. Taxpayers frequently claim discounts for both minority discounts and lack of marketability in closely held businesses, and they have long been accepted by the government and the courts.

Intuitively, it would seem that the sum of the values of all of the blocks of stock in the corporation should be equal to the value of whole. But that has proven not to be true. Both the Tax Court[21] and the IRS[22] have held that they are not. In Revenue Ruling 93–12, P owned all of the stock of X Corporation, all of which she transferred by making simultaneous gifts of 20% of the stock to each of her five children. The question was how to value each of the five gifts. The Service ruled that each of the gifts should be valued separately and that the relationships between and among P and her children should be ignored.[23] For this reason, P was entitled to a minority

---

[18]   37 TCM 1138 (1978).

[19]   See for example, *Estate of Jung v. Comm'r*, 101 T.C. 412, 435–437 (1993).

[20]   § 20.2031–2(e) (last sentence).

[21]   *Estate of Newhouse v. Comm'r*, 94 T.C. 193 (1990).

[22]   Rev. Rul. 93–12, 1993–1 C.B. 202.

[23]   The ruling held that the IRS would follow *Estate of Bright v. U.S.*, 658 F.2d 999 (5th Cir. 1981) and other cases that refused to aggregate interests held by family members in determining whether a particular block was controlling. In *Bright* the deceased and her husband owned 55% of

discount for each of the five gifts! Essentially, this ruling blessed the *creation* of minority interests as a tax planning tool, one that has been used very aggressively. The Tax Court has even endorsed this position, in cases where the minority interests were created on a deathbed with the *sole* purpose of reducing transfer taxes. In the *Estate of Frank*,[24] Anthony Frank owned 50.2% of the family corporation and his wife, Margaret, owned 13.5%. Both Anthony and Margaret were quite ill and Anthony had given their son a power of attorney to act on his behalf. Using that power, on October 24, 1988, the son transferred a portion of Anthony's stock in an amount equal to 18% of the corporation to Margaret. After the transfer, Margaret owned 31.5% and Anthony 32%. Two days later Anthony died. Two weeks later, Margaret died. Even though the transfer of the stock was clearly intended to eliminate Anthony's control premium and convert him into a minority shareholder, the Tax Court respected the transaction and gave both Anthony's and Margaret's estates discounts for lack of marketability (30%) and holding a minority interest (20%)!

In the following section we discuss how the availability of discounts has been extended to family owned entities that do not actually conduct a business, but may simply own investment assets, This type of entity is frequently a partnership or an LLC, and we refer to them collectively as family limited partnerships, or "FLP's."

Tax Planning and Discounts

Absent any of the discounts that we have described in this chapter, an interest in an FLP should be worth approximately the same percentage of the total entity's assets as the interest represents. So a 20% interest in an FLP holding assets worth $100,000,000 should have a fair market value of approximately $20,000,000. That would be its "net asset value" and that is typically the starting point for determining transfer tax valuation. Then the discounts come into play. They are typically claimed, and granted, for minority interests, lack of control, and lack of marketability, as we've discussed above. The discounts are often appropriate in the context of an entity actually doing business. There are important business reasons for operating in the corporate, LLC or partnership form, even when the owners are family members, reasons that have significance well beyond the transfer taxes. These include limitation of liability, easier transferability of interests, commercial practices (in the business world customers often feel more comfortable dealing with an entity rather than an individual). But what about an FLP that holds nothing but non-business property, often only investment assets? The reasons described above play no role in the creation of the entity. The entity is a legal fiction that is interposed between

---

several corporations as community property. The court held that her 27.5% interest should be valued without taking into account the stock owned by her husband.

[24] *Estate of Frank v. Comm'r*, 69 TCM 2255 (1995).

the assets and the owners of the entity, solely for purposes of estate tax avoidance. Yet taxpayers claim, and the government and courts often allow, the same type of discounts that are allowed for businesses.

The legal fiction exploited by FLP's is often very tenuous. Courts have refused to respect the entity if the taxpayer treats is as mere window dressing. If a taxpayer continues to deal with the property as if she owns it outright, and uses entity funds to pay her bills, courts have been willing to disregard the entity and apply principles of § 2036 to include the property in her estate without regard to any entity discounts.[25] If the owner of an LLC could require at any time that the LLC liquidate and distribute all of its assets to the owners, then there seems little reason to allow a discount from the asset value of an interest.

In this section we will discuss a few of the more aggressive ways that marketability and minority discounts are being used by estate planners. There are four examples below, each of which are based on the following basic facts:

Basic Facts: T and her husband, both 60 years old, are happily married and in excellent health. Over the years, they have been quite successful and currently own well over $100 million in publicly traded stock. They have three children and seven grandchildren. To date they have not used any portion of their unified credits. Whenever a gift is made, assume that it will be a split gift between T and her husband under § 2513. Further assume at all times that all parties pay taxes at rate of 20% on their investment income and that the Federal mid-term rate is 2.5%. Therefore, the appropriate rate under § 7520 is 3% (i.e., 120% of 2.5%).

Discounts and the Annual Exclusion

In order to take advantage of discounts, the first thing that is typically done is to form a family limited partnership ("FLP") or a limited liability company ("LLC"). By doing so, the owners will be able to segment their interests in the underlying property, so that they can give away "minority interests" in the entity, rather than simply transferring a portion the underlying property. This will have the immediate effect of increasing the annual gift tax exclusion under § 2503 by the amount of the discount. To illustrate consider the following example:

Example #2: In December of 2016, T and her husband formed an FLP by transferring $100 million worth of publicly traded stock (assume this consists of 10,000 shares of stock, each worth $10,000) to the FLP. In exchange, they receive 10,000 "units" of the FLP,

---

[25] See, e.g., Estate of Rosen v. Comm'r, 91 T.C.M. 1220 (2006).

each of which had a net asset value of $10,000. So the couple no longer owns the stock, but instead hold units of the FLP. In 2017 they give to each of their children and grandchildren four units of the FLP. They claim minority and lack of marketability discounts totaling 30%, valuing the units at $7,000 each.

Under § 2503, T and her husband are jointly entitled to an annual exclusion of $28,000 per donee. They have transferred property that had a value in their hands of $40,000 to each of the ten donees. Had they transferred actual stock worth that amount, the transfers would exceed their available annual exclusions by $12,000. But they didn't actually transfer the stock, they transferred units in the FLP that are not readily marketable, and that represent a minority interest in the entity. Applying the discounts, property that was worth $40,000 per donee without regard to the FLP is valued at $28,000 for gift tax purposes, and all of the gifts fall within the annual exclusion. The creation of the FLP and transfers of minority interests has allowed $12,000 of value per donee (totaling $120,000 in 2017 alone) to disappear from the transfer tax base.

GRATs and Discounts

In *Chapter Eight* we discussed how GRATs can be used to freeze the value of estate assets. Let's see what happens if we combine GRATs and transfers of minority interests in an FLP.

Example #3:   In 2018, T sets up a trust for the benefit of her children and grandchildren by transferring to it 1000 units of the FLP in exchange for a 2-year annuity of $3,658,276.[26] The value of the annuity using the § 7520 rate of 3% is precisely equal to $7,000,000. At the time of the transfer, the net asset value of the units is $10,000,000, but after application of 30% discounts their value is claimed to be $7,000,000.

First notice that this is a zeroed-out GRAT: there is no gift tax on the creation of this trust because the value of the annuity is equal to the discounted value of the units. Now let's see how this plays out under the extremely conservative assumption that there is a 3% return on all capital and the FLP makes current distributions of all of its earnings to its members. On these assumptions, the net assets of the Trust will be worth $3,182,700 in two years after completely paying off the annuity determined as follows:

---

[26] The trust will pay to T the amount of $3,658,276 per year for two years. After that T's interest in the trust will terminate, and the assets will be held for the benefit of her children and grandchildren.

Initial value	$10,000,000
2018 earnings	$300,000
2018 annuity payment	($3,658,276)
Balance at year end	$6,641,724
2019 earnings	$199,252
2019 annuity payment	($3,658,276)
Balance at year end	$3,182,700

In this transaction, T has successfully transferred over $3 million dollars without incurring one dollar of transfer taxes! Notice that because of the discounts, on the creation of the GRAT, T has economically transferred $3 million dollars to the trust on which the beneficiaries earned 3%.

Notice as well, there would no legal reason that T and her husband could not set up a GRAT for each of their 10 children and grandchildren to increase the tax-free transfer to $30,000,000.

The concept of minority discounts originated with interests in closely held businesses, where it is clear that an outsider would be reluctant to purchase a minority interest in the business without receiving some discount for lack of control and marketability. But estate planners, and indeed the courts, have pushed these discounts well beyond their original purpose, and allow taxpayers to theoretically, though not actually, reduce the value of their assets by placing them in a legal entity such as a partnership or an LLC. As we've just seen, a 30% discount (an amount routinely allowed by the IRS) they can change a $28,000 joint annual exclusion into a $40,000 one. Just imagine what that means for the exemption amount. For a married couple with $15,000,000 in joint assets, a minority discount would value their estate at $10,500,000, meaning they would have no estate tax liability whatsoever.

Calls for reform have been made for years,[27] and administration proposals have included reforms. Nothing yet has happened to place a curb on the discounts for family owned entities. Indeed, aggressive tax planners have been successful in creating discounts in other types of property, such as artwork, by fractionalizing the ownership of that property.[28]

---

[27] See, e.g., Laura E. Cunningham, *Remember the Alamo: The IRS Needs Ammunition in its Fight Against the Family Limited Partnership* 86 Tax Notes 1461 (March 31, 2000); *FLP Fix Must Be Part of Transfer Tax Reform* 112 Tax Notes 937 (September 11, 2006); FLPs, the Transfer Taxes and the Income Tax, 127 *Tax Notes* 805 (May 17, 2010).

[28] See, e.g., *Estate of Elkins v. Comm'r*, 140 T.C. 86 (2013), aff'd in part, rev'd in part, 767 F 3rd 443 (5th Cir. 2014). In *Elkins*, the decedent and his three adults children jointly owned 64 works of art. They entered into a "Co-tenant's Agreement" that significantly restricted each of their rights to "possession, partition, and alienation" of the art, including that no owner could sell her interest without the consent of all owners. The estate initially took the position that the art should

Intentionally Defective Grantor Trusts, or "IDGTs"

There is a set of income tax rules known as the "grantor trust" rules, found in §§ 671–679 of the Code. Those rules have a long history, and were added to the Code in 1954 to prevent wealthy taxpayers from reducing their income tax bills by shifting assets, and therefore taxes, to a trust, while still maintaining a level of control over the assets. They were enacted during a time of very high maximum income tax rates. By placing the assets in the trust, the taxpayers attempted to subject that income to the trust's lower tax. Given changes in the law since 1980, the rules no longer serve a significant purpose under the income tax.[29] Yet they provide an opportunity for estate planning that has become quite popular.

There is a transaction that exploits the fact that certain "grantor trusts" are treated differently under the income tax than they are under the gift tax. Under the statute, a "grantor trust" is a trust in which the grantor's retained control violates the grantor trust rules, so that the grantor is treated as the owner of the trust for income tax purposes. The powers that can run afoul of the rules are found in §§ 673–676. Some, like the power to revoke, or retention of a reversion, are treated similarly under the income tax and the estate and gift taxes.[30] But some are not. The proscribed powers that can make a trust a "grantor trust" include (1) the appointment of a trustee who is non-adverse person and who has broad discretion over how to distribute income and/or principal among the beneficiaries[31] and (2) the right of the grantor to reacquire the principal of the trust by substituting other property of equal value.[32] If a grantor transfers property to a trust that violates those rules, he will be treated as the owner of the trust and will be taxable on the trust's income, but the gift may be complete and the property will not be brought back into his estate. The ability to thread this needle is what gave birth to the "Intentionally Defective Grantor Trust," or "IDGT."

To illustrate, consider the following example:

Example #4: **On December 31, 2018, T transfers $10,000,000 of marketable securities (investments held outside the FLP**

---

be discounted by 44.75% because of the restrictions and the fractional ownership. The Service refused to permit any discount. Both the Tax Court and the Fifth Circuit disagreed and held that the fractional ownership in the works of art were entitled to a discount. The Fifth Circuit gave discounts on the works of art ranging from 50% to 80%.

[29] For a more extended discussion see Laura E. & Noël B. Cunningham, *"Tax Reform Paul McDaniel Style: The Repeal of the Grantor Trust Rules,"* in THE PROPER TAX BASE, STRUCTURAL FAIRNESS FROM AN INTERNATIONAL AND COMPARATIVE PERSPECTIVE—ESSAYS IN HONOR OF PAUL MCDANIEL, *Brauner & McMahon, eds., Wolters Kluwer, 2012.* For an excellent analysis of all of the issues related to intentionally defective grantor trusts, see Daniel L. Ricks, *I Dig It, But Congress Shouldn't Let Me: Closing the IDGT Loophole,* 36 ACTEC Journal 641(2011).

[30] For example, a revocable living trust is essentially ignored for income tax purposes during the grantor's life, and is included in the grantor's estate in full under § 2038.

[31] § 674(a) & (c).

[32] § 675(4)(C).

described in the basic facts) to a trust for the benefit of her children and grandchildren and appoints her brother Trustee. Under the terms of the trust, the Trustee is given broad discretion to distribute income and/or principal among the beneficiaries as he deems appropriate. At T's death, the principal is to be divided equally among her grandchildren. T retains the right to reacquire the principal of the trust and substitute other property with equivalent value.

On these facts, for gift tax purposes, T has made a completed gift. She has given up dominion and control over the securities transferred to the trust.[33] Under § 2513, T and her spouse will each be deemed to have gifted $5,000,000 and all gift taxes on the transfer will be offset by their unified credits. However, for income tax purposes this is a grantor trust, and all of its income will be taxed directly to T. So, for example, if the Trust earns $1,000,000 in capital gain income during its first year, this amount will inure to the benefit of the Trust and its beneficiaries; the trust would have a net asset value of $11,000,000, but it would owe no income taxes. T would be required to pay the taxes of $200,000 on the income. This is a rather bizarre result. Normally if a person pays the taxes of a loved one, this constitutes a gift. However, because § 674 imposes this liability on T, she is simply satisfying her own obligation, not making a gift. What this means is that during T's life, every year she will pay the income taxes on the Trust's income, thereby transferring assets to her grandchildren without making a taxable gift!

Example #5: **Same as *Example #4,* except that in January of 2019, the Trust purchases from T a 20% interest (2000 units) in the FLP for $14,000,000, its discounted value. Under the terms of the sale, the Trust issues a secured note for the entire purchase price. The note calls for interest payable annually at the rate of 3%, with the principal due in a balloon payment in 9 years. Once again, we will make the extremely conservative assumption that there is a 3% return on all capital and that the FLP makes current distributions of all of its earnings to its members.**

In 2019, the FLP earns 3% or $3 million on its capital and allocates and distributes its earnings to its members. The Trust receives its share of $600,000. In addition, the Trust earns 3% on the marketable securities that it owns, earning an additional $300,000. At year end, the Trust pays interest of $420,000 on the note, leaving it with net assets of $10,480,000.

Because the Trust is a grantor trust, it is ignored for income tax purposes, and viewed as an extension of T. Therefore, the installment sale is ignored; one cannot sell property to oneself. For this reason T is not taxed on any gain realized on the sale, and the interest payment by the Trust to

---

[33] § 25.2511–2.

T is also ignored. The sale, however, is respected for gift tax purposes, so no gift occurs. The bottom-line is that for 2019, the Trust has $900,000 of economic income, but will owe no income tax. Instead, T is responsible for the $180,000 in income taxes.

By selling the 20% FLP interest to the Trust, T has accomplished two major things. First, because of the minority discount, T has transferred $20,000,000 in assets to the trust, and has received a $14,000,000 note in exchange; because of discounts that is considered "adequate and full consideration," and there is no gift. T has effectively transferred $6 million of value (the amount of the discount) to the Trust without paying any gift tax. Second, T has paid $180,000 in income taxes that should be charged to the trust, again without the imposition of any gift tax. This means that the Trust will grow at a tax-free rate of return. Additionally, and not insignificantly, to the extent that the FLP earns more than 3%, the Trust could benefit enormously.[34]

Part E. Statutory Curbs on Valuation Techniques (§§ 2701–2704)

During the 1970s and the 1980s, estate planners commonly used a technique called an "estate freeze" to limit ". . . the value of property held by an older generation at its current value and [to pass] any appreciation in the property to a younger generation."[35] An estate freeze could take several different forms. In 1990, Congress addressed these transactions by enacting §§ 2701 to 2704. In *Chapter Eight* we explored § 2702, which deals with transfers to trusts in which the grantor retains an interest. The remaining three sections target valuation techniques used for closely held businesses, and we discuss them here. Although a detailed analysis of these three provisions is beyond the scope of this book, in this section we will briefly describe the estate freeze techniques that triggered their enactment, and how each of these provisions addresses these techniques.

Section 2701

Section 2701 creates special rule to value certain equity interests in corporations and partnerships that are transferred to a "family member"[36]

---

[34] For example, assume that the rate of return on capital for both the FLP and the trust is 10% for the full term of the note, and that the trust makes all interest payments when due and pays off the balloon payment at maturity. In that case the net asset value of the trust, free of all liabilities will be over $50 million after nine years, and neither T nor her husband will have paid a penny in transfer taxes.

[35] Staff of the Joint Comm. on Tax'n, 101st Cong., Federal Transfer Tax Consequences of Estate Freezes at 9.

[36] § 2701(e)(1). Family members include the transferor's spouse and the lineal descendants (and spouses) of both the transferor and her spouse.

if the transferor or an "applicable family member"[37] retains an "applicable retained interest."[38] Generally speaking, "family member" refers to T, T's spouse and their descendants while "applicable family member" refers to T, T's spouse and their ancestors. In the case of a controlled entity,[39] an "applicable retained interest" includes an equity interest that has distribution rights that are senior to those of the interest transferred.[40] Unless these distribution rights are "qualified,"[41] i.e., fixed and cumulative, if § 2701 applies, the value of the retained interest will be zero.[42]

Section 2701 was enacted to curb the use of the so-called "preferred equity freeze." To illustrate how this particular transaction could freeze the value of a family corporation, suppose, Parent (P) owns 100% of the only class of stock in X Corp., which is worth $10 million. P anticipates that the value of X Corp. will increase over time, and wants that value to inure to the benefit of her daughter, D. To accomplish this P recapitalizes X Corp, creating a new preferred stock, all of which it issues to P. The preferred stock has a par value of $10 million, and it has a first call on assets on liquidation, and entitles the holder to a dividend of up to 5% of the stock's par value before any dividends are paid to the holders of the common stock. The dividend rights are noncumulative, so that if no dividend is paid on the preferred stock in a given year, the holder has no right to those funds in a subsequent year.

Immediately after the recapitalization, all of the current value of the corporation is in the preferred stock, and the common stock has a negligible value. P then gives the common stock to D. Prior to the enactment of § 2701, the value of the common stock would have been treated as zero, resulting in no gift, while P has retained the preferred stock. Notice, however, that the value of P's preferred stock is fixed, if X pays dividends P will receive a return of 5%, but any return in excess of that will redound to the benefit of the common shares. And if X pays no dividends, all of the return will benefit the common shareholders.

Section 2701 changes this result dramatically. P transferred an equity interest to D, a family member, in a corporation controlled by P, and she retained a right to distributions (the preferred dividends) that are senior to those of the transferred common stock. Section 2701 is triggered, and because the preferred dividends are not cumulative, P's retained interest

---

[37] § 2701(e)(2). Applicable family members include the transferor's spouse and the ancestors of both the transferor and her spouse.

[38] § 2701(b).

[39] Control is defined in § 2701(b)(2). In the case of a corporation control means holding at least 50% (by vote or value) of the stock of the corporation.

[40] § 25.2701–2(b)(3).

[41] § 2701(c)(3). The treatment of qualified payments is similar the treatment we saw for "qualified interests" under § 2702(a)(2)(B). In both cases, Congress thought that the retained interests could be valued.

[42] § 2701(a)(3)(A).

(i.e., the preferred stock) is valued at zero and P treated as making a gift to D of $10 million.

Section 2703

Buy-sell agreements among the owners of small closely-held businesses are quite common and serve perfectly legitimate purposes. In an effort to keep ownership within the group (or the family), the agreement often restricts the transfer of proprietary interests to outsiders and sometimes sets a price (either fixed or by formula) at which the continuing owners can purchase the interest of the exiting owners or their estates. Imagine a law firm partnership, where the partners do not want a deceased partner's share to pass to her family but to stay within the existing partners. Their partnership agreement may allow the continuing partners to purchase the interest of a deceased partner, at a price determined by a formula in the agreement. In that case the partners are dealing at arm's length, and that agreement can provide a means of valuing the interest of a partner who dies.

In the context of family owned businesses, however, the same type of arm's length negotiation may not take place. All parties involved have an interest in arriving at a low estate tax value. As a result, estate planners often used these "buy-sell" agreements to reduce estates by setting the price to be paid for a deceased owner's interest. These agreements often provided that if an owner died, the entity (or to the surviving owners) would have an option to purchase the decedent's interest at a fixed price, which might be significantly below its fair market value. As long as the option was enforceable, the courts generally used the option price as the maximum possible value for the interest. In 1990, Congress reacted by enacting § 2703(a), which states that "the value of any property shall be determined without regard to (1) any option, agreement . . . at a price less than the fair market value of the property . . . , or (2) any restriction on the right to sell or use such property." Although this provision can apply to any property, it was targeted at buy-sell agreements.

There is an important exception to the general rule in § 2703(b), if the agreement meets three conditions:

(1) it must be a bona fide business arrangement,

(2) it cannot be a device to transfer the property to family members at less than fair market value, AND

(3) its terms must be comparable to similar arrangements entered into by non-family members in an arms' length transaction.

If all three conditions are met, the value of the property will be valued taking into account the agreement and/or the restrictions on the property. This protects the lawyers in our hypothetical firm.

Section 2704

Section 2704 imposes two additional rules on the valuation of family owned entities: § 2704(a) treats the lapse of certain voting or liquidation rights of a family owned business entity as a taxable transfer, and § 2704(b) provides that certain restrictions on the liquidation of a family owned entity are to be disregarded.

Section 2704(a) was directed at transactions like the following example, which is based upon a simplified version of the facts in *Harrison v. Commissioner*:[43]

Five months prior to his death, T joined with his two sons in creating a limited partnership (the "FLP"). T transferred $60 million in assets (consisting primarily of real estate, oil and gas interests, and marketable securities) to the FLP, and his sons transferred roughly $8 million each in similar assets of their own, T and his sons were general partners, and T was the sole limited partner. T's percentage interest as a general partner was relatively small, and represented only $1 million of the assets he contributed. The bulk of his share of the partnership was represented by his limited partnership interest, representing the remaining $59 million. The stated purpose of the FLP was to consolidate and preserve T's assets. T's assets had been managed for some time by one of his sons acting under a power of attorney, and the FLP transaction was entered into on behalf of T under that power. T was in poor health, and died 5 months after the partnership was formed.

According to the partnership agreement, any general partner, acting alone, could dissolve the partnership. The partnership agreement also provided that, on the death of a general partner, the surviving general partners would purchase the decedent's general partnership interest for its undiscounted fair market value, basically its "net asset value," if they wanted to continue the partnership. Otherwise, it would dissolve. The sons executed that purchase, paying $1,000,000 for the general partnership interest, which established its value for estate tax purposes. The more difficult question was how to value the limited partnership interest.

The parties stipulated that T's limited partnership interest's net asset value of $59 million was its fair market value immediately before T died, because of his right as a general partner to dissolve the partnership, and walk away with assets worth that amount. However, that right to liquidate did not survive T. It ceased, or lapsed, when he died. His estate did not

---

[43]   *Harrison v. Comm'r*, 52 TCM 1306 (1987).

have the power to liquidate, either as holder of his general partnership interest or his interest as a limited partner,

The government argued that, because of his right to liquidate, which T held up to the time of his death, the correct value of the limited partnership interest should be its undiscounted net fair market value of $59 million. The estate argued that, because that liquidation right lapsed at the moment of T's death, the interest should be discounted to reflect its lack of marketability and control. The court allowed a discount of $26 million, bringing the value of the limited partnership interest down to $33 million, and expressly noted that: "The difference between the two values is attributable entirely to the right which decedent had as a general partner up until his death to force a dissolution of the partnership."

Congress viewed this result as inappropriate. It did not think that the mere lapse of a voting or liquidation right in a family owned business entity should create a discount, especially when the lapse is designed to *create* the discount, and enacted § 2704(a). Under this provision, if

(i)   there is a lapse of any voting or liquidation right in a business entity, and

(ii)   the individual who held the lapsed right and his family controlled the entity,[44] both before and after the lapse,

then the lapse shall be treated as a taxable transfer by that individual. When the statute applies, it will treat the lapse as a gift or an amount includible in a decedent's estate. The amount of the transfer is the decline in value of the individual's interests in the entity caused by the lapse.[45] The effect of this is essentially to deny the discount. If we applied § 2704(a) to the facts of our illustration, the limited partnership interest would still be valued at the discounted amount of $33 million. But since T's right to liquidate the partnership lapsed when he died, and because he and his two sons controlled the partnership both before and after the lapse, T would be treated as making an additional $26 million transfer, includible in his estate.

Section 2704(b) provides that if there is a transfer of an interest in a business entity that the transferor's family controls immediately before the transfer, that any "applicable restriction" shall be disregarded in determining the value of the interest transferred. An applicable restriction is one that effectively limits the ability of the entity to liquidate and either 1) lapses (in whole or in part) after the transfer, or 2) could be removed by the transferor's family. There is an exception for commercially reasonable

---

[44]   §§ 2704(c)(1) & 2701(b)(2). Generally, in the case of a corporation control is holding at least 50% (by value or vote) of the corporation's stock, and in the case of a partnership control means holding of at least 50% of either the capital or profits interests in the partnership. In the case of a limited partnership, any interest as a general partner is considered control.

[45]   § 2704(a)(2).

restrictions and restrictions imposed by Federal or State law. To illustrate, suppose that that FLP is owned 70% by Parent and 15% each by her two children. The partnership agreement requires unanimous consent of all partners for FLP to liquidate; in the absence of this provision, state law would permit liquidation with the approval of 60% of the partnership interests. If Parent dies leaving her partnership interest to her two children, the restriction on her shares would be ignored in valuing her interest in Family Partnership, i.e., it would be valued as if she had the right to liquidate the partnership.

In August 2016 the Treasury issued proposed regulations under § 2704 intended to bolster the application of the statute, and in some ways expand it.[46] The proposals were met with hostility from the estate planning community. Public hearings were held on the proposals, and comments were overwhelmingly negative. The Service continues to keep the proposals under consideration, and their future is uncertain.

Moving Forward

We have completed our journey through the federal transfer taxes. We hope that you have gained a firm grasp of the basic principles that we have discussed here, and are better prepared to enter practice, where the real learning begins!

---

[46] Prop. Regs § 25.2704–1, –2 & –3, 80 Fed. Reg. No. 150, August 4, 2016.

APPENDIX

A BRIEF SURVEY OF WILLS AND TRUSTS

■ ■ ■

The federal transfer taxes are imposed upon donative transfers of wealth, i.e., transfers that are not made in exchange for consideration. We will study in more detail later what constitutes consideration for this purpose, but for the moment it is sufficient to focus on the idea that the taxes do not apply to commercial transactions, but only personal ones. Thus, the gift tax attaches when a transfer is made by gift, the estate tax attaches when transfers are made at death, and the generation skipping tax steps in and taxes certain interests that might otherwise fall between the cracks. Many of the principles studied in the law school Trusts and Estates course (sometimes called Wills and Trusts) come into play in studying the transfer taxes. Because some students may not have yet completed that course, in this Appendix we will briefly review some of the basic concepts that are covered there.

The Probate Estate

Assets held in the name of a decedent at death become the decedent's "probate estate." If a decedent dies with a valid will, the terms of that document dictate the distribution of the property in the decedent's probate estate. If the decedent dies without a valid will, then the intestate succession law of the state in which the decedent resided will dictate who will receive the decedent's probate estate. The probate process is the mechanism by which the decedent's assets are marshaled, creditors are satisfied, taxes are paid, if necessary, and the assets are distributed by court order to the will beneficiaries or heirs entitled to receive them. The estate tax will apply to the assets of the probate estate, but that is just the starting point for determining the decedent's "gross estate" for estate tax purposes.

Non-Probate Transfers

The wealth transferred by a decedent is not limited to the decedent's probate estate, and if the estate tax is to do its job of taxing all wealth transferred at death, it needs to reach beyond the probate estate. There are a multitude of "non-probate transfers" that are reached by the tax as well.

We will see that the estate tax statute contains provisions including these transfers in the gross estate, including such items as:

- Property held by the decedent and another in joint tenancy, which passes directly to the surviving joint tenant, bypassing the probate estate.

- Life insurance owned by the decedent, which will not be part of the probate estate unless the estate is the beneficiary of the policy.

- Retirement plans earned by the decedent, which will pass directly to the beneficiary named in the plan.

- Property held in a Revocable Living Trust created by the decedent. Such trusts have become popular mechanisms for probate avoidance, and frequently contain the bulk of a decedent's assets. The concept of trusts is further discussed below.

Introduction to Trusts

Irrevocable & Testamentary Trusts

Donative transfers can be made in a variety of ways. For example, assume D wants to make a lifetime gift (an "intervivos" transfer) to her child, or a bequest to her child at death (a "testamentary" transfer). There are a number of ways that she can accomplish this, the simplest being an "outright" transfer. To do this intervivos she would simply transfer funds or assets of a specific amount into her daughter's name. The testamentary transfer would be accomplished by a bequest in her will directing that certain funds or assets should pass into her daughter's name. Outright intervivos transfers will generally treated as gifts by D for purposes of the federal gift tax,[349] and outright testamentary transfers are subject to the reach of the estate tax.

There may be reasons, however, that D is reluctant to make an outright transfer of wealth to her daughter, either during her lifetime or at her death. First, she may have concerns about the daughter's ability to manage the funds. Second, she may want the bulk of the property to be preserved for another person, such as her daughter's children. These are non-tax reasons that D may prefer that her wealth does not pass to her daughter outright, but instead that is should pass "in trust." To the extent that D transfers wealth in trust, rather than outright, those transfers are equally subject to the gift and estate taxes.

What, then, is a trust? A trust is a legal entity, the salient feature of which is to separate legal title from beneficial title. To illustrate, if D

---

[349] In *Chapter Two* we study some exceptions and exclusions that often apply.

wishes to make a gift to her daughter in trust she will transfer legal title to the assets not to her daughter but to a "Trustee," with instructions on how to manage and distribute the trust assets. The document creating the intervivos trust is typically referred to as a "trust agreement." If D wants to make a testamentary transfer to her daughter in trust, the terms of the trust will be set out in her will (trusts created by will are called "testamentary trusts."). The Trustee (who can be an individual or a corporate entity such as a bank) holds legal title to the assets, which means that it or she can invest the assets, transfer them, etc. The Trustee does not hold beneficial title, however. This means that the Trustee cannot utilize the assets for its own benefit, but instead is circumscribed by the directions given by D (either in a trust agreement or in D's will) regarding the use of the property for the daughter's benefit. The trust can also dictate who will receive the property when the daughter's interest in the property ends. Because the terms of the trust are determined by D, they can take virtually any form. A typical trust might provide language such the following:

> So long as D's daughter is alive, the Trustee shall pay to or apply for her benefit the entire net income of the trust, together with as much of the principal as the Trustee determines necessary for her health, education, maintenance and support. On the death of the daughter, the Trustee shall distribute the trust to the daughter's descendants.

By separating the legal title from the beneficial title, D has ensured that the assets will be available to her daughter as needed, but has also ensured that any funds remaining at the daughter's death will pass to her descendants. Because D is the creator of the trust, she has much flexibility over its terms. She could instead direct the Trustee to distribute set dollar amounts to her daughter each year. She could provide that the trust will terminate after the daughter reaches a particular age. She could provide that the trust will continue after her daughter's death, with the daughter's children becoming trust beneficiaries at that point in time. The possibilities are endless. The trust has, in a very real sense, allowed D to retain a level of control over the assets long after her death. The infamous "Rule Against Perpetuities" puts a limit on how long D can exert that control.

While it is true that trusts are typically created for non-tax reasons, like D's concerns over her daughter's management ability, they are often created for tax reasons as well, as we will learn in this book. We will see that trusts are frequently drafted in a manner intended to accomplish specific tax purposes, and that there are certain "magic words" that are used to reach the desired result.

Revocable Trusts

We have seen that intervivos trusts are used as substitutes for outright gifts. As gifts are irrevocable, so are such trusts, either by the terms of the trust agreement or by local law.[350] Nevertheless, in some cases the grantor of an intervivos trust will reserve the right to revoke or amend the trust. Such trusts are commonly referred to as "revocable living trusts", and they are created for an entirely different purpose, which is the avoidance of probate.

As discussed above, assets held in a decedent's name must go through the probate process in order to vest title in the will beneficiaries or heirs. The probate process can be expensive, and time consuming. In the last 25 years or so the "probate revolution" has caused many individuals to create revocable living trusts. These documents serve a number of purposes, but are mainly designed to get the title to a decedent's assets out of her name during life, and instead into the name of a Trustee. Then, once the decedent dies, the assets can be transferred by the trustee to the objects of the decedent's bounty without the need for a probate process.[351] So long as the grantor is alive, the trust operates essentially as another pocket of the grantor; she can amend or revoke it at any time. But the trust also dictates who receives the assets on the grantor's death, and to that extent it operates as a substitute for the grantor's will. So it is sometime useful to think of irrevocable intervivos trusts as gift substitutes, and revocable intervivos trusts as will substitutes.

While a properly drafted revocable living trust can indeed avoid probate, tax savings are not the driving force behind creation of such trusts. The trust is essentially ignored for tax purposes as long as the grantor is alive, and once the grantor dies any provisions of the trust are governed by the same principles applicable to wills. Thus, although revocable living trusts are sometimes advertised as a tax saving ploy, in fact there are no tax benefits to them that cannot otherwise be obtained with a will.

Beneficial Trust Interests

As noted above, a trust separates legal title from beneficial title. The transfer taxes are concerned only with beneficial trust interests, transfers of mere legal title are not transfers of wealth subject to tax. We will devote much time to the rules governing the taxation of beneficial trust interests.

---

[350] A well drafted trust will always specifically say whether it is revocable or irrevocable. Local laws vary on the default rule if the trust does not specify, for example the rule in New York is that trusts are irrevocable unless the power to revoke is expressly reserved. Other states, such as California, have the opposite default rule. Because a will become irrevocable on the death of the decedent, testamentary trusts are necessarily irrevocable.

[351] The trust can also avoid the necessity of an expensive and unpleasant conservatorship or guardianship proceeding in the event the grantor becomes incompetent. In such instance the trustee has the ability to continue to apply the trust assets for the grantor's benefit without the necessity of a court proceeding.

Interests held by trust beneficiaries generally break down into two categories, present interests and future interests. Present interests are those that are currently enjoyable by the beneficiary, an example would be D's daughter's right to receive the income from the trust in the example above (such interests are generally referred to as "income interests").[352] The law of future interests has a long and complex history, though in the tax context we are principally concerned with two types: reversions and remainders.

A reversion is a right in the creator of a trust (called "grantor," "trustor," or "settlor") to receive the property back after the termination of another interest. It can be expressly reserved by the grantor, or it can occur by operation of law. An example of an express reversion would be as follows: G transfers property in trust providing for income to X for life, and on the death of X the property reverts to G if he is alive, and if not then to Y or his estate. G has retained an express reversion, if G survives X he will get the property back. G could also retain a reversion by operation of law if, for example, the trust fails to dispose of the property. If the trust provided for income to X for life, but did not state what should happen once X dies, then local law would typically provide that the property would revert to G, or to his estate.

A remainder is the right in someone other than the grantor to receive property upon the expiration of a prior interest. Remainders can be vested, which means the holder, or his estate, is certain to take possession at some point in the future, or they can be contingent, which means that they will only become possessory if the contingency is satisfied. So that if a trust provides for income to X for life, remainder to Y or his estate, then Y's remainder is vested. If, however, the trust provides income to Y for life, remainder to Y if he survives X, and if not then to Z or his estate, then both Y and Z have remainder interests that are contingent.[353]

Powers of Appointment

Consider the following trust: Grantor transfers property to T as Trustee, and directs T to pay the income to Isabel for life, together with as much of the principal of the trust as Isabel shall request from time to time. On Isabel's death, T is to distribute the principal of the trust as Isabel directs in her will, and if she fails to so direct, then to her issue.

What if Isabel directs the Trustee to distribute funds to her daughter? Has she made a gift? What if Isabel dies? At that point her income interest

---

[352] The term "life estate" is sometimes used to describe an income interest in a trust that lasts for the beneficiary's life.

[353] Those that have studied future interests may recall that a remainder may be vested subject to divestment. For tax purposes, those remainders are treated as contingent.

terminates. What property interests does she have in the trust for estate tax purposes?

Consider Isabel's rights with respect to this trust, and compare them to the rights she would have if T had transferred the property to her outright, rather than in trust. She is entitled to all of the income generated by the property. She has the right to take the property and give it away or sell it, and use the proceeds for whatever she likes. She has the right to decide who will receive the property after she dies. If Grantor had transferred the property to her outright it certainly would be an asset of Isabel's estate at death. Yet under our facts when Isabel dies she does not hold a "property interest" in the trust. What Isabel does die holding is a "power of appointment" over the trust. A power of appointment is a creature of local law. It gives the holder of the power certain rights with respect to the underlying property that may have real value, but that fall short of a "property interest" per se. Local law typically distinguishes between "general powers of appointment" on the one hand, and "special" or "non-general" powers of appointment on the other. A general power is one that gives the holder the right to direct (or "appoint") the property to herself, to her estate, to her creditors, or to the creditors of her estate. Any power that is not general is referred to as "special," or "non-general."

As we will learn in **Chapter Six**, even though Isabel's rights with respect to the trust are arguably equivalent to outright ownership of the trust property, the Supreme Court held early on that a "power" is not a "property interest" for purposes of the estate tax. In order to reach assets subject to a power Congress enacted another statute that specifically applies to powers of appointment. We will learn that the Code largely tracks local law in defining powers, with some modifications, and that for tax purposes the holder of a general power is essentially treated as if she held the property outright, while the holder of a non-general power is not taxed as if she owned those assets.